Contents

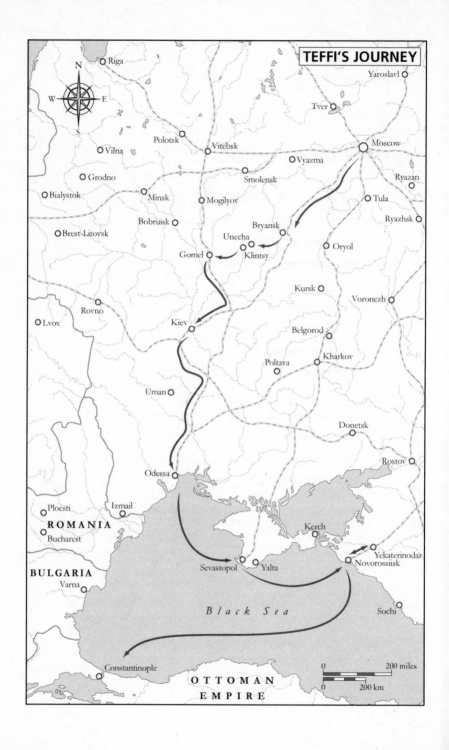

BEFORE A MAP OF RUSSIA

In a strange house, in a faraway land,
her portrait hangs on the wall;
she herself is dying like a beggar woman,
lying on straw, in pain that can't be told.

But here she looks as she always did look:
young, rich, and draped
in that luxurious green cloak
in which she was always portrayed.

I gaze at your countenance as if at an icon...
"Blessed be your name, slaughtered *Rus!*"
I quietly touch your cloak with one hand;
and with that same hand make the sign of the cross.

TEFFI

translated by
Robert Chandler

Introduction

Teffi, commenting in 1918 on the savage civil war that was decimating the Russian Empire in the wake of the October 1917 Revolution, put the blame squarely on the devil. Russia had improbably held together for so many centuries, she wrote:

> But suddenly some wily devil poked his stick somewhere near Moscow and began spinning Russia like a whirlwind top. "Whee-ee-ee!" The pieces are flying in various directions like sparks. The Crimea! The Caucasus! Poland! Little Russia! Lithuania! Finland! The Baltic region! Siberia! Kazan! Whee-ee-ee! More! More! Cities! Seas! Kingdoms! Principalities! Free lands! More! More! Soon only the stick will remain...[1]

Teffi was at the time one of the most widely read and beloved of Russia's writers. As one émigré commenter asserted: "There was scarcely ever another writer in Russia who had such an enormous circle of readers as Teffi." He added that, although she published almost exclusively in the liberal press, "both Russias" read her and she was a favourite of the last tsar, Nikolai II[2] (as she was of his Bolshevik successor, Vladimir Lenin). Her celebrity reached such heights that there even existed Teffi Perfume and Teffi Candies.

Teffi (pseudonym of Nadezhda Alexandrovna Lokhvitskaya) was born in 1872 into a distinguished St. Petersburg family. Her father, Alexander Lokhvitsky, was a professor of law and much published writer both in the academic and popular press, who, after the legal reforms of Tsar Alexander II in the 1860s, became a celebrated criminal lawyer. Teffi noted that he was "renowned for his wit"—a gift inherited by his daughter.[3] The second youngest of six children (five girls and one boy), she recalled that all her siblings wrote poetry[4]—and no less than four of the sisters became professional writers. One of them, Mirra Lokhvitskaya, achieved renown as a poet before her early death in 1905. Known as the Russian Sappho, she introduced unbridled female sexuality into Russian poetry and had close ties to the decadents and Symbolists. The only boy, Nikolai, pursued a military career and during World War I led the Russian expeditionary force to France, rising to the rank of lieutenant general.

Teffi's own writing career was delayed by her short and unhappy marriage to Wladyslav Buczynski, a Polish graduate of the St. Petersburg Law School and a landowner. They wed around 1890 and separated less than a decade later when Teffi abandoned her family at her husband's estate in the Mogilev Province (now in Belarus) and returned to St. Petersburg to pursue her literary calling. In 1901 her first publication—a serious poem that she herself judged "dreadful"—appeared under her maiden name, N. Lokhvitskaya.[5] After publishing two more unexceptional lyrical poems, at the end of 1901 her first satirical verses came out and for the first time she adopted the pseudonym Teffi.[6] For the next couple of years she signed her serious work with her real name—usually her married name, N. Buchinskaya—and her humorous pieces Teffi, but by 1904 she used her pseudonym exclusively.

By 1903 Teffi was reaching a broader audience, her feuilletons, stories, and verse (both satiric and serious) appearing regularly in the popular Petersburg newspaper, *Birzhevye vedomosti* (The Stock Exchange Gazette), as well as in other broad circulation newspapers and magazines. In 1907 her activities spread to the theatre when her one-act play, *The Woman Question*, was successfully staged at St. Petersburg's Suvorin Theatre.[7] It was followed by many more theatrical miniatures, which enjoyed great popularity over the next decade in St. Petersburg, Moscow, and throughout the Russian Empire. In addition, Teffi's talents extended to music. She wrote many songs—sometimes both words and music, at other times only the lyrics. These she sang to the accompaniment of her guitar (which she tenderly eulogizes in *Memories*) and many became part of the repertoire of well-known performers.

It has been said that Teffi invented her own genre—"the feuilleton that got by without politics"[8]—but this was not always the case. She, like many writers and intellectuals, actively supported the 1905 Revolution and she had quite close ties to the Bolsheviks. In March 1905, her poem "Banner of Freedom" (later entitled "The Bees") came out in the Geneva Bolshevik newspaper, *Vpered* (Forward).[9] In October, after the tsar issued his manifesto guaranteeing certain civil liberties including freedom of the press, Teffi wrote for the first legal Bolshevik newspaper allowed in Russia, *Novaia zhizn'* (New Life). The newspaper's literary contributors included a diverse collection of contemporary writers, ranging from the Symbolist Konstantin Balmont, to the realist Ivan Bunin, to the revolutionary Maksim Gorky, but Teffi was more deeply involved than most. She served as one of three non-Party members on the editorial board, who all, according to one of the Bolshevik participants, "made themselves out at the time to be Marxists or Marxist-leaning [*marksistvuiushchikh*]."[10]

In the first issue of *Novaia zhizn'*, Teffi's sketch, "October 18," vividly depicts—using visual iconography common in revolutionary art—the masses united in a "mighty and triumphant procession," their red banners outlined against the sky "like gigantic dark streams of resurrected triumphant blood."[11] She pictures the unity of all classes: "A soldier, a lady in white gloves, a worker, an officer," etc., and at the end returns to the banners, which "lead their people, their great host, forward, through the black night, to a new dawn, to a new life." Teffi published several more pieces in *Novaia zhizn'*, but relations between the literary staff and the Bolsheviks, strained from the start, became worse when Lenin arrived from exile in November 1905. Finally, when *Novaia zhizn'* became no more than a Party organ, the entire literary section, including Teffi, resigned. This negative experience left a permanent mark, and accounts for her hostility toward the Bolsheviks—and Lenin in particular—in 1917.[12]

Between 1906 and 1908 Teffi's political satire continued to appear in other opposition periodicals, but with time it grew milder, due in part to greater government restrictions, but also, no doubt, to fading revolutionary fervour. Russia was tired of all that solemnity, she wrote in 1910, and was longing for laughter:

Laughter is now in style [...] Books of humour go through three editions in three or four months and demand for them keeps rising. Humour magazines are alluded to even in speeches delivered under the bell of the State Duma. Theatrical entrepreneurs are longing for a good merry comedy and beg tearfully, "Why, write something, the kind of thing that makes your throat begin to tickle with laughter!"[13]

The demand for laughter coincided perfectly with Teffi's special gift, and it accounts for the renown she achieved during her final decade in Russia. The first print organ that spread her fame was *Satirikon* (Satyricon), the best Russian humour magazine of the early twentieth century, conceived of in 1908 by Arkady Averchenko (who in *Memories* is Teffi's travelling companion from Moscow to Kiev). With its very talented staff of writers and artists, *Satirikon* was a resounding success, and Teffi and Averchenko became its most celebrated writers. Her popularity grew still greater in 1909 when she became a feuilletonist for the Moscow-based *Russkoe slovo* (Russian Word), the most widely read and highly regarded newspaper in Russia, whose circulation reached over a million by 1917. Her Sunday columns—which included both topical feuilletons and stories—appeared in *Russkoe slovo* until it was closed by the Bolsheviks in 1917.

Teffi published her first books in 1910, and they reflect the two sides of her talent. The first, *Seven Fires*, is a volume of poetry plus a play written in orientalized prose; the second was entitled *Humorous Stories*.[14] The poetry received mixed reviews, but the stories were universally praised by critics, both in the elite and popular press. Mikhail Kuzmin, in his review in the prestigious *Apollon* (Apollo), favourably contrasted Teffi's natural Russian humour in the Chekhov manner to the "fantastic lack of verisimilitude" of Averchenko's "American" variety.[15] Teffi published no more books of poetry in Russia, but *Humorous Stories* was followed almost yearly by new prose collections, all of which were published in multiple editions and highly praised by critics, who often deemed Teffi the best humorous writer of the time. Typical are a reviewer's comments on her 1914 collection, *Smoke without Fire*; asserting that Teffi "undoubtedly occupies first place" among contemporary humorists, he declared her humour "purely Russian, sly and good-natured," and concluded: "Teffi's style is refined and simple, the dialogue—her favourite form—is lively and unforced; the action unfolds quickly, without superfluous details, and sincere merriment is effortlessly conveyed to the reader."[16] Some critics noted the sadness intermingled with Teffi's comedy, her "almost elegiac humour" depicting "grey, everyday life…"[17] Her more sombre side is reflected particularly in *The Lifeless Beast* (1915), her best collection of the teens, in which the serious mood predominates. Teffi's position as a woman writer—and more unusually, a woman humorist—aroused contradictory responses. One critic found "something typically feminine in that observant mockery with which she illuminates every trifle of everyday life," whereas her fellow Satyriconian, Arkady Bukhov, distinguished her from the usual run of despised women writers: "In general Teffi writes so cleverly and beautifully that even her enemies would not call her a woman writer."[18]

During the revolutionary year of 1917, political events began again to figure centrally in Teffi's stories and feuilletons.

Exultation over the February Revolution and the overthrow of
the monarchy is reflected in the story "The Average Man," whose
title character is now able to shout fearlessly "the policeman is a
fool." He explains to his wife: "I felt like it and I screamed. That's
the way I am. I! The free citizen Gerasim Ivanych Shchurkin."[19]
Such optimism was not to last long, however, in part because
of the Provisional Government's inability to implement its
liberal program during wartime, but, on a more fundamental
level, because Teffi's dream of class unity, expressed in 1905, was
clearly unrealizable. In a June 1917 feuilleton titled "Deserters,"
she criticized the intelligentsia for their anxiety over the violent
unrest among the peasantry. She accused them of expecting a
miracle—that "the same people [narod] who for centuries were
stupefied with vodka, oppressed, crushed by lack of rights, by
illiteracy, poverty, superstition, and hunger," would at once
reveal "a great and shining soul..."[20] Acknowledging the out-
rages, she nevertheless branded as "deserters" those who wished
to avoid "participation in the difficult and great exploit of building a new life." Even if their worst fears prove to be justified,
she concludes, "and instead of a triumphal chariot only black
corpses will be driven along our great path, may each one of
us be able to say: 'My forces were weak and small, but I gave
of them totally. And I did not renounce and did not flee. I was
not a deserter!'"[21]

Teffi's revolutionary sympathies, however, emphatically did
not extend to the Bolsheviks. Her disdain for Lenin and his party,
which dated back to 1905, is expressed powerfully in a feuilleton
of late June 1917, in which she gave a withering portrait of Lenin:
"Average height, grey complexion, completely 'ordinary.' Only

his forehead is not good, very prominent, stubborn, heavy, not inspired, not seeking, not creative..." The "sincere and honest preacher of the great religion of socialism" (as she rather surprisingly calls him) lacks "the fiery tongue of the gift of the Holy Spirit..., there is no inspiration in him, no flight, and no fire."[22] For Lenin's followers she expressed unadulterated contempt, but at once makes clear that she has not rejected socialism as such: "Leninists, Bolsheviks, anarchists and communists, thugs, registered housebreakers—what a muddle! What a Satanic vinaigrette! What immense work—to raise once more and cleanse from all this garbage the great idea of socialism!"

Teffi criticized the Bolsheviks for their inability to correctly judge the movement of history, but revealed a stunning lack of foresight when she asked rhetorically: "Is not the word 'Bolshevik' now discredited forever and irrevocably?" For only a few months later, on the night of October 24–25, they carried out their bloodless coup in Petrograd. In their effort to solidify their position, the Bolsheviks quickly acted to stifle the opposition press, shutting down *Russkoe slovo* and other unfriendly periodicals in late November 1917. The staff writers, including Teffi, did not succumb easily, however, for in January 1918, they opened another newspaper, which they called *Novoe slovo* (New Word). When it was closed on April 2, the determined journalists opened yet another newspaper, *Nashe slovo* (Our Word) on April 11, which lasted until July 6. *Satirikon* (now *Novyi Satirikon*, New Satirikon) eked out its existence until August 1918, with Teffi's works appearing to the very end.

Life in Petrograd grew intolerable, both materially and morally, during the months following the October Revolution. Aside from a pervasive atmosphere of fear among the Bolsheviks' political and class enemies, during the bitterly cold winter of 1917–18 the city was suffering from severe shortages of food and fuel. By March 1918, things had reached such a pass that Teffi declared Petrograd dead: "We live in a dead city... On the streets are the corpses of horses, dogs, and quite frequently of people... At night dark, frightened figures steal up to the horse corpses and carve out a piece of meat."[23] She writes of arrests: "Someone released from a Petrograd prison tells about executions... Nobody knows anything for certain, but in the dead city they are always talking about death and always believe in it."[24] In a piece written in Kiev the following October, Teffi quotes a typical conversation between two Petrograd acquaintances:

"He's arrested, arrested. It's not known where..."

"They've been executed, both of them..."

"It's said they were tortured... shhh... Somebody's listening in." And suddenly his face adopts an unnatural, carefree expression and his trembling lips whistle "Pretty Girls of the Cabaret."[25]

In May 1918, Teffi left hungry Petrograd for Moscow; the theatre magazine *Rampa i zhizn'* (Footlights and Life) noted her delight with "Moscow bread."[26] She probably came to Moscow that spring to attend rehearsals of *Catherine the Great*, an operetta she co-wrote with the comic poet Lolo (L.G. Munshtein, c. 1866–1947), which opened with great success in August. Another and more urgent reason for her departure from Petrograd, however, might have been a troubling incident that took place at the very beginning of 1918: An actress was arrested after a New Year's Day performance of works by Teffi and Averchenko, and only after a lengthy interrogation and a warning that "she must not dare to earn her bread through slander of the people's government," was she let go.[27] (In *Memories* Teffi reimagines this incident, also moving it to a later date.)

By September 1918, life in Moscow was also growing more dangerous. In contrast to Petersburg, as Teffi later wrote from Kiev, Moscow was "still alive," although just barely: "Mad motorcars race, with a whistle and a whoop. Rifle shots enliven the black silence of nocturnal streets. Moscow is being robbed and stabbed. It is still alive, still protesting, jerking its legs and pressing a foreign passport to its heart."[28] This was the situation confronting Teffi at the beginning of *Memories*.

In the title piece to Teffi's 1927 book, *The Small Town* (the title referring to the Russian colony within the larger Parisian metropolis), she expresses her disdain for émigré memoir writers. Aside from the usual categories of men and women, she writes, the town's population includes "ministers and generals," who spend their time amassing debts and writing memoirs.[29] "The memoirs," she adds, "were written to glorify their own name and to disgrace their comrades in arms. The difference among the memoirs consisted in the fact that some were written by hand and others on a typewriter."[30]

In the note that introduces her own *Memories*, Teffi signals at once that she has written a very different kind of book—one in which there are no heroes, no specific political line, no lofty conclusions. Her subjects instead are "ordinary unhistorical people who struck her as amusing or interesting."[31] The word "amusing" might at first seem jarring, given her grim subject matter, but in Teffi's view the funny and the tragic are not mutually exclusive. She writes in *Memories*, in a remark that could characterize her comic vision as a whole: "But life in Odessa soon began to pall. A joke is not so funny when you're living inside it. It begins to seem more like a tragedy." A number of critics noted that the humour only accentuated the horror. Mikhail Tsetlin, for example, wrote: "The laughter and bitterness in Teffi's book are so funny, and thereby it [the book] achieves a double impression: what nonsense and what sadness and what horror!"[32]

The author of *Memories* indeed makes no claim of heroism, warns us that she does not consider herself any more interesting than the others. For the most part Teffi portrays herself (as she often does in her writings) as a quite ordinary woman—frivolous, of limited understanding, guided more by emotions and naïve ideals than by abstract principles. But when need be she drops the mask, and the reader views events through her penetrating gaze. The closest thing to a hero in Teffi's dark comedy is the unlikely figure of "pseudonym Gooskin," her "impresario," who persuaded her to leave Moscow for a time and go on a reading tour of still Bolshevik-free Ukraine. An Odessan Jew whose non-sequiturs and mangling of the Russian language are a constant source of humour, Gooskin bears none of the external attributes of the hero, but during the treacherous trip from Moscow through the lawless western reaches of Russia it is his wiliness—his ability to outsmart the antagonist and lay low if necessary—that saves Teffi and her companions time and again.

Teffi parts ways with Gooskin in Kiev, and the remainder of the book traces her path down the map of the former Russian Empire, with stops in Odessa, Novorossiisk, Yekaterinodar. Everywhere she went she witnessed a similar dynamic: refugees like herself trying to rebuild cultural and social structures destroyed by revolution only to find them once again toppled by the forces of civil war. In Kiev, still occupied by the Germans in accordance with the Brest-Litovsk Treaty, Teffi encountered many literary and theatrical colleagues who, like herself, had fled from Bolshevik Russia and were now trying feverishly to start up theatres, newspapers, and other cultural institutions. At first it seemed like a "festival," she writes, but the second impression was of "a station waiting room, just before the final whistle." When the Germans, defeated in the World War, left in December 1918, and, after the brief rule of Ukrainian nationalists, the Bolsheviks began their approach in January 1919, the refugees fled further.

Many went to Odessa—Teffi among them. The new arrivals resumed their feverish social life, gambling and drinking through the night, while the eternally optimistic writers and journalists again set about starting a newspaper. The forces of destruction, however—at first taking the form of the notorious Odessan gangsters (made famous by Isaac Babel)—were never far below the surface. And when in April the Bolsheviks began their incursion, people resumed their exodus, Teffi barely escaping on a rickety ship, the *Shilka*, on which she hoped to sail to Vladivostok and from there to return home.

While on the ship Teffi witnessed the dissolution of her old world on a more individual level. A furnace stoker with whom she struck up a conversation on the deck one night revealed that he was in disguise—that he was actually a Petersburg youth who had visited her apartment, where they "talked about stones, about a yellow sapphire." Since then his entire family had perished and now he planned to go to Odessa to fight the Bolsheviks. Teffi remembers the evenings in Petersburg: "Languid, high-strung ladies, sophisticated young men. A table adorned with white lilac. A conversation about a yellow sapphire..." Then she imagines the execution awaiting this boy, who will "rest his weary shoulders against the stone wall of a black cellar and close his eyes..." If the stoker marks the demise of the aestheticized pre-revolutionary artistic world, a group of young officers who boarded the *Shilka* in the Crimean city of Sevastopol embodies the disappearance of the aristocratic military culture: "They were handsome and smart and they chatted away merrily, casually coming out with the odd word of French and singing French songs with perfect accents." Yet they were soon to be mowed down in battle, Teffi remarks, "to meet their death with courage and grace."

After the *Shilka* docked in the large port city of Novorossiisk, Teffi was invited to attend a performance of her works in Yekaterinodar, a last bastion of imperial pomp. On the train there she shared a car with "haggard" and "worn-out" soldiers and officers, who—in stark contrast to the jolly officers on the *Shilka*—bared the true, horrifying face of war. One of them told the story of a colonel who, after witnessing the torture of his wife and children, wreaked revenge on captured Bolsheviks time and again: "He would sit on the porch drinking tea and have the prisoners strung up in front of him, first one, then another, then another. While he carried on drinking tea." Another soldier declared him "insane," but his companion demurred, insisting that "In his world, in the world he lives in, he's perfectly normal." Within the bestial conditions of war, the usual rules governing human behaviour have been suspended. Although Teffi is obviously more sympathetic to the Whites, she shows both sides caught in the horror. Whether it is the female "commissar H" at the Russian border town (also "deranged"), who "sits on her porch, sentencing and shooting," or the crazed White colonel, the basest instincts have conquered these people. Later that night the voice of a soldier, in combat since the beginning of the World War, summed up the horror: "I can't go on anymore. Since 1914 they've been torturing me, torturing me, and now... now I'm dead. I'm dead..."

The contrast between these living corpses and the military elite Teffi then encountered at a theatre in Yekaterinodar could hardly be greater. After the dark vision of the fighting men, the generals and ministers seemed to be living a masquerade. The glitter was on full display: "Gold and silver lace, the glint of uniforms—true splendour." At the end of the performance, the author came out for a bow, Teffi commenting ruefully: "My last bow to a Russian audience on Russian soil." This gathering was also, in a sense, a "last bow" for the tsarist elite, soon to vanish forever from Russia.

Teffi conjures up a final, chilling image that encapsulates the annihilation of her old bohemian world, with its love of pose, of playing with life. As her train approached the Caucasus resort of Kislovodsk, she spied within the idyllic landscape "a scrap of rope. It is a gallows." She notes that it was there that they hanged "Ksenya G, the famous anarchist," whom she remembers: "Bold, gay, young, beautiful—always chic," one of an anarchist group whom everyone considered to be "fakes and braggarts. Not one of us had taken them seriously." But revolution played its tragic trick on Ksenya G and killed her in good earnest: She "had stood here, in this very spot, smoking her last cigarette and screwing her eyes up as she looked at her last sun. Then she had flicked away the cigarette butt—and calmly thrown the stiff noose around her neck."

Counterpoised to such visions of death and destruction, Teffi depicts too those who managed to survive the whirlwind of revolution more or less morally intact. A characteristic typical of Teffi's comic, anti-heroic world, and one that allowed some to endure, is a kind of lighthearted adaptability. Thus, there are the "elegant young men in smart suits" on the *Shilka* who, although they at first treat the demand that they haul coal as a joke, soon begin "entering into their new role"—not only carrying the coal, but adopting the stevedores' language and songs. They have, to be sure, only replaced one role with another, but that adaptability would prove essential for future émigrés, compelled again and again to reinvent themselves.

In general, though, women are the best survivors—not because of unusual valour or nobility, and certainly not because of political principles, but because of their ability to maintain such outward appearances as are necessary for human life, while at the same time adapting to shifting circumstances. With a combination of irony and affection, Teffi describes women running to the hairdresser or buying the last pair of shoes before their lives fall apart. "O sweet and eternal femininity!"

the narrator exclaims, comparing such women to edelweiss in a snowy wasteland. She tells of meeting one cheerful soul on a street in Novorossiisk who asks her to admire her dress made of "remarkably nasty muslin." The woman explains that it is made of "medical gauze," which, although not very strong, is "cheap, and it comes nice and wide." Teffi imagines that even "during Pompeii's last minutes, there had been edelweisses hurrying to fit in a quick pedicure."

A similar ability on a more serious level of necessity is manifested by a group of Armenian refugees camped out in tents along the Novorossiisk shore. They have been there for a long time and have suffered from all kinds of hardships, and yet they have adjusted to this life: They visit one another, argue, the children play music and dance. Teffi describes a woman who, judging from her torn silk dress, must have been rich but is now delighted because she has found a way to cover her tent with a shawl. Everything is relative, Teffi concludes. Those who can adapt, who can maintain life's forms even in the face of hardship, can survive. In her émigré stories it is typically the women who have learned this lesson well, who hold the family together while their husbands lie on the sofa, immersed in dreams of the past or in unrealizable schemes for the future.

During Teffi's stay in Novorossiisk there was a fierce windstorm (*nord-ost*), which becomes emblematic of all the destructive forces of nature that have crushed the refugees' lives, be it illness (the typhus epidemic then rampant in the city, the Spanish flu that Teffi barely survived in Kiev); the ferocious waves driving the *Shilka* passengers they knew not where; the internecine conflict itself, which, like a whirlwind, blew people "this way and that way, left and right, over the mountains or into the sea. Soulless and mindless, with the cruelty of an elemental force, this whirlwind determined our fate." People caught up in this whirlwind were no longer in control, Teffi writes, their movements and their ultimate destination often determined not by their conscious intent, but by chance. This was true of Teffi herself, whose plan to return to St. Petersburg from Vladivostok was thwarted when the *Shilka* was declared unseaworthy. People persuaded her to go abroad for the time being and to return to Russia in the spring. She thought: "'Spring,' 'motherland'— what wonderful words…" But not only did she not return in the spring—she was destined to live out her long life in exile.

After a period in Constantinople, Teffi reached Paris at the end of 1919 and, except for a short period in Germany in the early 1920s, lived in France until her death in 1952. Her weekly feuilletons and stories, published primarily in Paris émigré newspapers, as well as her many books, reestablished within the narrower circle of Russians abroad the immense popularity she had enjoyed in Russia. In her works she chronicled with her characteristic combination of humour and pathos—and at times with sharp, witty satire—everyday life in emigration. During her long decades in exile Teffi suffered the woes common among the Russian émigrés, especially of her ageing generation—financial need, serious illness, lack of acceptance in her adopted country, and permanent separation from her beloved homeland, to which she could return only in her vivid, amusing stories. There she looked back to Russia of the past with nostalgia and affection, but almost never with easy sentimentality—in fact, sometimes with quite the opposite emotion.

In her 1947 essay, "Baba Yaga," for example, Teffi treats as an inherent feature of the Russian character a violent drive to destruction not so very different from the elemental force that aroused such dread in *Memories*.[33] Her subject, Baba Yaga—the "terrible witch" from Russian folklore—is commonly considered to be the Russian "goddess of whirlwinds and snowstorms," Teffi writes, and she at first laments that, unlike the beautiful Venus and Diana, the Russian goddess is such a "hideous, vicious old woman." At the end, however, she evokes the lure of Baba Yaga's destructive might. When she overturns the sleigh of a winter traveller on his way to see his sweet Mashenka, he is enchanted by the "free and wonderful... song of the blizzard." The home and hearth promised by Mashenka mean nothing to him now: "Can he even remember her?... He feels both terrified and full of joy, and his soul sings and laughs. For never, never has it known such ecstasy." He cries to Baba Yaga: "You are a GODDESS. Take me into your death—it is better than life."

This celebration of the same elemental destructiveness so lamented in Teffi's *Memories* is unnerving, but it is telling that not long before she wrote "Baba Yaga," she touched upon an atrocity even greater than the Russian civil war—one that had only just been perpetrated by a "civilized" Western European country, Germany. In 1945, after seeing a film showing the Majdanek concentration camp, Teffi expressed particular horror at the orderliness of the Nazis' annihilation machine—the "rectangular little houses at a correct distance from one another" with "a big factory chimney"—the crematorium—protruding in their midst.[34] The fact that this "regular, clean little picture" was "thought up by man, created by human will" made it even "more horrifying than the heaps of skeletons." The latter, after all, have been seen before "on battlefields or in countries swept by the cyclone of revolution," but in such cases "chaos is the essential form, it cries out [that you are] stepping over the edge, over the brink of order, of common humanity." And so the Nazis' rationalization of evil and death makes even the chaos of the Russian civil war seem not as terrible.

—*Edythe Haber*

MEMORIES

T *he author considers it necessary to warn readers that in Memories they will not find famous historical figures or the deeply significant words such figures were said to have uttered. Nor will they find any elucidations and conclusions or refutations of this or that party line. They will find only a simple and truthful account of the author's involuntary journey across the entire expanse of Russia—a journey she made along with millions of other ordinary people.*

And readers will find in these pages, with very few exceptions, only ordinary unhistorical people who struck her as amusing or interesting, and incidents and adventures that seemed entertaining; and if the author has to speak of herself, this is not because she believes she is of interest to the reader, but only because she took part in the incidents described and absorbed the impressions made by these people and these events—and the removal of this axis, this living soul, would make the whole story go dead.

I

M oscow. Autumn. Cold.
        My Petersburg life has been liquidated. The *Russian
Word* has been closed down.[1] There is, it seems, no possibility
of anything.

Or rather, there is one possibility; it appears, day after day,
in the shape of a squint-eyed Odessa impresario by the name
of Gooskin, who is trying to persuade me to go with him to
Kiev and Odessa and give public readings there.

"Had any bread today?" is how he begins, in a tone of
foreboding. "Well, tomorrow you won't. Everyone who can
is going to the Ukraine. Only no one can. But *you*... You'll
be going there by train. I'll be paying you sixty percent of
gross takings. I've already telegraphed the Hotel London to
reserve you the best suite. The sun will be shining, you'll
be beside the sea, you'll read people one or two of your
stories... You'll take the money, buy yourself some ham
and some butter—and then you'll be sitting there in a café,
eating away to your heart's content. What's to lose? Everyone
knows me—just ask your friends. My pseudonym is Gooskin.
I could tell you my real surname too, but it's terribly long

and difficult. For the love of God, let's go! The best suite in the International!"

"But you said the Hotel London!"

"All right then, the London. Do you have something against the International?"

I ask around for advice. There truly are a lot of people desperate to get to the Ukraine.

"This pseudonymous Gooskin of mine," I demur. "There's something odd about him."

"What do you mean?" people of experience reply. "He's no odder than any of the others. They're all the same, these petty impresarios."

It's Averchenko who puts an end to my doubts.[2] It turns out that he's being taken to Kiev by some other pseudonym. He too is going to give public readings. We decide to go together. Averchenko's pseudonym is also taking along two actresses, to perform short sketches.

"You see!" says Gooskin triumphantly. "Now all you need do is apply for your permits and everything will go swimmingly— like a knife through bread and butter."

I have to say that I hate all kinds of public appearances. Why, I don't know. It's a quirk of mine. And as for this pseudonymous Gooskin with all his talk of percentages, or, as he himself puts it, "precentages"... But everyone around me is saying, "You're so lucky, you're going!" Or "Lucky thing, in Kiev they have pastries filled with cream!" Or even just "Lucky thing... with cream!"

It seems clearer and clearer that I have to go. Everyone wants to leave. And if someone isn't struggling to obtain the necessary permits, since they know they've got no hope of success, this doesn't stop them from dreaming. While those who remain hopeful are suddenly discovering that they have Ukrainian blood, Ukrainian connections, and ties of every kind.

"My third cousin had a house in Poltava!"

"And my surname, strictly speaking, isn't Nefedin, but Nekhvedin—from Khvedko, which is a Ukrainian root."

"There's nothing I love more than fatback and onion!"[3]

"Popova's already in Kiev. So are the Ruchkins, the Melzons, the Kokins, the Pupins, the Fiks, and the Shpruks.[4] Everyone's already in Kiev."

And then Gooskin begins to prove his worth:

"Tomorrow at three I'll be bringing you a commissar—the most terrible commissar of all from the frontiermost station of all. A wild beast of a commissar. He's just stripped the whole of the Bat. Stripped them bare—didn't leave them a thing."[5]

"But if they even strip bats, what hope have *we* got of slipping through?"

"That's why I'm asking him round. Just say a few pleasantries to him and ask for a permit. And then in the evening I'll take him to the theatre."

And so I begin the application procedures. First in some institution to do with theatrical matters. A languid lady with a Cléo de Mérode hairdo[6] adorned with a shabby copper band and liberally sprinkled with dandruff grants me permission to go on a reading tour.

Then long, long hours in an endless line in some place that's like a cross between an army barrack and a large prison. Finally a soldier with a bayonet takes my document from me and goes off to show it to his superior. Then a door is flung open—and out comes the superior himself. Who he is I don't know. I can only say that, in the language of the time, he is "draped in bullet belts."

"So you're Teffi, are you?"

"Yes," I confess. (There is, after all, no getting away from this.)

"The writer?"

I give a silent nod. He's going to say no. Why else would he have emerged so suddenly?

"Would you mind just writing your name in this notebook? That's right. With the date and the year."

I write with a trembling hand. First I forget the date, then the year. I am rescued by a frightened whisper from someone behind me.

"So," the superior repeats sombrely. He frowns. He reads what I have written. And then his stern mouth slides into a warm and confidential smile: "You see... I wanted your autograph."

"You flatter me!"

I receive my permit.

Gooskin now further proves his worth. He brings the commissar along. The commissar is indeed terrible. Not a human being, but a nose in boots. There are creatures called cephalopods. Well, he is a rhinopod. A vast nose, to which are attached two legs. One leg, evidently, contains the heart, while the other contains the digestive tract. And these legs are encased in yellow lace-up boots that go right up to his thighs. These boots clearly mean a great deal to the commissar. He is very proud of them and they are, therefore, his weak spot. There indeed lies his Achilles heel. And so the serpent prepares to strike.

"I hear you are a lover of the arts," I begin my oblique approach. And then, with sudden feminine naïveté, as if unable to control myself, I exclaim, "Ah, what wonderful boots!"

The nose blushes and puffs itself up a little.

"Hem... the Arts... I adore the theatre, although I have seldom had the opportunity—"

"What astonishing boots! Truly the boots of a warrior. I can't help thinking you must be an extraordinary man!"

"No, no, whatever makes you say that?" the commissar protests feebly. "Let's just say that ever since childhood I have loved beauty and heroism... and service to the people."

Heroism and service to the people—these are words best avoided. It is in the name of service to the people that the Bat has been stripped. Art and beauty are surer ground.

"No, no, don't deny it! I sense in you a profoundly artistic nature. You love the arts. You are a true patron of art; you do everything in your power to bring art to the people—into the thick of them, into their depths, into their heart of hearts. Your boots are truly remarkable. Only Torquato Tasso[7] could have worn boots like yours, and maybe not even him. You are a genius!"

That last word settles everything. I am given permission to take a flask of perfume and two evening dresses across the frontier—as tools of my trade.

In the evening Gooskin took the commissar to see the operetta, *Catherine the Great*. Lolo and I had written the libretto together.[8]

The commissar softened still more, gave free rein to his feelings and ordered Gooskin to inform me that "art is indeed of material significance" and that I could take with me whatever I needed: he would say nothing. He would be as quiet "as a fish against a brick wall."

I never saw the commissar again.

My last days in Moscow pass in a senseless whirl.

Bella Kaza-Roza, a former chanteuse from the Ancient Theatre, arrives from Petersburg.[9] These last days have brought out a peculiar talent in her: She always knows who needs what and who possesses what.

In she comes, a distant look in her dark rapt eyes, and says, "In the Krivo-Arbat Lane, in the fabric store on the corner, they've still got a yard and a half of batiste. You absolutely must go and buy it."

"But I don't need any batiste."

"Yes, you do. When you come back in a month's time, there won't be a scrap to be found anywhere."

Another time she rushes in, out of breath, and says, "You must make yourself a velvet dress this very minute!"

"?"

"You know very well that you simply can't go on without one. The owner of the hardware store on the corner is selling a length of curtain. She's only just taken it down. Fresh as can be—nails and all. It'll make a wonderful evening dress. You simply can't do without it. And you'll never get a chance like this again!"

The look on her face is serious, almost tragic.

I hate the word "never." Were someone to tell me that I'll never again get a headache, even that would probably scare me.

I do as I'm told. I buy the luxurious scrap of cloth with the seven nails.

Those last days were strange indeed.

At night we hurried past the dark houses, down streets where people were strangled and robbed. We hurried to listen to *Silva*[10] or else to sit in down-at-heel cafés packed with people in shabby coats that stank of wet dog. There we listened to young poets reading—or rather howling—their own and one another's work; they sounded like hungry wolves. There was quite a vogue for these poets, and even the haughty Bryusov would sometimes deign to introduce one of their "Evenings of Eros."[11]

Everyone wanted company, to be in the presence of other people.

To be alone and at home was frightening.

We had to know what was going on; we needed to keep hearing news of one another. Sometimes someone would disappear and then it would be almost impossible to find out what had happened to them. Had they gone to Kiev? Or to the place from which there was no return?

It was as if we were living in the tale about Zmey Gorynych, the dragon that required a yearly tribute of twelve fair maidens and twelve young men.[12] One might well wonder how the people in this tale could have carried on, how they could have lived with the knowledge that a dragon would soon be devouring the finest of their children. During those last days in Moscow, however, we realized that they too had probably been rushing from one little theatre to another or hurrying to buy themselves something from which to make a coat or a dress. There is nowhere a human being cannot live. With my own eyes I have seen sailors taking a man out onto the ice in order to shoot him—and I have seen the condemned man hopping over puddles to keep his feet dry and turning up his collar to shield his chest from the wind. Those few steps were the last steps he would ever take, and instinctively he wanted to make them as comfortable as possible.

We were no different. We bought ourselves some "last scraps" of fabric. We listened for the last time to the last operetta and the last exquisitely erotic verses. What did it matter whether the verses were good or terrible? All that mattered was not to know, not to be aware—we had to forget that we were being led onto the ice.

News came from Petersburg that the Cheka[13] had arrested a well-known actress for reading my short stories in public. She was ordered to read one of the stories again, before three dread judges. You can imagine what fun it was for her to stand between guards with bayonets and declaim my comic monologue. And then—miracle of miracles!—after her first few trembling sentences, the face of one of the judges dissolved into a smile.

"I heard this story one evening at comrade Lenin's. It's entirely apolitical."

Reassured by this, the judges asked the suspect—who was, of course, also greatly reassured—to continue her reading, "by way of revolutionary entertainment."

Still, all in all, it probably wasn't such a bad idea to be going away, even if only for a month. For a change of climate.

By now Gooskin was proving his worth more than ever. Perhaps more from nerves than from any real need. One morning, for some reason, he had been over to see Averchenko.

"It was awful," he told me, waving his hands in the air. "At ten o'clock this morning I hurried over to see Averchenko—and what did I find? He was snoring—snoring cats and dogs! He's going to miss the train!"

"But I thought we weren't leaving for another five days."

"The train leaves at ten o'clock. If he sleeps like that today, then what's to stop him from sleeping like that a week from now? He'll be sleeping like that his whole life. He'll be sleeping—and we'll be waiting. Wonderful!"

Gooskin dashed about. He got more and more agitated. He moved faster and faster. He flapped his hands in the air, like a broken belt drive. But had it not been for his frenzied energy, who knows how my life would have turned out? Wherever you are, O my pseudonymous Gooskin, I send you my greetings!

2

The day for our departure was constantly being postponed. First, there would be delays with someone's travel permit. Then it would turn out that our hope of hopes, our Nose-in-Boots, had yet to return to his frontier post.

My own preparations were more or less complete. My trunk was now full. Another trunk, in which I had packed a number of old Russian shawls (the latest of my crazes), had been stowed away in Lolo's apartment.

But what if the authorities suddenly declared some "Week of Poverty"—or, for that matter, a "Week of Elegance"—and all these shawls were confiscated?

In the event of trouble, I asked Lolo to state that the trunk was of proletarian origin, that it belonged to Fedosya, his former cook. And to make all this more convincing and to ensure that the trunk was treated with proper respect, I put a portrait of Lenin inside it, with the inscription, "Darling Fedosya, whose memory I shall treasure with the deepest affection. Your loving Vova."[14]

Not even these measures proved of any help.

Those last Moscow days passed by in a turbid whirl. People appeared out of the mist, spun around and faded from sight;

then new people appeared. It was like standing on a riverbank in the spring twilight and watching great blocks of ice float past: On one block is something that could be either a cart packed with straw or a Ukrainian peasant hut; on another block are scorched logs and something that looks like a wolf. Everything spins around a few times and then the current sweeps it away forever. And never will you learn what it really was.

Various engineers, doctors, and journalists made brief appearances. Now and then some actress or other would show up.

A landowner I knew passed through on his way from Petersburg to his estate in Kazan. From Kazan he wrote that the peasants had looted his home and that he had been doing the rounds of their huts buying back his paintings and books. In one hut he had seen a miracle: a portrait of me painted by Schleifer,[15] hanging in the icon corner next to Saint Nicholas the Miracle Worker. The woman who had been allotted this portrait had taken it into her head that I was a holy martyr.

Lydia Yavorskaya was cast up on our shores.[16] She arrived unexpectedly, as elegant as ever, and talked about how we must all join forces and organize something. Just what, I never understood. She was accompanied by some kind of boy scout in shorts, whom she referred to rather solemnly as "M'sieur Sobolev." The block of ice spun around, and they floated away into the mist.

Mironova made a no less sudden appearance. She performed a few pieces at a little theatre on the outskirts of town and disappeared too.

Then a woman I liked very much, an actress from some provincial town, floated into our circle. Someone stole her

41

diamonds, and she turned for help to a criminal investigations commissar. This commissar turned out to be someone kind and good-natured. He did what he could to help and then, learning that she would be spending the evening with a group of writers, asked her to take him along with her. He adored literature but had never set eyes on a living writer; nothing could make him happier than to glimpse us in the flesh. The actress asked our permission, then brought him along. Never in my life have I seen someone so tall. His voice was like a great bell high above us, but the words this bell sounded were surprisingly sentimental: well-known children's verses, and declarations that until this moment his life had been only a matter of mind—or "moind," as he put it—but that now his heart had awoken.

He spent day after day pursuing criminals and bandits. He'd set up what he called a museum of crime, and he showed us his collection of complex instruments for sawing through locks, snapping off door chains, and slicing silently through iron bolts. He showed us the small tool kits with which a professional burglar goes out to work. Each little case contained a small flashlight, along with a bite to eat and a small bottle of eau de cologne. I was surprised by the eau de cologne.

"Who'd have thought it? Such refinement. What makes them want to douse themselves with eau de cologne when they're in such danger, when every moment is precious?"

His explanation was simple enough. The eau de cologne was a substitute for vodka, which was no longer obtainable.

After catching a few of his bandits, the commissar would join our little circle in the evening. He would show deep feelings; he would express astonishment that we really were the people we said we were. And at the end of the evening he would walk me home. There was something rather frightening about walking at night, down the bleak streets, beside this extraordinarily tall figure. All around us were alarming rustles, stealthy footsteps, screams, sometimes shots. Yet none of these was as frightening as the giant who was my guard.

Sometimes the telephone would ring late in the evening. It was our guardian angel whose heart had awoken. He was phoning to check that everything was all right with us.

After we'd recovered from the shock of the sudden ringing, we would recite:

> Nightmare demons
> stalk the sinful;
> guardian angels
> talk to children.[17]

Our guardian angel kept an eye on us until the very moment of our departure. He took us to the railway station and guarded our luggage, which was clearly an object of interest to the Cheka officers there.

All of us who were leaving felt a great deal of sorrow. There was a sorrow we all shared, and then we each had our own individual sorrow. Sorrow lay somewhere behind our eyes, deep behind our pupils. There it glimmered—like the skull and crossbones on the forage caps of the Prussian Death's Head Hussars. But this was not something we spoke about.

I remember the delicate profile of a young harpist. About three months after we left, she was betrayed and executed. I remember my distress over my young friend Leonid Kannegisser. A few days before the assassination of Uritsky,[18] he'd heard that I was in Petersburg. He telephoned me and said that he very much wanted to see me—but only on neutral territory.

"Why not in my apartment?"

"I'll explain when we meet."

We agreed to meet for a meal at the home of some mutual friends.

When we met, Kannegisser said, "People are following me. I don't want to lead them to your apartment."

I put this down to adolescent posturing. It was a time when many young people were assuming mysterious airs and pronouncing enigmatic phrases. I thanked him and enquired no further.

He was very melancholy that evening, rather silent.

We recall all too often how, when we last saw some friend of ours, they had sad eyes and pale lips. And we always know, once it is too late, what we ought to have done back then, how we should have taken our friend by the hand and led them away from the shadow of darkness. But there is a mysterious law that does not allow us to disrupt the appointed order, the decreed rhythm. And this is in no way mere egotism or indifference— sometimes it would be easier to stop than to walk on by. The author of *The Life of Leonid Kannegisser* required us to walk on by, not to disrupt the decreed rhythm of his tragic novel. As if in a dream: You can see everything, you can feel everything, you almost know everything, but you're unable to stop. You're compelled to walk on.

Yes, we writers—in the words of a contemporary French colleague—are "imitators of God," imitators of his creative work.
We create worlds and people and we determine their fates, often
cruel and unjust. Why we act one way and not some other way,
we don't know. We simply have no choice.

I remember a young actress approaching me during a
rehearsal of one of my plays and saying timidly, "May I ask you
something? You won't get angry?"

"You may. I won't get angry."

"Why did that poor boy in your play have to be fired? Why
do you have to be so cruel? Couldn't you at least have found
him some other job? And then in another play there's a poor
travelling salesman who ends up with egg on his face. *Why*? It's
horrible for the poor man. Surely there's some way you can put
these things right?"

"I don't know… I can't… It isn't me who decides."

But her lips were trembling, and she was pleading so pitifully
and so touchingly that I promised to write a separate fairy tale in
which I would bring together all those I had injured in my plays
and stories and somehow compensate them for their suffering.

"Wonderful!" said the actress. "That will be paradise!"

And she kissed me.

"But there's a problem," I interrupted. "I'm afraid that this
little paradise of ours won't really comfort anyone at all. No one
will believe us. They'll know we've just made it up."[19]

The day comes. Our train is leaving this morning.

Since the night before, Gooskin has been rushing from me
to Averchenko, from Averchenko to his impresario, and from

his impresario to the actresses. He keeps going into the wrong apartments and phoning the wrong numbers. At seven o'clock he bursts in on me, panting, covered in sweat, like an overheated horse. He looks at me, then spreads his hands despairingly in the air.

"Of course! Wonderful! Late for the station!"

"Surely not! What's the time?"

"Seven o'clock, almost ten o'clock. The train leaves at ten. That's it—it's all over now."

Someone gives Gooskin a lump of sugar. Gnawing on it like a parrot, he calms down a little.

A horn sounds in the street below, from the motorcar sent by our guardian angel.

It's a wonderful autumn morning. Unforgettable. Up above— pale blue, and golden cupolas. Down on the earth—grey and heavy, and eyes glazed over in deep sorrow. Some Red Army soldiers herding along a group of prisoners. A tall old man in a beaver hat carrying a bundle wrapped in a woman's red calico kerchief. An old lady in a soldier's greatcoat looking at us through a turquoise lorgnette. A line by a dairy kiosk with a pair of boots displayed in the window.

"Goodbye, Moscow, dearest Moscow! It's not for long. Just a month. I'll be back in a month. In one month. And then… No, best not to think."

"When you're walking a tightrope," an acrobat once told me, "you must never imagine that you might fall. On the contrary. You have to believe that everything will work out—and you must hum some little song to yourself."

A jolly little tune from *Silva* is going round and round in my head. The words are stunningly inane:

Cupid can't be canned,
Cupid can't be kind.
Stupid Cupid turns a man
Blinder than blind.

What goose could have composed a jingle like this?

Gooskin is waiting outside the main entrance to the station, along with the commissar whose heart had awoken.

"Moscow, dearest Moscow, farewell! See you in a month!"

That was ten years ago.

3

Our journey got off to a fairly smooth start.

We were in a second-class carriage, each with a seat of our own. We were sitting the way passengers are generally meant to sit—no one was curled up underneath the seats or lying up above in the luggage rack.

My impresario, the pseudonymous Gooskin, became very agitated: Why was the train taking so long to leave? And then, when it finally did leave, he said it was ahead of schedule.

"And that's a bad omen. Goodness knows what will happen now!"

The moment Gooskin climbed into the carriage, his appearance changed bizarrely. Anyone would have thought he had been travelling for ten days—and in the most appalling conditions. His shoes were unlaced, his collar unbuttoned, and there was a round green spot beneath his Adam's apple—evidently from a copper stud. Strangest of all, his cheeks were covered in stubble—as if he had been three or four days without shaving.

Along with our own group, there were three other ladies in the compartment. They were talking very quietly, sometimes even in a whisper, about matters all too close to our immediate concerns: who had managed to smuggle their money and diamonds abroad, and how.

"Have you heard? The Prokins managed to get away with their entire fortune. They used their old grandmother as a mule."

"But how come the grandmother didn't get searched?"

"How can you ask? She's so unpleasant. Who would dare?"

"As for the Korkins, they were really smart. And all on the spur of the moment! Madame Korkina, who'd already been searched, was standing to one side. And then, all of a sudden—'Ow! Ow!'—she twists her ankle. She can't walk, she can't even take a single step. Her husband, who hasn't been searched yet, says to a Red Army soldier, 'Please pass her my stick. She needs it.' The soldier gives her the stick. And it's the stick they've hollowed out and stuffed with diamonds. How do you like that?"

"The Bulkins have a teapot with a false bottom."

"Fanichka took a huge diamond out of the country—you'll never believe this—by stuffing it up her own nose."

"All very well for her—she's got a fifty-carat nose. But we aren't all as lucky as her."

Then they told the tragic tale of how a certain Madame Fook cleverly hid a diamond in an egg. She made a small hole in the shell of a raw egg, put the diamond inside, and then hard-boiled the egg. Who could find her diamond now? So she puts the egg into her food basket and sits there calm as can be, smiling away. Along come some Red Army soldiers. They search the luggage. And then one of them grabs that very egg, peels it and wolfs it down before Madame Fook's very eyes. The poor woman travelled no further. She got off at that station and trailed around after that wretched Red Army soldier for three days on end, not once letting him out of her sight, as if he were a little child.

"And then?"

"What do you think? Nothing! She went back home empty-handed."

Then they started talking about all sorts of cunning ploys—things they did to trap spies during the war.

"They grew so crafty, those spies! Just imagine: They started drawing plans of fortresses on their backs and then colouring them over. Well, military intelligence aren't stupid either, they caught on to this pretty quick. They started washing the backs of any suspicious characters. Of course, there were unfortunate errors. Back home in Grodno they caught this gentleman—he was dark-haired and suspicious as they come, but after a good wash he turned out to be the most honest of blondes. Military intelligence was most apologetic…"

Peaceful discussion of these alarming topics made our journey both entertaining and informative, but we hadn't even been going three hours when the train stopped and everyone was ordered to disembark.

We get off the train, drag our luggage out, stand on the platform for about two hours, and then get onto a different train. This train is third class only and packed full. Some malicious-looking peasant women with pale eyes are sitting opposite us. They clearly don't like the look of us.

"Here they be on our train," says a woman with a pockmarked

face and a wart. "Here they be on our train, but where and why they're going, they haven't a clue."

"Like dogs off a chain," agrees the other one. She has a grimy headscarf and is using the corners of it, rather gracefully, to wipe her duck-like nose.

What irritates them most of all is a Pekinese dog—a tiny, silken ball lying on the lap of the older of our two actresses.

"A dog on a train! Look at her—a hat on her head and here she be on a train with a dog!"

"Should've left it at home. Nowhere for folks to sit and here she be with this hound of hers!"

"But she's not in your way," says the actress, her voice quivering as she defends her hound. "Anyway, it's not as though *you'd* be sitting here on my lap!"

"No, we'd not be travellin' around with dogs," the women continue relentlessly.

"I can't leave her at home on her own. She's delicate. She needs more care than a little child."

"Huh?"

"What d'ye mean by that then?" shouts the pockmarked one, leaping to her feet in fury. "Here, listen to this! This one here with the hat says our children's worse than dogs! We're not standing for this, are we?"

"Huh? Us? We be dogs and she ain't?"

Then this discussion—and there's no knowing where it might have led—is interrupted by a wild shriek. The shriek comes from the space at the end of the carriage. Everyone jumps up and rushes to investigate. The pockmarked woman goes as well, and, when she returns, she tells us in the most amiable of tones that a thief had been caught and that they'd been about to "drop 'im under the car"—only the thief had beaten them to it. He'd jumped off the moving train.

"Charming characters!" says Averchenko. "Try to ignore them. Think about something cheerful."

I do as he says. Tonight, the lights will be switched on at the theatre, people will gather and sit in their seats and will listen to:

> Cupid can't be canned,
> Cupid can't be kind.
> Stupid Cupid turns a man
> Blinder than blind.

Oh why do I have to remember this? This idiotic refrain—spinning round and round in my poor head!

The women carry on chatting happily about how jolly it would have been to throw the thief under the wheels and about how he must be lying on the ground now with a smashed head.

"Lynch every one of 'em! Yes, him and every one of his sort. Poke out their eyes, rip out their tongues, cut off their ears, and then tie a stone round their necks and—into the water with 'em!"

"Back in our village we'd drag 'em under the ice on a rope, from ice-'ole to ice-'ole…"

"Oftentimes they was burned on a fire."

Thank God they were diverted by the thief. Otherwise who knows what they'd have done to us?

> Cupid can't be canned,
> Cupid can't be kind.

"How awful!" I say to Averchenko.

"Sh!"

"I don't mean them," I continue. "I have torments of my own, I can't get *Silva* out of my head."

I shall think instead about how we might have been roasted, maybe that will do the trick. First I think about the pockmarked woman sitting opposite me. She'd be hard at it! She's thorough. She'd be blowing on the kindling. And Gooskin? He'd be shouting, "Please excuse me, but we have a legally binding contract! You are preventing her from fulfilling her part of our agreement, and you are bankrupting me as an impresario! First she must pay me a forfeit!"

The "stupid cupid" gradually withdraws. It fades and dies away.

The train pulls into a station. Women with bundles start bustling about. The thump of soldiers' boots. Bags, sacks, and baskets obscure the light of day. And then, on the other side of the glass, I see Gooskin. His face is twisted in terror. For the past few hours he's been in a different car. What on earth has happened to him?

He looks ghastly. White all over, gasping for air.

"Get out quick! We must take a different route. This route's out of the question. I'll explain later."

Well then, so be it. We get off the train. I'm rather slow, the last one out. When I finally jump down onto the platform, a ragged beggar boy comes up to me and says very clearly, "Stupid Cupid can't be canned. Fifty kopeks, please!"

"Wha-at?"

"Fifty kopeks! Stupid Cupid."

It's all over. I've gone mad. I'm hearing things. My weak nerves must have been incapable of withstanding the combination of *Silva* and the people's wrath.

I look around for our group; I need moral support. Averchenko is studying his gloves with extraordinary attentiveness and doesn't respond to my mute appeal. I slip the boy fifty kopeks. I still don't understand, but I have my suspicions.

"Admit it!" I say to Averchenko.

He gives an embarrassed laugh.

"While you were still in the carriage," he says, "I asked the boy if he wanted to earn a little money. I said a passenger in a little red hat was about to get off the train. 'You go up to her,' I told him, 'and say, "Stupid Cupid can't be canned!" She gives fifty kopeks to everyone who says that to her.' Well, he seems like a bright boy!"

Gooskin, who's been busying himself with our luggage, walks over. He is drenched in sweat.

"Wonderful!" he says in a ghastly whisper. "That bandit has gone and got himself shot!"

"What bandit?"

"That commissar of yours! What don't you understand? Well? He's been executed for robbery and bribe-taking. We can't cross the border here. We'll be fleeced—and then slaughtered to boot. We must cross somewhere else."

All right then, a different border crossing it is. About two hours later we get onto another train and set off in another direction.

We arrived at the border station in the evening. It was cold. We wanted to go to bed. But we were anxious: What did this place have in store for us? When would they let us through and how would we continue our journey?

Gooskin and Averchenko's impresario went off into the station building to assess the situation and conduct negotiations, giving us strict instructions to stay where we were. The omens did not bode well.

The platform was empty. Occasionally a dark figure would appear—maybe a guard, maybe a peasant woman in a soldier's greatcoat. This figure would cast a suspicious look in our direction, then disappear again. We waited for a long time. Finally, Gooskin emerged—escorted by no fewer than four men.

One of the four came rushing up to us. I shall never forget him: a thin, dark little man with a crooked nose, wearing a student's cap and a huge, magnificent beaver coat that trailed behind him like a royal mantle in some throne-room portrait. The coat was brand new, evidently only just ripped off somebody's back.

The little man ran up to us. With what seemed like a habitual movement he hitched up his trousers with his left hand, then raised his right hand high in the air with inspired rapture, and exclaimed, "Are you Teffi? Are you Averchenko? Bravo, bravo, and bravo! Here I am at your service, the commissar of arts for this shtetl,[20] here at your service! Our cultural needs here are immense. You, our dear guests, will stay with us and help me to organize a series of cultural evenings—you will give readings and the local proletariat will act out your plays, under your supervision."

The actress with the little dog gave a quiet gasp and sank down onto the platform. I looked around me. Dusk. A tiny station building with a small garden. Beyond it—miserable little houses, a boarded-up food stall, mud, a bare willow and a crow. And this Robespierre.[21]

"We would, of course, love to," Averchenko said calmly, "but unfortunately we have booked a theatre in Kiev for our performances, and we really do have to hurry."

"Out of the question!" cried Robespierre. Abruptly lowering his voice, he added, "You will never be allowed across the border unless I put in a special request on your behalf. And what might induce me to make such a request? The fact that you have responded to the needs of our proletariat. Then I will even be able to arrange for your luggage to be let through!"[22]

At this point Gooskin suddenly darted forward and said, "Mister commissar! Of course they agree. Even though I'm losing enormous capital from this delay, I shall personally undertake to persuade them, although I could see at once that they are already overjoyed at the prospect of serving our dear proletariat. But you must understand, Mister commissar—only one evening. But what an evening it will be! Yes, an evening that'll have you licking every one of your fingers in delight! Believe me! So tomorrow the public performance—and the following morning we go on our way. Well, that's all settled then—everyone's happy. But where are we to put our guests for the night?"

"You stay here. We'll sort everything out right away," cried Robespierre and rushed off, his beaver coat brushing away his footprints. He was followed by the other three figures, evidently his entourage.

"Now we're in real trouble," said Gooskin. "Slap into the hornet's nest. Executions every day. Only three days ago a general was burnt alive. And they make off with every last piece of luggage. We must get out of here fast."

"Maybe we'll have to go back to Moscow."

"Shush!" hissed Gooskin, before saying with frightening emphasis, "You think they're going to let you go back to Moscow so you can tell everyone there how you've been robbed? A likely story!"

Averchenko's impresario came back, his head pulled down into his neck, constantly looking around him and keeping as close as he could to the wall.

"Where've you been?"

"Carrying out a little reconnaissance. It's going to be difficult. There's no space anywhere. The shtetl is crammed with people."

I looked around in surprise. These words did not tally with the emptiness of the streets, the silence, and the deep-blue twilight, against which the solitary streetlamp made no impression.

"But where *are* all the people? And what are they doing here?"

"What do you think? They're stuck here. They're having to stay here for two or three weeks. They're not allowed to go on and they're not allowed to go back. The things I've heard! But not now... Shush!"

Like a bird with outstretched wings, our Robespierre—followed by his entourage—was flying down the platform in his beaver coat.

"Accommodation has been found for you. Two rooms. Evictions are being effected as we speak. The rooms were jam-packed. Children too. Everyone howling and wailing!

But I have a warrant. I am requisitioning for the needs of the proletariat."

Once again he hitched up his trousers with his left hand and stretched out his right hand, forward and up, as if pointing the way to distant stars.

"You know what?" I said. "This really isn't what we want. Can you please not evict them? We just can't take their rooms from them like this."

"I agree," said Averchenko. "You said they've got children there. It's not right."

Gooskin immediately gave a cheerful shrug.

"See what these artists of ours are like! There's nothing to be done about it. But don't worry—we'll find somewhere to put ourselves. Yes, it's just the way they are."

While cheerfully inviting Robespierre and the rest of our station audience to marvel at our eccentricity, he did, of course, share our feelings.

Robespierre didn't know what to do. And then, unexpectedly, someone else stepped forward. Until then he had been keeping modestly out of sight behind the other members of the entourage.

"I c-can of-offer my roo-oo…"

"What?"

"Roo-rooms."

Who was this man? But then, what did it matter?

We were led somewhere behind the station building to a small house that looked as if it had been built for some government employee. The stutterer turned out to be the son-in-law of someone who had once worked on the railway.

Robespierre was triumphant.

"There you are, I have provided you with accommodation. Get yourselves settled in, and I'll drop by in the evening."

The stutterer mumbled something and bowed.

We settled in.

The actresses and I were to share one room. The stutterer took Averchenko into his own room and the two pseudonyms were tucked away into some kind of storeroom.

The house was very quiet. There was a pale and exhausted-looking elderly woman who wandered about as if with her eyes shut. We could hear someone else moving about in the kitchen, but we never saw them. Very likely it was the stutterer's wife.

We were given some tea.

"We could get some h-h-am," the stutterer whispered, "while it's still light."

"No, it's already dark," the old woman murmured in response—and closed her eyes.

"Ma-mama. What if I go without a lantern? Just with matches."

"All right, if you're not frightened."

The stutterer shivered and stayed put. What did all this mean? Why did they only eat ham during the day? I didn't like to ask. It seemed best not to ask anything at all. Our hosts took fright at the simplest of questions and never gave a direct answer. And when one of the actresses asked the old woman if her husband was here, she looked horrified, raised a trembling hand, quietly shook a finger at her and stared out through the window into the blackness beyond.

We sat there, silent and tense. It was Gooskin who saved the day. After loud huffing and puffing he began, in a loud voice, saying some remarkable things:

"I can see that you've had rain here. It's wet outside. When there's rain, it always gets wet outside. When it rains in Odessa, it's Odessa that gets wet. It's never the case that it rains in Odessa but it gets wet in Nikolaev. Hah! Yes, where it rains, that's where it gets wet. And when there's no rain, then God only knows how dry it can get. And who likes rain, I ask you. Nobody does, and that's God's truth. Well, why would I lie? Hah!"

Gooskin showed true genius. He spoke simply and with animation. And so, when the door burst open and Robespierre flew in, now with an entourage of six, what he saw was a group of friends sitting cosily round a table, drinking tea and listening to an engaging storyteller.

"Magnificent!" Robespierre exclaimed. He hitched up his trousers with his left hand and, without taking off his fur coat, joined us at the table. His entourage squeezed in too.

"Magnificent! We start at eight. Capacity of the barrack—one hundred and fifty. Décor—pine cones. Posters to be posted in the morning. And now we can have a little talk about art. Who's most important—the director or the chorus?"

This floored nearly all of us but not our young actress. Like a warhorse at the sound of the bugle, she took off and began talking unstoppably, managing the most remarkable leaps and turns. We heard flashes of Meyerhold and his triangles of forces, of Yevreinov's *Theatre for Itself*, of Commedia dell'Arte, of actor-creators, of the slogan "Away with the Footlights!", of theatre as collective ritual and goodness knows what else.[23]

Robespierre was in seventh heaven.

"This meets our needs exactly! You will stay here with us and give us some lectures on art. Yes, that's settled."

The poor girl turned pale and looked at us in confusion.

"I have a contract... I can in one month... I'll come back here... I promise you!"

But now it was Robespierre's turn. He had his own reper-toire—an entire play in "beyonsense language."[24] The most complete possible development of a gesture. The audience to compose plays in its own right, then act them out on the spot. Actors to play the part of the audience, which requires greater talent than any ordinary, routine acting.

Everything was going smoothly. The only disruption to our peaceful scene of cultured comfort came from the little dog, which evidently sensed something sinister about Robespierre. Tiny as a wool mitten, it growled at him with the fury of a tiger, bared its pearly little teeth and then, all of a sudden, threw back its head and began to howl like some common guard dog on a chain. And Robespierre, who was being transported into mysterious realms on the wings of art, for some reason took fright and broke off in mid-sentence.

The actress took her little dog away.

For a minute, everyone fell silent. And then from somewhere not far away, over by the railway embankment, came an almost inhuman cry, like the cry of a goat, full of animal horror and despair. It was followed by three dry, even shots, distinct and businesslike.

"Did you hear?" I asked. "Whatever was that?"

But nobody answered me. It seemed no one had heard.

The pale hostess sat motionless, her eyes closed. The host continued to say nothing. His jaw was trembling convulsively, as if he even thought with a stutter. Then Robespierre started talking excitedly, in a much louder voice than before, about the evening we had been planning. Clearly he *had* heard something.

The entourage did not join in; they just went on smoking silently. One of them, a snub-nosed lad in a ragged brown soldier's tunic, pulled out a massive gold cigarette case with an embossed monogram. Out toward it stretched someone's calloused paw, with broken nails. On this paw was a beautiful cabochon ruby, shining darkly from its deep setting in a massive antique ring. Our guests appeared to be unusual people.

The young actress walked pensively around the table and stood herself against the wall. I felt her calling me with her eyes, but I didn't get up. She was looking at Robespierre's back, her lips twitching nervously.

"Olyonushka," I said, "it's time we went to bed. In the morning we'll be rehearsing."

We nodded a general goodnight and went to our room. Our quiet hostess followed us with a candle.

"Put the light out," she whispered. "You'll have to undress in the dark. And don't, for the love of God, pull down the blind."

We quickly got ready for bed. Our hostess blew out the candle.

"And remember about the blind. For the love of God."

She left the room.

I felt warm breathing, close beside me. It was Olyonushka.

"There's a hole in the back of that wonderful coat of his," she whispered. "And there's something dark all around the hole… something terrible."

"Go to sleep, Olyonushka. We're all of us tired and on edge."

The little dog was fretting all night, growling and whimpering. And at dawn Olyonushka said in her sleep, in a loud, spine-chilling voice, "I know why the dog's howling. There's a bullet hole in that man's coat, and there's dried blood all around it."

My heart was pounding so fast I felt sick. I'd known this all along, I realized, even though I'd barely glanced at the coat.

We woke up late. A cold grey day. Rain. Outside the window—sheds and barns. Further on—the embankment. All completely deserted. Not a soul to be seen.

Our hostess brought us tea, bread, and ham, then said in a whisper, "My son-in-law slipped out at dawn. We've hidden the ham in the shed. If you go outside at night with a lantern, they report you. And it's no better during the day. One glimpse of you—and along they come. It's searches day in and day out."

She was more talkative now. But her face was still saying as little as ever. It was like stone, as if she feared it might say more than she wanted it to.

Gooskin was knocking on the door.

"Are you nearly ready? Our… young friends have been round twice."

Our hostess left. I half-opened the door and motioned Gooskin in.

"Gooskin, tell me, is everything all right? Will we be allowed to leave this town?" I asked in a whisper.

"Smile, for heaven's sake, smile!" Gooskin whispered, stretching his mouth into a hideous grimace, like Victor Hugo's *L'homme qui rit*. "Smile when you speak. Someone may, God forbid, be watching you. They've promised to let us leave and to provide us with an escort. There's a twenty-five-mile border zone. It starts here. And it's in this zone that people get robbed."

"Who by?"

"Who do you think? By *them*, of course. But if we can get ourselves an official escort, from the headquarters of this hornet's nest, no one will dare to rob us. But there's one thing I *will* say—we must leave tomorrow. Otherwise, I swear to God, I shall be astonished if ever the day comes when I see my dear Mama."

This was all rather complicated, and certainly not comforting.

"You must stay at home today. Don't go out anywhere. Say you're tired and rehearsing. Everyone is rehearsing and everyone is tired."

"You don't happen to know where the owner of this house is, do you?"

"I don't know anything for sure. He may have been executed, or he may have made off somewhere, or he may be sitting right here beneath our feet. Because why else would they be this scared? The doors and windows are open all day and all night. Why don't they dare close them? Why must they keep proving that they've got nothing to hide? But none of this has anything to do with us. Why are we talking about it? Is someone going to pay us for all our talking? Or grant us some kind of honorary citizenship? Things have been going on here that—well, heaven forbid that they should happen to us! What made that young fellow start stuttering? He's been stuttering for weeks on end.

If we're not going to end up the same, we'd better get out of here—with our trunks and a proper escort."

We heard a chair move in the dining room.

"Quick, rehearsal time!" shouted Gooskin, backing out of the room. "Come on, sleepy feet, get up now! Heavens, it's eleven o'clock and they're still snoring cats and dogs!"

Olyonushka and I stayed in all day, saying we were tired. Averchenko, his impresario, and the actress with the little dog took on the task of making conversation with the shtetl's apostles of political and cultural enlightenment. They even went out for a walk with them.

"Most interesting!" Averchenko said on his return. "You see that smashed-up shed? Apparently, a couple of months ago the Bolsheviks were having a hard time of it here, and some chief commissar of theirs needed to get out fast. He jumped up onto a locomotive and ordered a railwayman to take him away. But the railwayman just rammed the locomotive into the wall of the depot—under full steam. The Bolshevik was boiled alive."

"And the railwayman?"

"Never found."

"So… could this be our missing host?"

4

Overcast and wet, the day dragged on forever.

We huddled together in our "ladies' room," where Averchenko had joined us. As if by unspoken agreement, nobody said anything about our present concerns. We reminisced about our last days in Moscow and about the people with whom we had spent those last days. Not a word about either our present or our future.

How, we wondered, was our lofty protector doing? Was our exalted guardian still living with an awoken heart or was his life once again only a matter of *moind*?

I remembered how, on the eve of our departure, I had gone to say goodbye to a former baroness and found her stooping to a rather lowly task—cleaning the floor. Lanky and sallow, with the face of a thoroughbred horse, she was squatting down and examining the floorboards with distaste through a turquoise lorgnette. Between two fingers of her other hand she gingerly held a scrap of wet lace, using it to flick water about.

"I'll mop it up later, when my Valenciennes has dried out."

We also reminisced about the bread of our last Moscow days. One kind, made out of sawdust, had crumbled like sand;

the other kind, made out of clay, had been bitter, greenish and always damp...

Averchenko glanced at his watch.

"Well, it's already five—not long till our evening."

"I think someone just tapped on the window," said Olyonushka, on her guard.

It was Gooskin.

"Madame Teffi, Monsieur Averchenko!" he shouted loudly. "You must absolutely come out and stretch your legs a bit. To be in good voice, I swear you must have a clear head before the start of the evening."

"But it's raining!"

"Only a little drizzle. You absolutely must come out, I'm telling you."

"Maybe there's something he needs to say to us," I whispered to Averchenko. "You go first and see whether or not he's on his own. If Robespierre's there too, I'm not going. I just can't."

What I dreaded more than anything was having to shake this man's hand. I could answer his questions and even meet his eye, but I knew that I couldn't bring myself to touch him. My aversion to this creature was so intense, so beyond my control that I couldn't answer for myself. I couldn't be sure that I wouldn't scream or make a scene or do something irreparable, something that would cost me dear, something our whole group would have to pay for. I knew that physical contact with this reptile was more than I could bear.

Averchenko appeared at the window and beckoned me out.

"Don't go to the right," our hostess whispered to me in the hall, while pretending to look for my galoshes.

"Let's keep to the middle of the street," whispered Gooskin. "We're just out for a walk, for a breath of fresh air."

And so we set off, with a measured, easy walk, glancing more and more frequently at the sky. Yes, we were just stretching our legs, getting a breath of fresh air.

"Don't look at me," muttered Gooskin. "Look at the rain."

He looked to either side. He looked behind him. A little calmer now, he said, "I've managed to find out a thing or two. The person who runs the show here is a woman, commissar H—" After pronouncing her name, which sounded like the bark of a dog, he continued, "She's just a young girl, a student, a telephone operator. Her word is the law. And she's deranged, a mad dog, as the phrase goes. A beast," he spat out in a tone of horror. "She does as she pleases. She conducts the searches, she sentences, and she shoots. There she sits on her porch, sentencing and shooting. What goes on at night by the embankment—that's someone else's doing, that's not her. She herself just sits on her porch—and she's without shame. I can't even speak about such things in front of a lady, no, I can't, I would rather speak only to Monsieur Averchenko. He's a writer, so he'll be able to put it in some poetic manner. Well, suffice it to say that the simplest Red Army soldier will sometimes go and find a quiet place to answer the call of nature. But she—she just answers the call there and then, with no embarrassment at all. It's horrible!"[25]

He looked from side to side.

"Let's walk the other way for a while."

"Is anything being said about us?" I asked.

"They're still promising to let us through, but commissar H hasn't had her say yet. A week ago there was a general, on his way to the south. All his papers were in order. She searched him and found real money—a *kerenka*[26]—sewn into his trouser stripes. So she says, 'Don't waste good bullets on him, just beat him with your rifle butts!' So they beat him. 'Still alive?' she asks. 'Hm,' they say, 'seems like it.' 'Douse him with kerosene and put a light to it.' So they doused him with kerosene and set him on fire. Don't look at me, look at the rain—we're just having a breath of fresh air. This morning they searched some industrialist's wife. She'd brought all kinds of stuff with her. Money. Furs. Diamonds. She was travelling with her steward. Her husband's in the Ukraine. She was on her way to join him. They took away everything she had. Literally. Left her only the clothes she stood up in. Some old woman gave her her own shawl. It's still not clear if they'll let her leave or… Heavens! We shouldn't have come this far! Turn around, quick!"

We had almost reached the railway embankment.

"Don't look! Don't look that way!" Gooskin said in a loud whisper. "Quick! Turn around quick! We haven't seen a thing. Just keep going, keep walking quietly along… After all, we're just out for a walk, stretching our legs. We've got a concert tonight, we just need to stretch our legs." A smile on his pale lips, he was doing his best to sound convincing.

I'd turned around at once and almost not seen anything. I hadn't even quite understood what I wasn't meant to be seeing. A figure in a soldier's greatcoat was bending down, picking up stones and throwing them at a pack of dogs that seemed to be gnawing at something. This was at the foot of the embankment, but some way away. One dog ran off on its own, dragging something along the ground. All this took only a moment… but it seemed to be dragging… probably I imagined it… dragging an arm… yes, some shreds of clothing and a hand, I could see the fingers. Only that's not possible. A dog can't gnaw off an arm…

I remember a cold clammy sweat on my temples and upper lip, and a wave of nausea that made me want to snarl like an animal.

"Come along now, come along!" said Averchenko, taking me by the arm.

"The hostess did warn me," I wanted to say, but I couldn't unclench my teeth. I couldn't speak.

"We'll get you some steaming hot tea!" Gooskin shouted. "That'll sort out the migraine in no time at all. There's nothing like something nice and cold to sort out a migraine. Ri-ight?"

When we reached the house, he whispered, "Not a word to our actresses, not a word. After all, we can all scream blue murder—but there still won't be time to put the world to rights. We've got to leave in the morning. Ri-ight?"

Gooskin's "Ri-ight?" was not a question and did not require an answer. It was his style, a rhetorical flourish. Though sometimes it seemed that there were two Gooskins—one would speak and the other, in a surprised tone, would then ask for confirmation.

The house was a picture of peace, with lamp and samovar. The older actress was giving her little dog some milk; Olyonushka was rehearsing a monologue for the performance to come.

What was I to read? What kind of audience would we have? Robespierre had said that they would be "enlightened spirits who had cast off the chains of the ages." Did this mean they had all done forced labour? They would, moreover, be "true judges and connoisseurs of art." What sort of art? Averchenko thought that Robespierre was thinking of the music of criminal slang.

But what was I to read?

"You must read poems of tender feeling," said Olyonushka. "Poetry ennobles."

"I think I'll read that little police-station sketch of mine," said Averchenko. "Not so very ennobling, but it'll strike more of a chord with the audience."

Olyonushka disagreed. On tour in the western provinces, she had read my poem about a beggar woman: "Around the country walked Fedosya, around the land the cripple wandered," and so on (a piece much loved by actors and recited by them ad nauseam).

"And what do you think happened?" Olyonushka went on. "In the interval, this old Tatar comes backstage to see me. He's quite a simple man, and with tears in his eyes he says, 'Dear Miss Actress please read about that cripple woman again.'[27] The poem's about Christ,"—Olyonushka now sounded more impassioned than ever— "so it's the last thing a non-Christian should have wanted to listen to, yet he was truly moved."

"Olyonushka, dear," I said, "I don't think your simple old man will be there tonight. Read something about an airplane—or roast mutton."

Suddenly, from the entrance room, came the sound of Robespierre's ecstatic voice.

I left the room.

★

Evening. Eight o'clock.

Time to set out to our much-vaunted show.

What to wear? A serious question. We think long and hard, then decide on skirts and blouses.

"If we wear anything at all smart, we'll get robbed," says the actress with the little dog. "Better not to let them even suspect that we own any decent dresses."

"You're right."

We have to go on foot, over fences, across the railway line, and past some sheds. It's raining. Where the mud's thin, it slurps. Where it's thicker, it squelches. In the darkness it seems almost to boil and bubble.

Olyonushka suddenly stops dead, squealing that her galoshes have been "swallowed up."

Gooskin is swinging a shaded lantern over the road, as if censing the rain and the night.

How bleak it is—this dark road to the "Club of Enlightenment and Culture."

"What would they want with anything better?" says an unfamiliar voice. "Nobody ever goes there anyway."

Someone is slurping and squelching right beside me. A stranger. We must watch our words.

But even if we manage to get there, how can we appear on stage with clumps of mud all over our legs?

Averchenko's impresario suggests we take off our shoes and stockings and walk barefoot. When we get to the club, we can ask for a bucket of water, wash our feet and put our shoes and stockings back on. Or the other way round—we can carry on through the mud in our shoes, ask for water when we get there, wash our feet and then appear barefoot on stage. Or best of all—wash our stockings at the club and put them on wet. Who's going to notice?

"So you know how to wash stockings, do you?" asks a grim voice.

Gooskin ploughs through the mud in his clodhoppers and goes on censing the rain with his lantern. I catch a glimpse of bare feet—Olyonushka's. But I can't bring myself to take off my shoes. Robespierre has walked down this road today. Most likely he will have spat somewhere.

"Is this yours?"

Someone hands me something round and black. What is this filth?

"It's your galosh... with your shoe inside it."

"Gooskin!" I cry. "I can't go any further. I'll die."

Gooskin walks briskly up to me.

"You can't? All right, I'll carry you, on my shoulders."

I hear this as a metaphor. He is telling me, I think, that I am ruining everything and that it is he who has to shoulder the burden.

"Gooskin, I really can't. Look at me. I'm standing on one leg like a heron. My shoe's all covered in mud. How can I put it on now? Robespierre has passed this way. He may have spat on the ground right here... Gooskin, save me!"

"That's why I'm telling you to get up on my shoulders. I shall carry you."

I still find this hard to take in.

"You're so huge, Gooskin. I'll never be able to climb up that high."

"Well, you can start by climbing onto that little fence. Or even… I can see a short little fellow over there, he's probably quite young. Why not use him?"

Was I to ride on Gooskin? Like Gogol's Vakula—the blacksmith who once rode on the devil?[28]

I had taken part in many performances. I had ridden to them in carriages, in motorcars, and in cabs, but never on my own impresario.

"Thank you, Gooskin. But you really are too huge. I'll start to feel dizzy up there."

Gooskin is nonplussed.

"Well then… do you want to wear my boots?"

At this, even without the advantage of height, I start to feel dizzy.

As happens in moments of supreme tension, my whole life flashes like forked lightning before my inner gaze: childhood… first love… war… third love… public acclaim… second revolution and—and to crown it all—Gooskin's unforgettable clodhoppers. In the back of beyond, in the mud, in the dead of night—what an inglorious end! Because there is no way, you must understand, that I can come out of all this alive…

"Thank you, Gooskin. You are a man of high moral standing. But I'll get there on my own two feet."

Which, of course, I do.

We stand around for a while in the cubbyhole that serves as a dressing room for the "Messrs and Mesdames Artistes." While someone wipes our shoes clean with newspaper, we peek at our audience through a crack in the wooden wall.

The barrack probably holds about a hundred people. On the right, supported by timbers, is some kind of gallery or hayloft.

In the front rows of the stalls are what one might call the top brass and aristocracy. All of them in skins (I am talking, of course, not about their own human skin but about the skin of calves and sheep—about the leather jackets and tall boots with gaiters so loved by our revolutionaries). Many are draped in bullet belts or are carrying guns. Some carry two revolvers as if, rather than being about to watch a performance, they are preparing for some military operation—a quick sortie, a dangerous reconnaissance, a skirmish with numerically superior forces.

"There, in the front row," whispers Gooskin. "Yes, look, her in the middle!"

I see a dumpy, short-legged girl with a sleepy-looking face, a face as flat as if she were squashing it against a pane of glass. An oilskin jacket with cracked folds. An oilskin hat.

"A beast!" Gooskin hisses in my ear, in the same tone of horror as before.

A beast? I can't see it. I don't understand. Her legs are too short to reach the ground. She's wide. Her flat face looks washed out, as if a sponge has been drawn across it. There's nothing to catch your attention. No eyes, no eyebrows, no mouth. All her features are smudged, somehow blurred together. Nothing you could call diabolical here. Just a boring lump. The sort of woman you see in line at dispensaries for the poor, or at domestic service employment bureaus. Her eyes look so sleepy. Why do I seem to recognize them? I feel I've seen them before. A long time ago... in our village... the peasant woman who washed the dishes. Yes, that's it, I remember now. When chickens had to be slaughtered, she always put herself forward. The old cook never had to ask her—she just went out into the yard and got on with it. Every time. Those very same eyes, yes, I remember them clearly.

"No!" Gooskin whispers. "Don't stare at her like that. Not for so long. How can you?"

I shake my head impatiently, and he steps away. And I go on looking.

She slowly turns her face toward me and, unable to see me through the narrow crack, looks straight into my eyes, vaguely and sleepily. In the same way that an owl, dazzled by daylight but still sensing a human gaze, will somehow always look— blindly—straight at the source of this gaze.

And so we freeze in this strange union.

I say to her, "I know. Your life, beast, was nothing but boredom. Boredom and monstrous ugliness. You would never have got far on such stumpy little legs. The difficult path of human happiness requires longer legs than yours. You would have plodded dismally on until you were about thirty and then you would probably have hanged yourself with some old braces or poisoned yourself with boot polish—and that would have been the end of your story. But what a splendid banquet fate turned out to have prepared for you! You drank warm, sharp human wine. You've drunk deep and long, until you're intoxicated. Good, isn't it? You've quenched your thirst, your sick, black sensual thirst. Not in the shadows, with a sense of shame, but brazenly, wholeheartedly, glorying in your mad lust. Your comrades in leather jackets and revolvers are just murdering thieves, a criminal mob. You disdainfully toss them a few scraps—furs, rings, money. It is perhaps for this very selflessness, for your 'devotion to an ideal' that they respect and obey you. But *I* know better. I know that there is no worldly treasure for the sake of which you would renounce your black work. Your lowly, black work means more to you than anything in the world, and you reserve this work for yourself.

I don't know how I can look at you and not cry out like a wild animal, wordlessly, not out of fear, but out of horror on your behalf—horror that the divine potter, in an hour of fury and revulsion, an hour beyond the reach of reason, should have shaped so terrible a fate for a piece of human clay."

The barrack was packed. Red Army soldiers and some sinister riffraff. A few women, most of them in soldiers' greatcoats. Two stocky commissars in leather jackets kept exchanging glances and taking turns to exit the barrack with an unwavering revolutionary stride and then return to their places, adjusting their bullet belts as if, having swiftly consolidated the conquests of the revolution, they could now afford to reacquaint themselves with its artistic achievements.

Our Robespierre had for some reason gone rather quiet and was hanging about somewhere off to one side. He was without his entourage and was doing none of his usual excited gesticulating.

It was time for us to begin.

I returned to the Messrs Artistes' dressing room to find that our program for the evening was now settled. For the evening to go with a swing—Gooskin had suddenly realized—we absolutely had to have a master of ceremonies. It was a pity we hadn't thought of this earlier, but our stutterer, thank God, had unexpectedly come to our rescue.

"Well I never!" I whispered to Averchenko. "Poor man. God knows what he'll end up saying."

"We couldn't really say no to him," said Averchenko with a laugh. "And maybe it'll be the best part of the evening."

The first number was to be a short sketch performed by Averchenko's impresario and the actress with the little dog.

We pushed the stutterer out to announce, "Sketch by Averchenko, performed by... s... s... s..." He then gave up the struggle and retired backstage.

Understanding this as a request for silence, the audience showed no surprise.

The actress with the little dog began cheeping like a frightened bird. In these surroundings it seemed strange indeed to hear her lines about flowerbeds, waltzes, distant cousins, a lovesick professor, and Verdi's *Aida*.

I was keeping an eye on the audience. The two commissars continued exchanging glances and striding in and out of the barrack. Everyone else just sat there, as if waiting for the moment, after the final resolution had been carried, when they could go back home. But I do remember a look of interest on one broad face. Now and again it bared its teeth in a kind of smile. Then this broad face beneath a soldier's cap would appear to recollect itself, furrowing its brow and squinting fiercely. I felt that the authorities must have forgotten to explain to the poor audience that no particular understanding of cultural matters was being required of it—they had been summoned to the barrack simply to be entertained.

The stutterer refused to relinquish his assigned role. We kept begging him not to exhaust himself, but he insisted on going onstage before each number and coming out with all sorts of nonsense. He introduced me as Averchenko, Averchenko as "an actress in transit," and everyone else simply as "eh... eh... eh..."

Gooskin, for his part, was behaving like a true impresario—pacing up and down with his hands behind his back, thinking, scheming, muttering under his breath. Sometimes he went and whispered a few words to somebody. Finally we glimpsed this somebody: an unknown gentleman in sky-blue satin pantaloons, a red velvet kaftan and a dashing Cossack hat on the back of his head.

Elbowing us out of the way, this figure ran out onstage and began singing, "Sleep, Fighting Eagles."[29] His voice was appalling but very loud.

The stutterer, who had only just got through his 'eh... eh... eh' and hadn't yet left the stage, was rooted to the spot, his mouth twitching violently.

"Who is it?"

"What's going on?"

"He can't sing," we said anxiously. "His voice is quite dreadful."

Gooskin looked away in confusion, then replied, "Yes, he sings like the day he was born."

"Gooskin, what's going on? Who is this man? Why has he suddenly started singing?"

Gooskin looked around.

"Shh… *Why has he started singing?* He wants to get across the border to the Ukraine. He's taking yarn with him. What else can he do?"

The singer got the last note hopelessly, hopelessly wrong. More wrong than anyone could have done on purpose. And the audience at once began roaring and clapping their approval. They loved his Fighting Eagles.

Sweating and happy, the singer reappeared backstage.

"Well, it seems your yarn's safe for the time being!" And Gooskin, his hands behind his back, added his usual rhetorical question: "Ri-ight?"

At the end of the evening we all went back onstage for our curtain call. Our surprise singer darted to the front of the stage and began bowing and pressing his hand to his heart as if he were some famous star.

The audience went wild, clapping long and loud.

"Bravo! Bravo!"

And then from somewhere up on the right, from the gallery-hayloft, I heard a few voices quietly but insistently calling my name.

I looked up.

Women's faces, infinitely weary, hopelessly sad. Crumpled little hats, worn-out dark dresses. Craning down toward me, the women were saying:

"Sweetheart! We love you! God grant you get out of here soon!"

"Leave this town, sweetheart, leave this town!"

"Leave as quick as you can!"

Never, at any of my performances, have I heard such chilling words from an audience.

And what tense desperation, what determination there was in those voices, in those eyes. Speaking to me so openly, they were taking no small risk—though the top brass had already left and, with all their clapping and shouting, the small fry were making such a racket they probably wouldn't be able to hear anything.

"Thank you!" I said to them. "Thank you! One day, perhaps, we'll meet again."

But they had disappeared. I could no longer see their pale faces. I heard only one more word: a short and bitter "No."

5

Early morning. Rain.

Waiting in front of our house were three carts. Gooskin and Averchenko's impresario were loading our luggage onto them.

"All right, Gooskin? All set for the journey?"

"Yes! We've got all our passes. And we've been promised an escort." Gooskin sighed, then continued in a whisper, "Though it's the escort that frightens me most!"

"But we need an escort—without one we'll be robbed."

"Isn't it all the same who we're robbed by? Whether we're robbed by our escort or by somebody else?"

I agreed that it was, probably, all the same.

Two more carts pulled up. In one of them was a family with children and dogs. In the other, half-sitting, half-lying, was a very pale woman wrapped in a flannel shawl. Beside the cart was a man in a sheepskin coat. The woman looked very ill. Her face was completely still, her eyes staring straight ahead. Her companion was casting quick, anxious glances at her and seemed to be trying to stop anyone from noticing her, edging around the cart as he tried to shield her from our view.

"Dear, oh dear!" said the all-knowing Gooskin. "That's that industrialist's wife—the one who was robbed."

"But what's happened to her? Why does she look so ill?"

"She got stabbed in the side with a bayonet. But the two of them are doing their best to look as if she's fit and healthy and has nothing to complain about, as if she's just sitting there, journeying merrily along to the Ukraine—so I say we should go along with that and go sit with our things. Ri-ight?"

More carts appeared. In one of them sat last night's singer, wearing a ragged little coat. The picture of innocence—and three suitcases (filled with yarn?).

We were going to be quite a caravan. So much the better—safety in numbers.

Finally our escort turned up—four young men with rifles. One of them barked, "Let's get going! No time to waste!"—and off we went.

As we were leaving the shtetl, we were joined by a few more carts. Now at least a dozen strong, our caravan moved slowly on, the escort walking beside us.

It was all very dismal. Rain. Mud. Only damp hay to sit on. Ahead of us—the enigmatic border zone, all twenty-five miles of it.

We had covered about three miles. We were in the middle of nowhere, with only a ramshackle barn to our right, when all of a sudden we glimpsed six men in soldiers' greatcoats, walking in single file across an empty field. Walking slowly, as if just out for a stroll. Our convoy came to a stop, though the greatcoats had given no indication of wanting anything from us.

"What's up?"

I looked on as Gooskin jumped off the cart and walked briskly across the field, not toward the greatcoats, but toward the barn. Apparently in no hurry, the greatcoats turned toward the barn too—and everyone disappeared from sight.

"Diplomatic negotiations," said Averchenko, walking over to my cart.

These negotiations lasted for some time.

Our guards, for some reason, took no part in them. On the contrary, having lost their air of authority and military bravura, they seemed to be hiding behind our carts. All very strange.

Gooskin returned, gloomy but calm.

"Tell me," he said to my carter. "Are there going to be any turnings off this road?"

"No-ope," my carter replied.

"If there's a turning soon, then those young greatcoats will be able to cut across and intercept us again."

"No-ope," my carter said reassuringly. "Not in weather like this—they're already on their way home to bed."

Eight in the morning seemed early for bed, but we were happy to take his word for it.

The carter pointed to the right with his whip—there on the horizon were six figures, moving away from us.

"Right, let's get going," said Gooskin. "There may be more people wanting to talk to us."

The guards emerged from behind the carts and, with renewed bravado, walked on beside us.

It was all very dismal.

We kept going, with few stops. To relieve the tedium, we swapped places now and again to pay social calls on one another.

Unexpectedly, one of the guards started talking to us. I replied rather coolly and then said in French to Olyonushka, who was sitting beside me, "Best not to get into conversation with them."

The guard gave a slight smile and said, "What makes you say that? I've known you for a long time. You read to us once at the Technological Institute."[30]

"But… what on earth's brought you to these parts?"

He laughed. "Did you really think we were Bolsheviks? We'd been hanging around there for days, waiting for a chance to get out. There are four of us—two students and two former officers. Today, when it turned out you needed an escort, none of the Bolsheviks would volunteer—they didn't want to miss out on their daily plunder. We saw our chance. We volunteered. We had a word with the right people and said we'd help out—and so we have. The only thing that really bothered them was my friend's gold tooth. They wanted to pull it out. But in all the rush I think they simply forgot about it."

We went on further.

We came to a copse. A wooden fence was blocking our way. Two German soldiers were standing by a gate. Not far from the gate was a barrack.

"Not the most welcoming of *Guten Tags*!" I said.

"Quarantine!" Gooskin explained gloomily. "Wonderful!"

Out came a somewhat more important German, wearing a somewhat darker greatcoat. He told us that we had to spend two weeks in quarantine.

Gooskin explained in his outlandish German that we were the most famous writers in the world and that we were "all so well that God help us—and Herr Officer too, of course!" And why would the officer want to waste quarantine space on us when there were others who needed it more?

But the German failed to understand what was in his best interests. He went back, slamming behind him the small wicket gate through which he had first emerged.

"Gooskin! We're not going to have to turn back, are we?"

"Pah!" Gooskin answered contemptuously. "Back! Why turn back when we need to go forward? There's always a way—you just have to look for it. All of you stay where you are! I'll make a start."

His hands behind his back, he started pacing up and down, looking attentively into the sentries' faces. He walked past them once, then again, then a third time.

"What the hell's he playing at?" Averchenko wondered aloud.

Trustingly and obediently, our entire caravan waited.

After walking past the sentries a fourth time, Gooskin made up his mind. Stopping beside one of them, he said, "Well?"

The sentry, of course, said nothing, but his eyes slid to one side. Once, twice, a third time... I looked across the road and caught sight of another German behind some bushes, innocently examining a branch of an elder tree. Gooskin didn't look at this German but, like some bird of prey, began slowly circling around him. Then they both disappeared deeper into the wood.

Gooskin was not gone for long. Emerging from the wood, he announced loudly, "Nothing for it. We must all turn back."

And so we obediently turned back. Obediently but with good cheer, because we had faith in the genius of Gooskin.

We went back the way we had come. After about a quarter of a mile, we turned off into the wood. Gooskin then jumped down from the cart and strode off, looking alertly around him.

We glimpsed a German greatcoat. Somewhere in the bushes. Gooskin homed in on it.

"You stay where you are!" he shouted out to us. "I won't be long!"

This round of negotiations did not take long. Gooskin reappeared, now accompanied by two friendly Germans who, with both words and gestures, were explaining the path we should follow to avoid the quarantine post.

We did as they said and happened on another German. This time it took only a couple of minutes to reach an understanding. Next we happened on some peasant or other. We thrust a few coins at him too, just in case. The peasant took the coins, but he stood there for a long time, gazing after us and scratching behind his left ear with his right hand. It seemed we needn't have bothered.

In the evening we saw the lights of Klintsy, the large Ukrainian shtetl that was our goal. Our caravan was already bumping along the cobbled street when, for the last time, Gooskin jumped down, ran up to a passerby and held out some money to him. First surprised, then frightened, the passerby shied away and refused the money.

And we understood that the zone, this enigmatic border zone, now truly did lie behind us.

Klintsy was a large shtetl with a railway station, cobbled streets, stone houses, and even, here and there, electric lighting.

Klintsy was full of people like us. Getting across the border was evidently not the end of the story. It did not entitle a person to roam freely about the Ukraine. Here too one had to run around getting all kinds of papers and documents from all kinds of bureaus and offices. All this took time—and so Klintsy was packed full of travellers.

We wandered about, seeking a haven. One by one, carts peeled off and disappeared. In the end, all that was left of our caravan was its head: our own little family of carts—wet, dirty, and despairing.

It was slow going. Gooskin walked beside us on the pavement, knocking on doors and shutters, asking if we could stay the night. Beards and hands were thrust out of windows. Gesturing and waving in different ways, they all refused us.

We sat there in silence, blank and downcast, chilled to the marrow. It was as if Gooskin had loaded three carts with worthless junk and was now trying to sell this junk to people who merely shooed him away.

"Yes," said Olyonushka, as if guessing my thoughts. "He's carting us around as if we were young calves! But then why shouldn't he? We're not much different from calves—all we want is something warm to drink and a place to lie down for the night."

Eventually, by the gates of a newly built two-story house, Gooskin entered into so animated a dialogue with an elderly Jew that our carters stopped the horses. Experienced as they were, they understood that this might be leading to something. The dialogue was intensely theatrical. One moment—all sinister whispers; the next—frenzied yells. Both parties spoke at the same time. And then, at a moment when they were both waving their arms in the air and shouting what seemed like the most terrible of curses, making Olyonushka cling to me and shout, "They're going to throttle each other!"—at this alarming moment Gooskin calmly turned toward us and said to the carters, "Well, go on. What are you waiting for? Drive into the yard."

While the old man began to open the gates.

The house we now entered was, as I have said, new. It had electric lighting, but the layout of the rooms was unusual—the front door opened straight into the kitchen. We, as honoured guests, were taken further, but the owners themselves—the family who must have built this mansion—appeared to have got stuck in the kitchen. The whole of this huge family huddled together there, on beds, chests and benches and on blankets spread out on the floor.

The head of the family was an old woman. Next came the old woman's husband—the tall bearded man who had let us in. Then the daughters. Then the daughters' daughters, the daughters' husbands, the son of the son's wife, the son's daughters and some kind of a shared grandson whom they were all bringing up together, with much love and shrieking.

The first thing we did, for form's sake, was to ask the old woman how much she would be charging us. This truly was just for form's sake—there was nowhere else we could have gone.

The old woman pulled a mournful face and threw up her hands: "Ach, don't talk money! How can anyone make money out of the misery of others? Out of the misery of those who have nowhere to lay their head! We have enough space and we have all we need (here the old woman turned to one side and spat, to ward off the evil eye), so what do we want with your money? Go and rest, my daughter's daughter will give you a samovar and anything else you need. But first of all, get yourselves dry. And don't worry about anything. What do I want with money?"

Moved by her words, we made eloquent protests.

I studied this remarkable woman. As her faith required, she was wearing a wig—or rather, a piece of black cloth with white stitching to represent a parting.

"No," Averchenko said to Gooskin. "We can't possibly take advantage of such magnanimity. We absolutely must make her see reason."

Gooskin smiled enigmatically.

"Huh! You really don't need to worry on that score. Believe me!"

None of us was more deeply moved than Olyonushka. With tears in her eyes, she said to me, "You know, I think God has sent us on this journey to show us that there are still kind, magnanimous people in the world. Here we have a simple old woman. She is not rich but she is gladly sharing with us her last mite. Though we are complete strangers to her, she has taken pity on us!"

"An astonishing old woman," I agreed. "And, most astonishing of all, she doesn't really… she doesn't have a particularly nice face."

"Yes, it just goes to show. One really mustn't judge by appearances."

We were both so moved that we even turned down the offer of fried eggs. "Poor old woman… giving us her all and everything!"

Meanwhile Gooskin and the old man, wasting no time, set about the complex task of trying to obtain all the necessary passes and documents—so we could be sure to be on our way in the morning.

First, the old man went off somewhere on his own. Then he came back to fetch Gooskin and take him along too. They came back together—and Gooskin went off again on his own. Then Gooskin came back and announced that the authorities required me and Averchenko to present ourselves to them, without delay.

It was already eleven o'clock and we wanted to go to bed, but what could we do? Off we went.

We had only the vaguest idea what kind of authority to expect. Commandant, commissar, Cossack junior officer, clerk, provincial governor… "Here we are—at your bidding!" We were long accustomed to being without rights; we no longer even enquired where we were being dragged to, whom we had to see next or why. Olyonushka was right—we were little different from calves.

We came to an official-looking building. Something between a post office and a police station…

In a small whitewashed room, an officer was sitting at a table. By the door stood a soldier. A new kind of uniform, which meant they must be Ukrainians.

"Here you are!" said Gooskin and stepped aside.

Our patron—the old woman's husband—took up position by the door, looking very alert indeed. At the first hint of trouble, he'd be off in a flash.

The officer, a young blond fellow, turned toward us, studied us attentively and, all of a sudden, broke into a broad, joyful, and astonished smile.

"So it's true? Say who you are."

"I'm Teffi."

"I'm Averchenko."

"The Teffi who used to write for the *Russian Word*?"

"Yes."

"Ha-a! I used to read it all the time! And I used to read Averchenko too, in *Satirikon*.[31] Ha-a! Well this is a miracle! I thought this scoundrel here was lying. And then I thought he might not be. And that this might be my one chance to set eyes on you. I've never been in Petersburg and, to be honest, this was a chance I couldn't let slip. Ha-a! Well, I'm overjoyed. I'll send you both your travel passes this very day! Where are you staying?"

At this point the old woman's husband moved away from the door and recited his address, testifying to its authenticity with the words, "So help me God!"

We thanked the officer.

"So we can leave tomorrow, can we?"

"If you want to. Unless you'd like to stay here for a little while. We've got everything here and plenty of it. We've even got champagne."

"Now that does sound good," Averchenko said wistfully. "Almost too good to be true!"

The officer rose to show us out. Only then did we notice the distraught look on Gooskin's face.

"But you've forgotten the most important thing of all!" he said in a tragic whisper. "The most important thing of all! My own travel pass. Mr. Officer! I too am from their company, and there are three others. They can't possibly get by without me! They'll tell you that themselves. What will become of them?

I tell you, it will be like the last day of Pompeii, right here on your doorstep!"

The officer looked at us questioningly.

"Yes, yes," said Averchenko. "He's accompanying us—and there are three others. Everything he says is true."

"I shall be glad to be of service."

We said our goodbyes.

Gooskin complained bitterly all the way back: "How could you? Forgetting Gooskin's pass! The most important thing of all! Wonderful! Ri-ight?"

Back home, calm, content, and sleepy, we sat down around the samovar that had been heated by one of the daughters' daughters. Now that the intensity of our feelings about the self-sacrificing old woman had subsided a little, Olyonushka and I accepted the offer of fried eggs.

"Well, we can at least get her to allow us to pay for our food, even if she refuses to accept money for anything else. We don't want to have to starve to death just because she's such a wonderful person."

"And that Gooskin's so unpleasant. Smirking like an oaf and telling us we don't need to worry on that score. What does he care?"

Our room was nice and warm. After the cold wind, our cheeks were burning. It was time to go to bed—almost twelve. Then a young man burst in. I think it was the son of the son's wife.

"Someone from the office is here—asking for Pan Averchenko."[32]

"They haven't changed their minds, have they?"

"And we thought everything had been settled!"

Averchenko went out into the kitchen. I followed.

There, surrounded by a frightened crowd of the daughters' daughters stood a Ukrainian policeman.

"Here are your travel passes. And the officer also wishes to give you this."

Two bottles of champagne!

Who'd have thought there could be such magic in a visit from a Ukrainian policeman?

We clinked our cups of warm champagne.

How high the wheel of fortune had raised us! Electric lighting, corks flying toward the ceiling, and cups—yes, we were drinking from teacups—foaming with champagne.

"Oufff!" Gooskin let out a sigh of contentment. "I have to admit it, I was scared halfway to death!"

Morning in Klintsy.

The day is somewhat grey, but quiet and reassuringly ordinary—just like any other autumn day. And the rain too is ordinary, not like the despairing rain, the rain as bitter as tears, that only two days before had been watering those bloodied remains by the embankment.

We stay in bed late. Our bodies are worn out, our souls dozing...

But we can hear voices from the kitchen. People bustling about. Plates clattering, somebody being scolded, somebody being told to get out of the way, somebody else defending them, several loud voices all shouting at once... The sweet symphony of simple human life...

"And where are the plates, I ask you. Where are the plates?" a high solo soars above the chorus.

"*A vuide Moshke?*"[33]

Then an intricate duet, something like "*Zoher-boher, zoher-boher!*"[34]

And a rich contralto solo:

"*A mishigene kopf.*"[35]

Ever so cautiously the door begins to open. A small dark eye examines us through the narrow crack. And disappears. A grey eye appears a little lower down, then disappears too. Then, much higher up—another dark eye, enormous and astonished.

The daughters' daughters were, it seems, waiting for us to awake.

It was time we got up.

Our train wasn't leaving until the evening. We would have to spend the whole day in Klintsy. This, we feared, would be boring. The town was so very calm—and calm was something we were no longer used to. We could not have complained of boredom two days before this.

One of the daughters' daughters came and asked us what we would like for lunch.

Olyonushka and I looked at each other and said with one voice, "Fried eggs."

"Yes, fried eggs and nothing else."

The daughter's daughter went out again, looking surprised and maybe even displeased. The kind old woman must have been wanting to spoil us.

"Yes," said Olyonushka, "for us to abuse her generosity would be unforgivable."

"Of course. And there's certainly nothing cheaper than eggs. Although one doesn't really want fried eggs two days running."

Olyonushka glanced at me reproachfully, then looked down at the floor.

Averchenko appeared, bringing something wonderful—a whole pile of apples.

Olyonushka then went out for a walk herself. She came back full of excitement and said, "Guess what I've brought?"

"Don't know."

"Guess!"

"A cow?"

"Don't be silly. Guess."

"I can't. The only thing I can think of is a cow... Or a candelabra?"

"Nothing of the sort," she said triumphantly—and placed a bar of chocolate on the table. "There!"

The actress with the little dog went over to the table, her eyes on stalks. Her little dog was no less surprised—it sniffed the chocolate and gave a little yelp.

"Where's it from?" we began to interrogate her.

"You won't believe it—you'll think I'm joking. I simply bought it at a little stall. And nobody asked anything at all. I didn't need any papers, and I didn't have to line up. I just saw it in the window, went in and bought it. Real Boreman's chocolate.[36] Look!"

How strange life can be—someone walks down the street, feels like eating some chocolate, goes into a shop and—"Yes Madame, here Madame, as you wish Madame." And there are people everywhere. They can see and hear everything that's going on, yet nobody seems in the least bothered—as if all this is completely normal. Who'd have believed it!

"And it was just an ordinary stall?"

"Yes, just an ordinary little stall."

"Hmm! And you don't think it's some trap? Well, let's try some of this chocolate. And when we've finished it, we can buy some more."

"Only I probably shouldn't go there again myself," said Olyonushka. "Let someone else go—otherwise it might look suspicious…"

Olyonushka was right. One can't be too careful.

Once the first surge of delight and elation had passed, we all began to feel bored again. How were we going to pass the time until evening?

The little dog was whining. Her owner was darning her gloves and grumbling about something.

Olyonushka was in one of her moods: "No, this really can't be the right way to live. We should learn how to live without trampling the grass. Today we're having fried eggs again, which means still more destruction of life. One should plant an apple tree and live only off its fruit."

"Olyonushka, darling," I say. "Just now you polished off a good dozen apples in one sitting, without even thinking about it. A single apple tree won't last you very long, will it?"

Olyonushka's lips were trembling. She was about to start bawling.

"You're laughing at me. Yes, I ate a dozen apples, but so what? What ups… what really upsets me… that I've sunk so low… lost all self… self-control…"

At this point she began to sob. She truly did lose all self-control. Her mouth fell open and, like a child, she began to howl: "Boo-hoo, boo-hoo!"

Averchenko didn't know what to do.

"Olyonushka!" he said gently. "Don't get so upset! It won't be long till we get to Kiev. Then we can plant your apple tree for you."

Olyonushka carried on weeping inconsolably.

"Honest to God, we will. And the apples will ripen just like that—Kiev has a wonderful climate. And if there aren't enough for you, then we can buy a few more. Just now and again. Just now and again, Olyonushka! All right, we won't buy any more apples, only please stop crying!"

"It's all the old woman's fault for being so saintly," I said to myself. "Olyonushka now sees all of us—herself included—as vile, callous, and petty-minded. Ach, ach, ach…"

The door gave a quiet creak, interrupting my troubled thoughts.

Another eye!

The eye peeps in, then disappears. A quick scuffle behind the door. Another eye, very different. It peeps in, then disappears. And yet another. This eye is bold enough to allow a nose to follow it into the crack.

A voice behind the door asks impatiently, "Ri-ight?"

"There," replies the eye. And disappears.

What on earth was going on?

We watched.

There was no doubt. People were taking turns to peep into our room.

"Maybe Gooskin's making them pay to see us," said Averchenko.

I walked quietly up to the door and flung it open.

About fifteen people, maybe even more, sprang back and did their best to squeeze behind the stove. They were clearly not part of the family—the daughters' daughters and other family members were all going about their household chores with particular zeal, as if to emphasize that they had nothing to do with these outsiders. As for Gooskin, he was standing alone, innocently picking bits of loose plaster from the wall.

"Gooskin! What's going on?"

"Oh, nothing much—just people being inquisitive! 'What do you want to look at writers for?' I asked them. 'If you really must look at something, then look at me. So what if they're writers! You're not going to see inside them and on the outside they're no different from me. Ri-ight? How could they be any different?"

Had Gooskin been selling tickets? I wondered. Or had he been letting everyone in for free—like a pianist practising on mute keys so that his fingers don't lose their agility?

We went back inside, closing the door more firmly.

"I don't know," said Olyonushka. "Do we really have to deprive them of their entertainment? If they're that interested, why not just let them look?"

"Yes, you're right," I agreed quickly, afraid she might start bawling again. "Really, we should have put on even more of a show for them. We could have got Averchenko to stand on his head. Then we could have held hands in a circle and danced round him, while your fellow actress sat with her little dog on top of the wardrobe calling out 'Cuckoo! Cuckoo!'"

In the afternoon, after the first serving of fried eggs (there would be yet more before our departure), the old woman's husband came and entertained us. In all my life I have never met anyone so gloomy. He neither trusted the present nor had faith in the future.

"It's nice and peaceful here in Klintsy."

He hung his head dejectedly.

"Peaceful enough. But who knows what tomorrow will bring?"

"The apples you have here are delicious!"

"Good enough. But who knows what tomorrow will bring?"

"You have a lot of daughters."

"A lot of daughters—yes. But who knows…"

Since none of us knew what tomorrow would bring, we were unable to reply. And so our conversations with this old man always took the form of brief questions and answers, dense with philosophical implication, somewhat like Plato's dialogues.

"You have a lovely wife," said Olyonushka. "And you are, I think, all kind and good people!"

"Kind, good. But who…"

With a sudden gesture of despair he turned around and walked out.

After our second serving of fried eggs we packed our things; the husbands of the daughters' daughters dragged our luggage along to the station; we said emotional goodbyes to everyone and went out onto the porch, leaving Gooskin to handle the most delicate aspect of our departure—payment. We told him he really must get the family to accept our money. If he failed, the best thing he could do—Olyonushka and I were agreed—was to put the money on the table and make a swift exit. And we added that if the saintly old woman chased after him, he should run all the way to the station without a backward glance. We'd meet him on the platform. She was, after all, an old woman; she wouldn't be able to catch up with him.

We waited anxiously.

Through the door we could hear their voices—Gooskin's and the old woman's, one at a time, then both together.

"No!" Olyonushka said in distress. "He's simply not up to it. Matters like this require tact and sensitivity."

Then a sudden wild shriek. Gooskin.

"He's gone mad!"

He was shrieking loud, wild words.

"*Gelt?*" we heard. "*Gelt?*"

And the old woman began to shriek too. The same word: "*gelt.*"

And then silence.

Gooskin rushed out. He looked awful. He was bright red, soaked in sweat, his mouth all twisted. His bootlaces were undone and his collar had broken free of its stud.

"Let's go!" he commanded grimly.

"Well, did she take the money?" Olyonushka asked with timid hope.

Gooskin's whole body began to shake: "Did she take the money? Just try stopping her! I'd understood long ago that she was out to fleece us, but to fleece us so royally—may never the sun set again if ever I have heard the like of it!"

When angered, Gooskin would launch out into the most complex of rhetorical figures. There were occasions when we really had no idea what he was talking about.

"I told her in plain language—you, Madame, must have woken yourself up, Madame, from the wrong side of bed, Madame. So I suggest we wait until you've slept your way through it. Yes, I put it to her straight."

"But did you pay her the right amount?" we asked anxiously.

"Indeed I did! A lot more than the right amount. Do I look like the kind of person who doesn't pay? No, I'm the kind who pays."

He said all this with pride. And then, a little inappropriately, he muttered, "Though really, of course, it's you who'll be paying."

6

We left Klintsy in a freight car.

At first, this seemed fun. We sat in a circle on top of our luggage, as if gathered around a campfire. We munched chocolate and chatted.

Climbing up into the carriage was especially entertaining. There was no step or ladder of any kind and, since our car was toward the rear of the train, it always stopped beyond the end of the platform. You had to lift your foot almost to the height of your chest and then lever yourself up while those already inside seized hold of your arms and pulled.

But all this soon lost its appeal. The stations were empty and dirty. The signs, looking as if they had been nailed up in a hurry, were written in Ukrainian, and the unexpected spelling and unfamiliar words made everything seem like the work of some practical joker.

New to us as it was, this language seemed as inappropriate for official use as, say, the language of a Russian peasant. As surprising as if, in some official Russian institution, you were to see a sign saying, "No barging in without prior announcement," or, inside a train carriage: "Don't stick your mug out,"

"Don't lean your noddle against the glass," or "All tittle-tattle strictly prohibited."[37]

But even these entertaining signs and notices ceased to amuse us.

The train moved slowly, and the stops were many and long. The station buffets and cloakrooms were all closed. It was evident that a wave of popular fury had swept through these parts and that the newly enlightened population had not yet returned to the mundane tasks of everyday life. There was filth everywhere, and a vile stench, and the authorities' appeals to "misters" and "misses" to observe the wise old rules of station etiquette had clearly gone unheeded. These now liberated souls were above such concerns.

I don't know how long all this lasted. I remember that we managed somehow to get hold of a lamp. But the fumes were unbearable: "the stench of hellfire," as Gooskin put it.

So the lamp was put out.

It began to get cold. Wrapping myself up in my sealskin coat, which until then I had been lying on, I listened to the hopes and dreams of Averchenko and Olyonushka.

It's not for nothing that I just mentioned my sealskin coat. A woman's sealskin coat represents an entire epoch in her life as a refugee.

Were there any of us who did not have a sealskin coat? We put these coats on as we first set out, even if this was in summer, because we couldn't bear to leave them behind—such a coat was both warm and valuable and none of us knew how long our wanderings would last. I saw sealskin coats in Kiev and in Odessa, still looking new, their fur all smooth and glossy. Then in Novorossiisk, worn thin around the edges and with bald patches down the sides and on the elbows. In Constantinople—with grubby collars and cuffs folded back in shame. And, last of all, in Paris, from 1920 until 1922. By 1920 the fur had worn away completely, right down to the shiny black leather. The coat had been shortened to the knee and the collar and cuffs were now made from some new kind of fur, something blacker and oilier—a foreign substitute. In 1924 these coats disappeared. All that remained was odds and ends, torn scraps of memories, bits of trimming sewn onto the cuffs, collars, and hems of ordinary woollen coats. Nothing more. And then, in 1925, the timid, gentle seal was obliterated by invading hordes of dyed cats. But even now when I see a sealskin coat, I remember this epoch in our lives as refugees. In freight cars, on the decks of steamers, or deep in their holds, we spread our sealskin coats beneath us if it was warm or wrapped ourselves up in them if it was cold. I remember a lady waiting for a tram in Novorossiisk. Cheap canvas shoes on her bare feet, she was standing there in the rain, holding a little baby in her arms. To make it clear to me that she wasn't just anyone, she was speaking to the baby in French with the rather sweet accent of a Russian schoolgirl: "Seel voo ple! Ne plur pa! Voysi le tramvey, le tramvey!"

She was wearing a sealskin coat.

Seals are remarkable beasts. They can endure more than most horses.

The actress Vera Ilnarskaya once almost drowned wearing her sealskin coat.[38] She was on the *Gregore* when it sank off the Turkish coast. None of her belongings could be salvaged, of course—apart from the sealskin coat. The tailor to whom she then took it declared that, since the seal is a sea animal, immersion in its native element appeared only to have made the coat better and stronger.

Dear, gentle beast, comfort and defence in difficult times, banner of our lives as refugee women: A whole epic could be written about you. I remember you and salute you.

So, there we all were, being jolted about in a freight car. Wrapped in my sealskin coat, I was listening to the hopes and dreams of Averchenko and Olyonushka.

"First of all, a warm bath," said Olyonushka. "But just a quick one, followed immediately by a roast goose."

"No," said Averchenko. "First, some appetizers."

"Appetizers are piffle. And anyway, they're cold. We want something hot and filling straightaway."

"Cold? No, we'll order hot appetizers. Have you ever had the toasted rye bread with bone marrow they serve in the Vienna? No? In that case, your opinion's hardly worth listening to. A wonderful little dish, and it's certainly hot."

"Is that something like calves' brains?" Olyonushka asked in a businesslike tone of voice.

"No, it's not like brains, it's bone marrow—the marrow from inside a bone. You really don't know very much about anything, do you? And then at Kontan's, on the counter with the appetizers, there on the right, between the mushrooms and the lobster, they always have some hot *vorschmack*[39]—it's amazing. And in Alberto's, on the left, near the *mortadella*, they have an Italian salad... And at Medvedev's, right in the middle, in a small pan, they have those little… those little dumplings with mushrooms, they're hot too."

"All right," said Olyonushka. "But that's enough about appetizers. So, all these little dishes from all of these restaurants will already be on the table, but I think we need roast goose too, with cabbage. No, with buckwheat, buckwheat's more filling."

"Not with apples?"

"I said buckwheat's more filling. You love to argue with me, but you really don't know very much about anything. At this rate we're never going to find anything we can agree on."

"And where will all this take place?" I asked.

"Where? Oh, somewhere…" Olyonushka replied vaguely, then resumed her businesslike manner. "We can also get some Kislovodsk-style kebabs, from Orekhovaya Balka."

"Now you're talking," Averchenko agreed. "And in Kharkov I once had some very tasty tomatoes with garlic. They'll be perfect with the kebabs."

"On our estate they used to make burbot pie. Let's have that too."

"Excellent, Olyonushka."

Something dark and bulky stirred in the corner. It was Gooskin.

"Excuse me, Madame Teffi," he asked in an ingratiating tone. "I'm curious… do you like domplings?"

"What? Do you mean dumplings? What kind of dumplings?"

"My mama makes fish domplings. She'll make you some when you come to live with us."

"Live with you?" I asked, my heart sinking under the weight of terrible forebodings. "When am I going to live with you?"

"When?" Gooskin answered calmly. "When we get to Odessa."

"But you said I'll be staying in a hotel, at the London!"

"Yes, of course you will. Who's saying anything different? Nobody's saying anything different. You'll be staying at the London, but in the meantime, until the luggage... the cab driver... until we're done with all those shysters, you'll just have a little rest at Gooskin's and Mama will give you some of her domplings."

In my morbid imagination I immediately saw a tiny room, divided in two by a calico curtain. A cupboard. On top of the cupboard—Gooskin's clodhoppers and a collar that had seen better days. And behind the curtain—Mama, cooking "domplings."

"He's up to something," Averchenko whispered to me. "Once we're in Kiev, you must try and find out a bit more."

Encouraged by my silence, Gooskin began to elaborate his plans: "We can put on a show in Gomel too. Honest to God, and we'll be going through Gomel anyway. Gomel, Shavli. And every show will be a sell-out—I swear to it."[40]

Gooskin was quite something. A true impresario. A man one could go a long way with.

"Gooskin," Averchenko began, "am I right in thinking you've taken a great many artistes on tour?"

"Well, yes, I have. I've taken a choir. I've taken a whole theatre company. I've taken a... But what hasn't Gooskin taken on tour?"

"So, with so many shows—and all of them sell-outs—you must have earned millions?"

"Millions? Huh! Just give me the remainder. Give me the remainder from twenty thousand and I'll be more than happy."

"What remainder?" I whispered to Averchenko. "What on earth is he talking about?"

"He's saying he's earned so little that if everything he'd ever earned were subtracted from twenty thousand, then he'd be happy to take the remainder."

Goodness! My Gooskin was no simpleton.

"Gooskin, how come you've earned so little?"

"Because I am Gooskin, not Ruslansky. I see to it that an artiste is looked after properly, that he has the best suite in the best hotel and that the staff don't knock him about. Whereas Ruslansky, he thinks that the best suite is for the impresario. Once I said to him, 'Listen, Goldgrubber, you're no more of a lord than I am, so why is it I don't mind sleeping in the corridor while you always have to have the very best suite—and as for your artiste, he just gets left out on the street, lying beneath an umbrella?' Ruslansky, who does Ruslansky think he is? Once I gave it to him straight. I said, 'When one of Gooskin's tours comes to an end, the artiste says, "What a shame I wasn't born a day earlier, so I could have spent one more day with Gooskin!" But when one of Ruslansky's tours comes to an end, the artiste says to him, "Goldgrubber, may you rot like a rat in hell."' Yes, like a rat in hell. And then the artiste calls Goldgrubber a louse, but that really isn't something I should repeat to you. Ri-ight?"

But at this point our conversation was interrupted. The train stopped and the door to our freight car slid open with a grinding screech. A loud voice commanded, *"Heraus!"*[41]

And a second voice bleated, in Ukrainian, "Everybody out!"

"Wonderful!" said Gooskin—and out he went into the murky darkness.

We too leaped out into the thin, slippery mud—into the unknown.

Some soldiers pushed us aside and climbed into the car. They briskly threw out our luggage, then bolted the door.

Night, drizzle, soldiers, dim lights from hand-held lanterns.

And so there we were, once more on a station platform, in the rain.

We stood huddled together, like sheep in a blizzard—heads together, tails facing out. We waited obediently. Gooskin was our shepherd and we trusted him to look after us.

I can't say we felt particularly upset by all this. Of course, supper and a warm room for the night would have been more pleasant than standing on an open platform in the drizzle, but by this time our wants had grown modest. We were confident that nobody—nobody whatsoever—was intending to have us shot, and this confidence filled our souls with a happy, surprised contentment. The drizzle was quite cosy and not really even so very wet. Life on this earth truly wasn't so bad.

Our luggage was piled up beside us on a little station cart. A German soldier was guarding it.

The station was poorly lit. But somewhere in the distance we could see bright light shining through a glass door. Dark figures were going in and out. Behind that door must be where fates were determined.

A tall, dark shadow strides toward us. Gooskin.

"Once more it's the torments of Tantalus," he says helplessly. "Here I am, dancing around in the rain with no idea whom to bribe."

"What do they want from us, Gooskin?"

"They want to put us in quarantine. Why, I ask you, can't they just let their quarantine stay empty for a while? I told them we've already done time in quarantine. And they say, 'Show us your papers—we want to see when you left Moscow.' They see it was only a week ago. 'So where are your two weeks of quarantine?' they ask. Well, what could I say to that? What do you think I said? I said I'd go and change some money. What other answer can Gooskin give to a question like that?"

"What can we do?"

"We'll find a way. The bitten child fears the fierce flame. We have to find out whom to bribe. Why else have they dreamed up this quarantine? I just have to find another Jew, someone who can point out the way to me."

Gooskin walks off.

"Ladies and gentlemen," I say, "we have to try and speak to the soldier. Olyonushka, let's start talking to each other in German. Then the soldier will feel more sympathetic toward us. All right?"

"I've forgotten all my German!" says Olyonushka. "I can only remember a few grammatical rules."

"That'll do! Let's hear your rules—and put some feeling into them!"

"*Ausgenommen sind: binden, finden, klingen*," Olyonushka began. "*Gelingen, ringen…*"[42]

"A bit jollier, Olyonushka. Livelier!"

"*Nach, auf, hinter, neben, in, stehen mit dem accusativ*," Olyonushka chirps on.

"*Mit, nach, nächst, nebst,*" I answer, nodding my head in confirmation. "Look, the soldier's beginning to stir. Quick, give him some more!"

"*Ausgenommen sind: binden, band, gebunden. Dringen, drang...*"

"*Zu, aus...*"

The soldier is now looking at us with wan curiosity.

"Yes, you've got through to him, you've kindled his sense of patriotism. So, what next?"

"Maybe we should sing a duet? *Das war in Schöneberg?*"[43]

"No, I don't think singing would be quite right."

But what is our soldier staring at? Ah, he's looking at my suitcase.

I walk over to him. Aha! My old suitcase has a Berlin label on it. That's what he's looking at. Well, now he'll be easy prey.

"Berlin! What a wonderful city," I say to him in German. "Have you ever been to Berlin?"

No, he hasn't.

"Oh, when all this is over, you really must go. Oh! Oh, what a wonderful city! The Kempinski restaurant, the Wertheim department store! The beer and the sausages! Oh, oh, oh, what beauty!"

The German smiles, his patriotic feelings now blazing merrily.

"Have *you* been to Berlin?" he asks.

"Of course I have! And here's the proof—my own suitcase. Berlin! Oh, Berlin!"

And now—to business.

"Yes, that was a good time—before the war. Now, though, things are so much more difficult. Here we are in the rain and we don't know what to do. We have, of course, spent time in quarantine, though not long, because we're all terribly healthy. That's why we were allowed out. But we didn't think to ask for any documents. What do you think we should do?"

The soldier adopts a severe expression, looks away from me and says, "Lieutenant Schwenn."

He repeats the words, quietly but no less seriously, "Lieutenant Schwenn."

Then he turns on his heels and walks away. Victory! I run off to find Gooskin.

Hurrying about between the flickering beams from the lanterns is a shadowy figure. It is, of course, Gooskin.

"Gooskin! Gooskin! The soldier said 'Lieutenant Schwenn.' Do you understand me?"

"Huh! I've already heard that from at least a dozen people. Schwenn's in there, with the officer in command. We have to wait."

I go back to the others.

The soldier's patriotism is now blazing so ardently that he can no longer quiet it. "Lieutenant Schwenn!" he repeats, looking away from us. "*Nun?* Lieutenant Schwenn."

Eventually I say, "*Schon!* Already!"[44]

The soldier's eyebrows and ears twitch a little. Then he calms down.

Gooskin comes back.

"Well?" I ask.

"A complete trifle! So cheap I felt well and truly ashamed! Ri-ight? But you have to go and talk to the officer yourselves. He's the one who issues passes. He'll give you one all right, but you must ask in person."

Along we go, with no idea what we're going to say to this officer.

We find him at his desk, a German with an entourage of junior Ukrainian officers.

"Why the hurry?" ask the Ukrainians. "Why not stay here for a while?"

"We've got no choice. We have to hurry. We're performing the day after tomorrow in Kiev and we really must be there on time."

Some of the officers have heard of us. They smile shyly and make little jokes.

"Instead of making us wait here, you should take some leave and come to see our show in Kiev," says Averchenko. "We're inviting all of you. Come along. Yes, you really must!"

The young officers look excited: "A show? And you'll be performing? Oh, if only we could!"

"Quarantine? How can there even be any question of quarantine?" Gooskin interrupts. "These are Russian writers! They're so brimming with health that God forbid—have you ever heard of a Russian writer getting ill? Huh! See what a Russian writer looks like!"

And he proudly exhibits Averchenko. He even pulls his coat open.

"Does *he* look like he's sick? No, certainly not. And the day after tomorrow, they're putting on a show. Such a show that I would certainly go flocking to it myself. A show that will go down forever in the canals of history. And if we really do need some quarantine, then we can find it in Kiev. Honest to God! We'll find one of your quarantines and stay there for a while. Why not? Ri-ight?"

"Please say a word on our behalf to your German," I ask the officers.

They click their heels, whisper among themselves for a few minutes, then put some documents in front of the German. At which point Gooskin turns to me and says with great seriousness, "And whatever you do, please be sure to say that it was I who went into quarantine first of all. Otherwise they might try and keep me here! And it's five months now since I last saw my mama."

Turning to the astonished officers, he pronounces in the most solemn of tones, "For five months now I have been located outside my mother."

Once again we were on a train.

In Gomel, some kind people had suggested we go to Kiev by steamer: "You'll go past an island that's been taken over by some kind of armed band. They've got machine guns. They shoot at every steamer that goes by."

Cosy as this sounded, we had chosen to go by train.

Our first-class carriage was entirely adequate, but there were few passengers and nearly all of them rather strange—peasants, it appeared, in peasant smocks. They sat without saying a word, moving only their eyebrows. There was also a bearded man with a gold tooth who didn't look in the least like a peasant. His overcoat was rather grubby, but his hands were smooth and podgy. The wedding ring on his ring finger had sunk deep into the flesh.

A strange lot. But there was no sign of any malice in their stares. It was not like when we were leaving Moscow; then people had looked at us with real fury—the intelligentsia suspecting we might be from the Cheka while the workers and peasants had seen us as capitalist landlords still drinking their blood.

"Well, not long now till Kiev," said Gooskin, who was keeping us entertained with soothing chatter.

"In Kiev, I shall introduce you to a friend of mine," he said to Olyonushka. "A very nice, profoundly cultured young man. Lotos."

"What?"

"Lotos."

"An Indian?" Olyonushka asked reverently. In her eyes I glimpsed a vision of yogis, of an apple tree she had planted and the fruit it was bearing.

"What makes you think that?" said Gooskin, offended on his friend's behalf. "He's a salesman, a salesman for Lotos. Optical glass. He's from an aristocratic family. His uncle had a pharmaceutical warehouse in Berdyansk. He wants to get married."

"And you, Gooskin? Are you married?"

"No."

"Why not?"

"My demands are excessive."

"What are your demands?"

"First, she needs to be buxom." Gooskin lowered his eyes, paused and added, "*And* of course, she must have a dowry."

"And tell us, Gooskin! What's your first name? The way we keep calling you by your surname feels a little strange."

Gooskin gave an embarrassed smile.

"My name? You're all going to laugh."

"Heavens, what makes you think that?"

"Honest to God, you will. I'm not telling you."

"Dear Gooskin, we won't laugh! We give you our word. Tell us!"

"Olyonushka," I whisper. "Don't be too insistent. Maybe it sounds like some rude word."

"Don't be silly… Please tell us, Gooskin. What's your real name?"

Gooskin blushed. With a helpless shrug of the shoulders, he said, "My name is… I'm sorry, it's a bit of a joke! Alexander Nikolaevich! Well, now you know."

We had indeed been expecting anything but this.

"Gooskin! Gooskin! You're killing us!"

Gooskin laughed louder than any of us.[45] He was wiping his eyes with a rag of indescribable colour that, in more elegant times, had probably been a handkerchief.

7

The closer we get to Kiev, the more animated the train stations.

Station buffets begin to appear. Walking along the platforms are people with oily lips and shiny cheeks, still chewing. On their faces is a look of amazed satisfaction. Posters on the walls bear witness to a demand for culture: "A Stupendous Dog Show—After the Method of the Renowned Durovs"[46]; "A Troupe of Lilliputians"; "With a Full Local Repertoire—an Actress from the Alexandria Theatre."

"Well, life's literally taking a full swing at us here!" says Gooskin. "Look at these posters! Nicely done. Ri-ight? I'd certainly go flocking to these shows myself!"

German policemen are everywhere—squeaky clean, brightly polished, and tightly packed with Ukrainian fatback and bread.

We have to change trains twice more. We have no idea why.

On a platform in one of the bigger stations, Averchenko, Gooskin, and the actress with the little dog, all conspicuously tall, are standing in the middle of a waiting crowd. A breathless figure with eyes darting about in bewilderment, with a bowler hat on the back of his head and an unbuttoned coat billowing like a lopsided sail, suddenly runs up to them and says, "Excuse me for asking—you're not the Lilliputians, are you?"

"No," Averchenko replies modestly.

The man with the lopsided sail is swept further on down the platform.

Gooskin doesn't show the least surprise.

"He's obviously waiting here for a troupe of Lilliputians, and they're late. What are you laughing at? It happens often enough—companies arriving late. Ri-ight?"

To Gooskin the question had seemed entirely normal.

With each change of trains the class of passenger changes too. Respectably and even elegantly dressed people start to appear—"ladies and gentlemen." By the last stretch of the journey, everyone but ladies and gentlemen has disappeared.

"Where have they all gone?"

A shifty character with a suitcase disappears into a station cloakroom—and then out comes a pillar of society: a lawyer, a landowner, a hydra of counterrevolution, with neatly combed hair, wearing a clean collar, and carrying in his gloved hand the same little suitcase. I recognize faces. The man with the podgy fingers has now combed his beard and put a frown on his face; picking some lint off the sleeve of his wool overcoat, he voices his indignation over some recent outrage: "It's a disgrace! The liberties they take!"

Well, if we've got to the point of disgraceful liberties, then we must, at last, be on solid ground.

Kiev is very close.

Gooskin puzzles us with an unexpected question, "Where are you all planning on staying?"

"In a hotel."

"In a hotel?" he repeats—and smiles enigmatically.

"What's the matter?"

"I've heard the hotels have all been requisitioned. And the private apartments are all so crowded I wish I could say the same of my purse! Ri-ight?"

I don't know anyone in Kiev and have no idea what to do if I can't get into a hotel.

"Gooskin, this is, in point of fact, your responsibility," says Averchenko. "Since you are the impresario, you should have arranged rooms. You should have written to someone."

"And who would I write to? The Ukrainian Hetman?[47] Yes, I suppose I could have written to him—if I'd wanted to get myself well and truly written off. It would be better, I think, if Madame Teffi went to speak to the Hetman. Something might come of that. Yes, something would be sure to come of it—though it might not be anything good. Still, I can see already that Madame Teffi has no intention of going anywhere herself. She's just going to sit and wait at the station while Gooskin runs around looking for an apartment. Once again Gooskin has so much work on his hands that he can't get a breath in edgewise."

"What are you getting so upset about? This is clearly one of your responsibilities!"

"Responsibilities?" Gooskin repeats thoughtfully. "Yes, responsibilities. Well, find me the fool who enjoys his responsibilities! Ri-ight?"

"If worst comes to worst, I think I can help," Olyonushka joins in timidly. "I have friends in Kiev, maybe we can all stay with them…"

Olyonushka looks unhappy and anxious. I realize she's trying "to live without trampling the grass."

On a bench across the aisle, the actress with the little dog is hissing at Averchenko's impresario, "Why is it that others can and you can't? Why can't you ever get anything done?" Then, in answer to her own question: "Because you are a complete idiot."

I say quietly to Averchenko, "Your actor friends don't seem to be getting on very well. That Fanichka and your impresario have been at each other's throats throughout the journey. Putting on shows with those two will be hard work."

"Yes, they have their differences," Averchenko says calmly. "But what do you expect? Their affair's been going on a long time now."

"Their affair?"

I prick up my ears.

"I'm ashamed of you," the actress is hissing. "You never shave, your tie's all torn, your collar's grubby. All in all, you look like a gigolo fallen on hard times."

"Yes, you're right," I say to Averchenko. "There are clearly deep and powerful feelings at play."

The impresario mutters back, "If I were a man who enjoyed scenes, madame, I would tell you that you're a vulgar cow, and vicious too. Bear that in mind."

"Yes," I repeat. "Deep and powerful feelings, on both sides."

It's my duty, I feel, to cheer everyone up.

"Ladies and gentlemen," I say, "why are you all looking so downcast? Remember how in the freight car you were dreaming of a bath and a good dinner? Just think—this time tomorrow we'll probably be all clean and dressed up, sitting in a good restaurant and eating wonderful delicacies to the sound of music. There'll be a gleaming white tablecloth, crystal glasses, flowers in vases…"

"I really don't like restaurants," Gooskin interrupts. "What's so special about them? When my mama serves up plain broth at home, it goes down much better than the most expensive liver in the grandest of restaurants. Ri-ight? Of course, in a very expensive restaurant everything is in order, they do you a real parade. After you're done gnawing your chicken bones, they bring you some warm water, and even soap, so you can wash your hands and face. But to go to a restaurant like that, you have to be stinking rich. Whereas in an ordinary restaurant you simply wipe your hands on the tablecloth. And where's the fun in that? No, I don't like restaurants. What's so special about eating soup and having some idiot sitting next to you eating, pardon me, fruit compote."

"What's wrong with that?" Averchenko asks in bewilderment.

"*What's wrong with that*? You must be joking! Do you really not understand? Where do you think he spits out the stones? He spits them out onto your plate. He's not a juggler—they're not all going to land on his own plate. No thank you! I've seen more than enough restaurants to last me this lifetime."

Our train arrives at a station.

Kiev!

The station is crammed with people and the whole place smells of borsch. The new arrivals are in the buffet, partaking of the culture of a free country. They slurp away with deep concentration. With their elbows jutting out to either side as if to ward off any encroachment, they seem like eagles hovering over their prey. But how can anyone behave otherwise? Your reason may affirm that you are completely safe, that your borsch is your own property and that your rights to it are protected by the iron might of the German state. You may think you understand this, but your subconscious doesn't. Your subconscious sticks out your elbows and sends your eyes out on stalks. "What if an unfamiliar, vile spoon reaches over my shoulder," it says to itself, "and takes a scoop for the needs of the proletariat?"

We sit in the buffet with our luggage and wait for news about where we'll be staying.

The podgy man with the beard and the wedding ring is eating his fill at the next table.

On a plate in front of him is a steak. Hovering above him is a waiter's frightened face.

The man with the beard is laying into this waiter: "I said to you, you scoundrel, in plain Russian—steak with fried potatoes. Where are the potatoes? Where, I'm asking in plain Russian, are the potatoes?"

"Excuse me, sir, they are being fried now, sir. At this moment we only have boiled. Please be so good as to wait, sir. They'll only take a minute, sir!"

The bearded man chokes with indignation: "*Please be so good as to wait, sir*! You expect me to wait while my steak gets cold! I don't believe it—it's a disgrace!"

A young porter, his lips pursed, is leaning against the wall and watching the "gentleman" and the waiter. The porter's face says a great deal. This whole little scene is a gift to the Bolsheviks. What do they want with propaganda posters about capitalist hydras and counterrevolution when people are putting on shows like this on their behalf?[48]

The buffet is stuffy and it looks like there will be a long wait. I leave the station building.

The cheerful, sunny day will soon have faded. But the streets are full of life, with people hurrying from store to store… And then I see a wonderful and unprecedented scene, like a dream from a life forgotten, something improbable, exhilarating and even awe-inspiring—in the door of a bakery stands an officer with epaulettes on his shoulders, eating a cake! An officer with e-pau-lettes on his shoulders! Eating a cake! So there are still Russian officers in the world who can stand outside on a bright sunny afternoon with epaulettes on their shoulders. Instead of hiding away in basements like hunted animals, sick and hungry, wrapped in rags, knowing that their very existence threatens the lives of their loved ones…

Just imagine—daylight, sunshine, people everywhere, and in the officer's hand, an unseen, unheard-of luxury, the stuff of legend—a cake!

I close my eyes and open them again. No, it isn't a dream. So it must be real life. But how very strange this all is…

Might we all have grown so unaccustomed to life that we can never find our way back into it again?

My first impression is that the whole world (the whole of Kiev) is brimming with food, bursting with food. Steam and smoke billowing out of every door and window. Shops crammed with hams, sausages, turkeys, stuffed suckling pigs. And on the streets, against the backdrop of these stuffed suckling pigs—*le tout Moscou et le tout Pétersbourg.*

8

For a moment all this seems like a festival.

But soon it begins to feel more like a station waiting room, just before the final whistle.

The hustle and bustle is too restless, too greedy to be a true festival. There is too much anxiety and fear in it. No one is giving any real thought either to their present or to their future. Everyone just grabs what they can, knowing they may have to drop it again at any moment.

The streets are swarming with newcomers. People have grouped together in the oddest of combinations: a Moscow city councillor with an actress from Rostov, a balalaika player with a lady who had been an eminent public figure, an important courtier with a smart, young provincial reporter, a rabbi's son with the governor of a province, an actor from a small cabaret with two elderly ladies-in-waiting… And they all appear somehow bewildered—they keep glancing around, clutching at one another. Never mind who your companion may be—at least there's a human hand, a human shoulder, close beside you.

The seven pairs of clean beasts and seven pairs of unclean beasts must have felt something similar in Noah's ark. They had only just met, they were still introducing themselves, giving one another a friendly sniff—and then there they were, all feeling seasick together as they were rocked about by the rising waters.

Promenading along Kreshchatik[49] are many of those who had gone missing without a trace. Here is the public figure who, only a month before, flaring his nostrils impressively, had declared that we must not leave, that we must work and die at our posts.

"But how come you've left your post?" I call out unkindly.

"It had come to be too much of a whipping post, my dear!" he replies, doing his best to brazen it out. "First let me get my strength back a little. And then—who knows?"

And all the while his eyes dart anxiously about. Here, there, and everywhere.

Kreshchatik bustles with life. It is a place for both business and pleasure. In the middle of the pavement stands a well-known, all-knowing journalist. Like the host at some grand reception, he nods this way and that way, shakes hands to his left and to his right, walks a few steps with particularly eminent figures, grants others only a casual wave.

"Ah! At last!" he calls out to me. "We were expecting you here last week."

"*We?*"

"Kiev!"

The crowd carries me forward and Kiev shouts after me, "See you tonight! You know, at—"

That's all I manage to hear.

"We all dine there," says a voice beside me.

It's a lawyer I know. He too had disappeared from Petersburg without warning.

"How long have you been here?" I ask. "Why didn't you come and say goodbye before you left? We were worried about you."

He gives an embarrassed shrug.

"You know, the way it all happened… It really was most absurd…"

I hear cheery greetings from all sides—more than I have time to acknowledge.

I come across a colleague of mine from the *Russian Word*. "You wouldn't believe it!" he says. "The city's gone mad! Open any newspaper you like—you'll find all the best writers from both Moscow and Petersburg! The theatres have been taken over by the finest of artistic talents. The Bat is here. Sobinov is here. There's going to be a cabaret with Kurikhin in it. Ozarovsky's staging special evenings of short plays. New plays are expected from you too. You'll be asked to write for *Kiev Thought*. Vlas Doroshevich is here already, I've heard, and Lolo's expected any day. We're soon going to have a new newspaper—financed by the Hetman and edited by Gorelov. Vasilevsky's thinking of starting a newspaper too. We won't let you go. Life's in full swing here."[50]

I remember Gooskin's words about life "taking a full swing at us."

"People here don't know what's hit them," my companion continues. "Now they've seen what visitors are being paid, the local journalists are talking of going on strike. 'We're the only ones you can rely on,' they say. 'Any day now our visitors will be moving on.' And the restaurants are simply inundated by all the new customers. Cultural 'corners' and 'circles' are springing up in every square. Yevreinov will be here soon—we'll be able to open a 'theatre of new forms.' And we really need a Stray Dog.[51] This is a matter of the utmost urgency whose day has well and truly dawned."

"I'm only passing through," I say. "I'm being taken to Odessa to give some readings."

"Odessa? Now? What do you want to go to Odessa for? It's chaos there. You should wait until things have settled down a little. No, we're not letting you go."

"*We?*"

"Kiev."

Heavens!

Next I see a round, familiar face—a woman I know from Moscow.

"We've been here for ages," she says proudly. "We are, after all, a Kiev family. My husband's father used to have a house here, right on Kreshchatik. Yes, we're true Kiev natives... You know, they have very decent crêpe de chine here... My dressmaker—"

"Will you be going to Mashenka's tonight?"[52] interrupts the loud bass of an actor. "She's here for a few guest appearances... The coffee there is divine. Made with cream and cognac..."

Everyone eats and drinks. Everyone drinks, eats, and nods in agreement: Quick! Quick! All that matters is to have one more drink and one more meal and then to snatch up more food and drink to take with you! The last whistle is about to sound.

Olyonushka arranged for me to stay with some friends of hers. The eldest of the three girls worked in an office; the younger two were still in high school.

All three were in love with a tenor at the local opera; they were very sweet, gobbling away in their excitement like little turkeys.

They lived in a wing of a large house. The yard was so densely stacked with firewood that you needed a perfect knowledge of the approach channel in order to manoeuvre your way to their door. Newcomers would run aground and, their strength failing, start to shout for help. This was the equivalent of a doorbell and the girls would calmly say to one another, "Lily, someone's coming. Can't you hear? They're in the firewood."

After I had been there about three days, someone quite large got caught in the trap and began letting out goat-like cries.

Lily went to the rescue and came back with Gooskin. In only three days he had grown so much stouter that it took me a moment to recognize him.

"I thought you were still at the train station. I've been trying to find you somewhere to stay."

"You really thought I'd just wait in the station buffet for days on end?"

"I thought… something of the kind," said Gooskin, evidently feeling too lazy to lie with any conviction. "If you're going to find anywhere to stay here, you have to arrange it through a special bureau. Otherwise you don't have a chance. But, of course, if you were to make a request in person and, at the same time, provide evidence of ill health…"

"But I'm not in the least ill."

"So you're not ill? So what! You've probably had measles at some time in your life. They'll write 'has suffered from measles, must have accommodation under a roof.' Yes, something scientific like that. Well, what do you think of Kiev? Have you been to Kreshchatik? And why are there so many blondes here—can someone explain that to me?"

"It sounds as if you don't like blondes!" giggled one of the girls.

"Why do you say that? Brunettes are good too. I don't want to offend anyone, but blondes have something heavenly about them whereas brunettes are more down to earth. Ri-ight?" Turning to me, Gooskin added, "Well, we need to organize an evening for you."

"But everything about Odessa's already agreed."

"Oh… Odessa…"

He smiled mysteriously and left—plump, sleek, and sleepy-looking.

That evening I saw Averchenko and told him my concerns about Gooskin.

"I don't think you should go to Odessa with him," Averchenko replied. "Pay him his cancellation fee and get rid of him as soon as you can. He's just not the right person to put on a literary evening. Either he'll send you out on stage with a circus dog or he'll start singing himself."

"That's exactly what I'm afraid of. But what should I do?"

"Have a word with my own impresario. He's as honest as they come, and I think he has a lot of experience."

Averchenko, a thoroughly honourable man himself, imagined everyone else to be honourable and spent his whole life surrounded by crooks. Still, where was the harm in asking for a little advice?

"All right, ask this fine fellow of yours to come round."

The fine fellow came round the next day and outlined a surprising plan: "First of all, don't do any evenings in Kiev yourself because that might be detrimental to my plans for Averchenko. One literary evening is interesting enough, but when there's literature raining down on all sides, the audience will fragment and takings will plummet."

"Very good," I said. "You need to look after your own interests. But I was hoping for some advice about *my* affairs."

"With regard to your own affairs, I have some very subtle advice. Yes, in these matters you have to be very subtle indeed. First, travel on to Odessa and let Gooskin arrange an evening for you there. There's a concert hall, I'll tell you which one— there's a concert hall in Odessa where no one can hear a word you say. So, go along there for your evening and read in a terribly weak voice. The audience will, of course, be dissatisfied and they will, of course, get angry. Then you must send a note to the papers—I'm sure you have contacts in the press—yes, you must send a note saying that the evening's a waste of time. Tell people they could have more fun at home. Then arrange a second evening in the same hall. And again read in a barely audible voice—let the audience get really furious. Then I'll show up in Odessa with Averchenko, hire a small hall and get wonderful reviews everywhere. And then you just say to Gooskin, 'See what a mess you've made of everything. Everyone is up in arms. I think we have to terminate our agreement.' How can he object under circumstances like that?"

I looked at him for a while without a word, and then said, "Tell me. Did you come up with this scheme all by yourself?"

He looked down at the floor with modest pride.

"So, you're advising me to turn my own evenings into catastrophes and then publish damning reviews about them? This certainly shows originality on your part, but why does all this originality have to be at the expense of poor Gooskin? He is your colleague, your fellow impresario—why do you want to ruin him? Do you really not understand what effect this would have?"

The impresario took offence.

"Well, it seems my scheme doesn't appeal to you. In that case, you must find some other way to get rid of Gooskin. Once you've found a way to do that, you and I can come to an agreement. And then everything, I guarantee you, will be perfect."

"I don't doubt it! Never in my life have I met anyone so ingenious as you are."

He smiled, flattered.

"No, really, that's too much!"

9

Not wanting to impose on Olyonushka's young friends for too long, I set about finding somewhere else to stay. This was a long, tedious, and confusing business. It meant many hours in lines waiting to get myself registered, returning day after day to check up on things, unravelling one tangle after another.

Eventually, I obtained a room. It was in a huge hotel with a leaking roof and broken windows. The ground floor was occupied by the Bat. The first floor was empty and undergoing refurbishment. My own room was on the second floor, which was also empty.

It was a corner room; there were two windows on one side to catch the north wind, and two on the other side for the west wind. They were all double-paned, and the glass had been knocked out so skillfully that at first you didn't even notice: on the inner window it was the bottom left and top right panes that were missing, while on the outer window it was the bottom right and top left panes. At first glance, everything looked fine and you had no idea why letters were flying about the room and the dressing gown on the hanger kept flapping its sleeves.

The room was furnished with a bed, a table, a washstand, and two rattan armchairs. The armchairs were exhausted, worn out by life, and during the night they liked to stretch out their arms, legs, and backs, creaking and groaning.

I moved in on a cold, dry autumn day. I looked around and said to myself, for no apparent reason, "I wonder which of the doctors round here specializes in Spanish influenza. Because I'm going to have Spanish influenza with pulmonary complications."

With Gooskin, everything was resolved—or rather dissolved—quite happily. After receiving an advance from *Kiev Thought*, I paid him his cancellation fee and he left for Odessa entirely content.

"You're not going to be working with Averchenko's impresario, are you?" he asked jealously.

"You have my word that I won't be working either with him or with any other impresario. I hate making any kind of public appearance. I've only ever given readings at charity events, and always with great reluctance. You can rest assured. All the more so because I really don't like Averchenko's impresario."

"Well, you surprise me to death! A man like that! Just ask people in his home town of Konotop! In Konotop literally everyone adores him. Peskin the dentist once hit him with a ham bone. Because of his wife. Of course, there may be something a bit poultry about his behaviour, and he may even seem rather unattractive... Such swarthy features... And maybe it wasn't because of his wife that Peskin hit him—maybe it was to do with some business disagreement. Or maybe he didn't hit him at all, the man may just be lying—well, I'm sure his dog will believe him!"

And so Gooskin and I parted amicably. After we had finished all our goodbyes, he poked his head through the door again and asked anxiously, "Do you eat curd fritters?"

"What? When?" I asked in surprise.

"Some time," Gooskin replied.

And so we parted.

Olyonushka was the next to leave. She had been offered work at a theatre in Rostov.

Just before leaving, she said she wanted to have a heart to heart with me, to ask my advice about a matter of great complexity.

I took her to a patisserie where, dripping tears into her hot chocolate and whipped cream, she told me her story: Vladimir was terribly in love with her and he lived in Rostov. But Dmitry, who lived here in Kiev, was also terribly in love with her. Vladimir was eighteen and Dmitry was nineteen. Both were officers. She loved Vladimir, but she had to marry Dmitry.

"*Why?*"

Olyonushka sobbed and almost choked on her cake: "I must! I simply m-m-m-ust!"

"Wait, Olyonushka. And please don't howl like that. If you want to know what I think, you must tell me everything."

"It's not easy," said Olyonushka, still weeping. "It's all quite awful! Awful!"

"Stop it, Olyonushka! Stop it! You'll make yourself ill."

"I can't, the tears just keep coming…"

"Well, at the very least, stop eating cakes. You're on your eighth now, you'll make yourself ill."

Olyonushka gave a despairing shrug. "What do I care? I'd be only too happy to die—it would solve everything. But yes, you're right. I *am* starting to feel a little sick…"

Olyonushka's story was indeed emotionally complex. She loved Vladimir, but he was someone bright and cheerful and always lucky in life. Whereas Dmitry was very poor and some-how always unlucky. Everything was going wrong for him and she didn't even love him. All this meant that she simply *had* to marry him. It just wasn't right for someone to have to suffer so much: "It'll be the death of the poor man!"

At this point her howls became so alarming that the elderly owner of the café came out from behind the counter, shook her head sympathetically and gently stroked Olyonushka's hair.

"She's a kind woman!" sobbed Olyonushka. "You must give her a good tip!"

Three days later we saw Olyonushka off on her way to Rostov.

The trains were all crammed with people, and it was only with difficulty that we managed to get her a seat. We sent a telegram to the ticket office in Kharkov, to reserve a sleeping berth for her in the night train from there to Rostov, and we gave her a letter to show when she reached Kharkov.

A week later we received a letter from Olyonushka, telling the awful story of how a certain determined officer had insisted on his right to die.

There had been only one berth left in the sleeper from Kharkov, and this was duly assigned to Olyonushka. But an officer standing just behind her in the line demanded that he himself should be given this berth. The man in the ticket office argued with him, showing him our telegram and explaining that the berth was reserved. But the officer remained intransigent. He was an officer, he said, and he had been fighting for the fatherland. He was exhausted and needed to sleep. In the end, Olyonushka gave up her berth to him and crossly took a seat in a second-class carriage.

In the middle of the night she was woken by a terrible jolt and almost thrown from her seat. Cardboard boxes and suitcases flew down from the overhead luggage racks. The frightened passengers all rushed to the end of the carriage. The train was not moving. Olyonushka jumped down and ran toward the front of the train, where there was a crowd of shouting people.

Under full steam, their locomotive had collided with a freight train. The two front cars had been smashed to splinters. Having so eloquently asserted his right to die, the unfortunate officer was being retrieved from the wreckage piece by piece.

"So you don't always help someone by giving in to them," Olyonushka concluded.

The thought that the officer had died "because of her" was evidently causing her great distress.

A month after this we received a telegram: "Vladimir and Olyona ask you to pray for God's blessing."

We understood that they had married.

I began work at *Kiev Thought*.[53]

These were wild and hectic times. The air was full of confused rumours about Petlyura.[54]

"Who is this man anyway?"

"An accountant," said some.

"An escaped convict," said others.

Whether he was an accountant or a convict, he had also worked for *Kiev Thought*, if only in a modest capacity. Apparently he had been a proofreader.

The place where we newly arrived "scribes" met most often was the house of the journalist Mikhail Milrud.[55] He was a wonderful man. And we were given a warm welcome by his kind and beautiful wife and their three-year-old son Alyoshka. Alyoshka had been born into the world of journalism, and the games he played were always linked to political events. He would be a Bolshevik, a White, a member of some unidentified "band" or, later on—Petlyura himself. On one occasion, under cover of the scraping of chair legs and the tinkle of teacups and spoons, "Petlyura" crept up to me on all fours, let out a wild shriek, and sank his sharp teeth into my leg.

Milrud's wife had never before been involved in any kind of charitable work. Nevertheless, when crowds of hungry soldiers—former prisoners of war released from camps in Germany—began to arrive in Kiev and representatives of various organizations took to pontificating about our duty to society and how dangerous it would be to create a class of angry and embittered young men, who would be only too ready to listen to Bolshevik propaganda, she at once began cooking cabbage soup and buckwheat. Without the least drama, without making any political demands of anyone, she would go quietly along to the barracks with a few servants and feed up to twenty soldiers a day.

More and more people kept arriving in Kiev.

I met some old acquaintances from Petersburg—a very senior official, almost a government minister, and his family.

The Bolsheviks had tortured and killed his brother, and he had only just managed to escape them himself. Shaking with hatred and sounding like an Old Testament prophet, he would repeat, "I will not know peace until with my own hands, there on the grave of my brother, I have slaughtered enough Bolsheviks for the blood to seep down into his coffin."

He is now working quietly in an office in Petersburg. It appears he has, after all, managed to find peace, with or without seeping blood.

Vasilevsky appeared, with plans for a new newspaper. People got together, conferred, and drew up agendas.

Then Vasilevsky disappeared. [56]

In the weeks before Petlyura's arrival people were disappearing all the time. Anxiety was in the air. Even the slightest tremors registered on the sensitive membranes of the most alert souls—and these souls quickly took their bodies somewhere calmer and safer.

I had an unexpected visit from a tall young man in a strange dark-blue uniform—one of the Hetman's retinue. With great eloquence he tried to persuade me to become involved with a new newspaper that the Hetman was setting up. He said that the Hetman was a colossus and that I must support him with my *feuilletons*.

I thought that if this colossus had nothing more reliable by way of support, he must be in a somewhat shaky position. Moreover, the prospective staff of this newspaper were a motley crew. There were names I did not want to appear beside. Either the colossus had a poor grasp of the world of journalism or he just wasn't so very particular.

I promised to consider the proposal.

The young man went on his way, leaving behind a check for an unbelievably large advance—mine should I choose to accept.

After he left, I wrapped myself, like Sonya Marmeladova, in a *drap de dames* shawl and lay all day on the couch, mulling this over.[57] The check lay on the mantelpiece. I tried not to look in its direction.

Early the next morning I put the check in an envelope and sent it back to the representative of the colossus.

Some people accused me of being "excessively quixotic" and even of harming my fellow scribes since my refusal cast a shadow over the newspaper and thus made it awkward for other, more sensible, writers to join it.

But these sensible people were not, in any case, able to enjoy their life of comfort and ease for long.

Petlyura was approaching.

10

L olo joined us in Kiev.

As a native of the city, he became *Levonid* (Leonid); his wife—the actress Vera Ilnarskaya—became *zhinka Vira* (wifey Vira).

They were emaciated and exhausted. They had managed to get out of Moscow only with great difficulty—and with considerable help from our guardian angel, the giant commissar.

"When he came round after your departure," wifey Vira told me, "he was like a forlorn dog howling beside a burned-down house."

Soon we heard rumours that our commissar had been executed.

I saw Doroshevich a number of times.

He was living in an enormous apartment. He was ill and haggard. He had aged and was clearly finding it almost unbearable to be separated from his wife—a pretty, empty-headed little actress who had stayed behind in Petersburg.

Doroshevich would stride up and down his huge office and say with assumed nonchalance, "Yes, yes, Lyolya should be here in about ten days."

It was always ten days—ten days that lasted until his death. I don't think he ever found out that his Lyolya had long ago married another man—a splendid figure of a leather-clad Bolshevik commissar.

Doroshevich would have probably gone to Petersburg to fetch her had he not been so utterly terrified of the Bolsheviks.

He died in hospital, alone, in Bolshevik Petersburg.

But throughout our time in Kiev he kept pacing up and down his office, tall, thin and weak from illness, as if, with the very last of his strength, he was determined to stride forward—toward his own, bitter death.

While I was working for the *Russian Word*, I rarely saw Doroshevich. I lived in Petersburg and the editorial office was in Moscow. There were just two occasions in my life when, so to speak, he looked my way.

The first was at the very start of my newspaper career. The editors were eager to assign me to "topical *feuilletons*." There was a fashion then for these little squibs—castigating the city fathers for the unsanitary state of coachmen's yards, lamenting the "desperate plight of the modern washerwoman." You were allowed to touch on politics, but only in the lightest and most inoffensive of tones, lest the editor get it in the neck from the censor.

And Doroshevich had intervened on my behalf.

"Let her be. Let her write what she likes—and how she likes."

Then he had said something very kind: "You don't use an Arab thoroughbred to haul water."

The second occasion was during a very complicated and difficult time in my life.

At such times, you always find yourself alone. Your closest friends tell themselves that it will be best if they keep their distance: "After all, she has enough on her plate as it is."

This display of tact leaves you with the feeling that nobody cares about you in the least: "Why are they all avoiding me? They must all think it's *me* who's to blame!"

Afterward it emerges that everyone was on your side all the time. They were with you all the time in spirit. Everyone was deeply concerned, but no one dared to approach you.

But Doroshevich was different. He came up from Moscow. All of a sudden.

"My wife said in a letter that you seem in a very bad way. I felt I really must see you. I'm leaving tonight, so let's talk now. It's not good for you to get so upset."

He talked for a long time—with real kindness and from the heart; he even offered to champion me in a duel if I thought that would help.

More publicity, I answered, was the very last thing we needed.

He made me promise that if ever I needed help, advice, or friendship, I would send him a telegram, and he would get on a train to Petersburg without delay.

I knew very well that I would never summon him, and I wasn't even entirely confident that he would come if I did, but his kind words were a comfort and a support. They created an opening, a chink of light in a black wall.

This startlingly chivalrous gesture—so at odds with his reputation as someone self-satisfied, hardheaded, and enamoured only of himself—had truly moved me, which made it all the more painful to watch him now, pacing up and down his huge room and blustering away: "Lyolya should be here in about ten days. Anyway it will only be a few weeks, if not days, before the Bolshevik regime collapses. Maybe it's not even worth her leaving Petersburg. It's not the safest of times to travel. I keep hearing rumours about some kind of armed bands…"

This was a reference to Petlyura.

My premonition about Spanish influenza proved remarkably accurate.

I fell ill in the night. A 104-degree fever swept down on me like a hurricane. In my semi-delirium I remembered only one thing: that at eleven o'clock, Meskhieva, one of the actresses from the Bat, was coming to pick up some little songs of mine she was going to sing in a concert. And all through the night she kept knocking at the door, and I kept getting up to let her in and then realizing that this was delirium, that nobody was knocking, and that I was still in my bed. And then there she was, knocking at my door yet again. I forced my eyes open. It was light. A loud, clear voice was calling, "Still asleep? Then I'll come round again tomorrow."

Then quick footsteps, receding down the passage. Tomorrow! But what if I couldn't get up? Would it be twenty-four hours before anyone even knew I was ill? The hotel had no staff and nobody was due to visit me.

Horrified, I leapt out of bed and drummed on the door.

"I'm sick," I called out. "Come back!"

She heard. Half an hour later some frightened friends of mine hurried round, bringing what someone with influenza

needs more than anything—a bouquet of chrysanthemums—
and telling me, "Well, you're over the worst now!"

News of my illness got into the papers.

And since no one really had anything to do, since few
people wanted to start anything new until "the death throes of
Bolshevism" were well and truly over, my predicament evoked
the most intense sympathy.

From morning until night my room was crowded with
people. They must have all found it very entertaining. They
brought flowers. They brought sweets, which they then ate
themselves. They talked and smoked. Young couples arranged
trysts on one of the windowsills. Everyone swapped theatrical
and political gossip. There were people I didn't know at all, but
they smiled and helped themselves to food and drink the same
as everyone else. Sometimes I felt superfluous amongst this
merry crowd. Fortunately, though, they soon ceased to pay
me any attention.

"Perhaps there's a way to send them all packing?" I said
timidly to Vera Ilnarskaya, who was nursing me.

"Oh no, dear, you mustn't do that—they'd be offended. It
would be awkward. Just put up with it all for a while. You can
have some rest when you get better."

I remember one evening in particular. My guests had all
gone out to have dinner. Only Vera was still left, along with
someone unknown to me, who was saying, in what seemed
an endless drone:

"I have an estate outside Warsaw, just a small one of course..."

"I have an income from this estate, just a small one of
course..."

Was I, or was I not, dreaming all this?

"I have meadows on this estate, just small ones of course…"

"I have an aunt in Warsaw…"

"Just a small one, of course," I interrupted, surprising even myself. "But how about, if only for the sake of variety, going and calling a doctor? Yes, I can see you're someone most kind and obliging, go and fetch me a doctor, just a small one of course…"

Were those last words his or mine? I wasn't sure. I hope they were his.

The doctor came. He marvelled for a while at the state of my room.

"What's been going on in here? Have you been holding a ball?"

"No, it's just… visits from well-wishers."

"Out! Out with the lot of them! And the flowers too—get rid of them! You have pneumonia."

I was triumphant.

"Why so cheerful all of a sudden?" he asked, scared.

"Yes, it's what I said! Just what I said was going to happen!"

He must have thought I was delirious, and he most certainly was not going to share in my joy.

After I'd recovered, when I went outside for the first time, Kiev was all ice. Black ice and wind. The few pedestrians I saw were barely able to make their way along the streets. They were falling like ninepins, knocking their companions off their feet too.

I remember an editorial office I used to visit from time to time. It was halfway up an icy hill. Trying to get to it from below was hopeless—I'd manage ten steps, then slide back down again. Approaching it from above was no better; I would gain too much momentum and slide straight past. Never in my life had I encountered such ice.

The mood in the city had changed; it was no longer celebratory. Something had been extinguished. Everyone was on the alert, ears pricked, eyes darting about. Many people had quietly disappeared, to destinations unknown. There was more and more talk of Odessa.

"Things are looking up in Odessa, I've heard. Whereas round here… Peasants, armed bands… They're closing in on us… Petlyura or something…"

Kiev Thought did not fear Petlyura. Petlyura was a former employee. He would, of course, remember this.

He did indeed. His very first decree was to close down *Kiev Thought*. Long before he entered the city, he sent his minions ahead with instructions.

Kiev Thought was perplexed, even a little embarrassed.

But close it did.

11

Then true winter set in, with snow and severe frosts.

My doctor said that living in an unheated room with broken windows after a bout of pneumonia, however amusing it might seem, was not conducive to good health.

And so my friends found me a room in a *pension* for high-school girls run by a very respectable lady. They promptly gathered up my belongings and moved both them and me to this new room. They worked selflessly. I remember how Vera Ilnarskaya, who had made herself responsible for the small accoutrements of my everyday life, threw into a single cardboard box a lace dress, my silk underwear, and an uncorked bottle of ink. Verochka Charova (from the Korsh Theatre in Moscow) took charge of twelve withered bouquets that she considered of sentimental value. Tamara Oksinskaya (from the Saburov Theatre) collected together all the visiting cards heaped on the windowsills. Meskhieva carefully packed the remaining sweets and empty bottles. All in all, my move was arranged briskly and efficiently. The only things they forgot were my trunk and all my dresses in the wardrobe. But the little things were all there and that's what really matters, because it's little things that are most often forgotten.

My new room was astonishing. The kind lady who rented it out to me had evidently furnished it with all the objects that had embellished her journey through life. There were antlers and horns of all kinds, canes, woollen pom-poms, and nine or ten small tables, their stout, heavy marble tops supported by frail, splayed, stick-like little legs. It was impossible to put anything down on these tables. You could only marvel from a distance at human ingenuity: Who would have thought it possible to rest such a weight on something so insubstantial? Sometimes one of the tables would collapse of its own accord. You'd be sitting there quite peacefully and then you'd hear a sigh from the other end of the room—a table swaying for a moment before crashing down to the floor.

There was also a grand piano which—amid all this clutter—we did not immediately notice. It was awkwardly located. First you had to squeeze past some horns and an _étagère_—only then, hemmed in by three small tables, could you sit down at it.

We decided to make everything a bit nicer and more comfortable: to drape a shawl over the unused door, to move the piano to the opposite wall, and to hang the portraits of various aunties behind the wardrobe.

No sooner said than done. There was a rumble of tables, a glassy tinkle—and one of the aunties broke free from the wall all by herself.

"Good God! What was that? If the landlady hears, I'll be straight out on the street."

Blonde curly-haired Lilya, who had come to welcome me on behalf of the high-school girls, also offered her help. She immediately broke a vase full of pom-poms and collapsed in horror onto the divan, right on top of the second aunty, who had been taken down and carefully placed there out of harm's way.

A crunch and a snap. Howls. Squeals.

"Somebody sing something to drown all this racket!"

At this point everyone got down to the really important task—moving the piano.

"Wait!" I cried. "There's a little bronze dog on top of the piano, on a malachite stand. I'm sure the landlady really treasures it. Let me take it out of the way. Yes, leave this to me—you good people just smash things."

I took hold of the little dog and carefully began to lift. What a weight! And then—what was that terrible crash? And why did this dog suddenly feel so light? There it was, still in my hands. The malachite stand, however, now lay at my feet, smashed to bits. Who would have thought that the dog hadn't been glued to the stand!

"That'll fetch the landlady all right," Lilya whispered in horror.

"Whose fault is that? Why didn't you sing like I asked you to? You saw me picking up that little dog—that was your cue to start something choral. Well, you'd better get on and move the piano or we'll be here all night."

We pushed the piano out into the room, rolled it along on its casters, tucked in its long tail, and finally got it into position.

"Wonderful. Over here will be just right. Meskhieva, I'll compose a new song for you."

I fetched the stool, sat down, and tried to play a chord…
What on earth? The piano refused to play. We rolled it along a
little bit further and banged a few times on the lid. It remained
silent as silent can be.

A knock on the door.

"Sh!"

"Somebody sing something!"

But we couldn't not answer the door.

It wasn't *her*. It was an engineer I knew. He'd come to wish
me well in my new lodgings.

"Why are you all looking so tragic?"

We told him everything, including the tragedy of the grand
piano.

"The piano? I can sort that out for you in no time. First, we
just need to take out the keys."

"Darling, you're the answer to our prayers."

He sat himself down, twiddled something around—and
out came the keys.

"There! And now back they go!"

But the keys didn't want to go back.

The engineer went very quiet. He took out his handkerchief
and wiped his brow.

A terrible suspicion began to dawn on me.

"Wait! Look me in the eye and tell me the truth. Have
you ever before in your life removed the keys from a grand
piano?"

"Yes!"

"And have you ever got them back in again?"

Silence.

"Tell me the truth! Have you ever got them back in again?"

"N-n-no. Never."

Dreary, uneventful days.

The life that had bubbled up so noisily and excitedly had now subsided.

Returning to Moscow was impossible. Kiev was cut off from everywhere to the north. Those who were quicker and more alert had already left. Everyone, however, now had their plans. Remaining in Kiev was out of the question—and we all knew this.

Once, I was talking to the famous clairvoyant, Armand Duclos, in the foyer of a theatre, after a show. A soldier on duty by the door came up to us and said, "Tell me, Mr. Duclos, will Petlyura be here soon?"

Armand frowned and closed his eyes.

"Petlyura... Petlyura... three days from now."

Three days later, Petlyura entered the city.

Armand Duclos was extraordinary.

Before I left Moscow, I had been to several of his séances. His answers to the questions put to him were extremely accurate.

Later when we got to know each other, he admitted that he usually started these sessions with little prearranged tricks—but after a while he would start to feel strange. He would slip into a trance and find himself answering a question this way or that way without knowing why.

He was very young, not more than twenty. A pale, thin boy with a beautiful, tired face. He never talked about his background, but he spoke French quite well.

"I was alive many, many years ago. Then I was called Cagliostro."[58]

But he lied lazily and without enthusiasm.

I think he was simply a Jewish boy from Odessa. His impresario was an energetic young student. Armand himself was quiet and sleepy and had no business sense at all. His own success meant nothing to him.

While Armand was still in Moscow, Lenin had taken an interest in him and twice summoned him to the Kremlin; Lenin wanted to know what fate held in store for him. When we asked Armand about these meetings, he was evasive: "I don't remember. I remember only that Lenin has success till the end. As for the others, some have success and some don't."[59]

His impresario told us how alarming all this had been. He was well aware that "when something came over him," Armand would quite forget who he was dealing with.

"Well, thank God that's all behind us!"

Only a few months later, Armand was executed.[60]

The last act of our Kiev drama.

Petlyura was entering the city. There was a wave of arrests and searches.

Nobody wanted to go to bed at night. We all wanted to stay together, usually in Milrud's apartment. We would play cards to keep awake and we were always listening out to see if anyone was coming. If there was a knock or a ring at the door, we hid the money and cards beneath the table. Armand often used to join us.

"No, I can't play cards," he said. "I mean, I know every card in advance."

He then lost three nights in a row.

"How strange. When I was a little child, no one dared play with me."

"But who wants to play cards with children?" we would reply.

Quiet, always rather sleepy, he neither argued nor laughed. He was a strange boy.

"I'm always half asleep. And this sleep exhausts me. It drains my blood and saps my strength."

His beautiful face was indeed very pale. He was telling the truth.

Petlyura's men were now patrolling the streets. Unbelievably polite gentlemen in soldiers' greatcoats would click their heels and tell us which streets to avoid so as not to get caught in one of their raids.

"But who are you?" we would ask.

"We're the peasant bands you all kept talking about," these gentlemen would reply with proud humility and heavy Ukrainian accents.

The shops ran out of stock, then closed. People hid or fled. There were more and more soldiers' greatcoats to be seen.

Milrud's apartment was searched. Apparently little Alyoshka sprang out of the playroom with a ferocious cry:

"I'm Petlyura! Don't you dare!"

And the patrol respectfully withdrew.

There was a victory parade. Vinnichenko bowed to the crowds. Never had he received such ovations for any of the plays he had written.[61]

Fine fellows in new overcoats made from German cloth rode by on strong, sturdy steeds.

Muscovites said mockingly, in Ukrainian, "Long live Ukraine, from Kiev to Berlin."[62]

And then—after a last quick walk, a last quick look—we packed our cases. Time to leave.

Not far from the city, we heard the boom of cannon.

"Where?"

"Behind Bald Mountain, I think. Seems the Bolsheviks are approaching."

"Well, there's no knowing when all this will be over. Have you got a travel permit?"

"Odessa! To Odessa!"

12

I went to say goodbye to the Lavra.[63]
"God knows when I'll be here again!"

Yes, God knows…

The Lavra, the very heart of devout old Russia, was empty.
No pilgrims: no old men with little knapsacks; no old women
with little bundles tied to their walking sticks. The monks going
about their business looked troubled and anxious.

I went down into the caves. I remembered my first visit, many
years ago, with my mother, my sisters, and our old nanny. A
checkered and eventful life lay between me and the long-legged
girl with blonde pigtails I had once been. But my feelings of
awe and fear had not changed. Just as I had crossed myself and
sighed long ago, so I crossed myself and sighed now—moved
by the same beautiful and ineffable sorrow emanating from the
age-old vaults that had heard so many ancient Russian prayers
and seen so many, oh, so many Russian tears…

An old monk was selling little crosses, prayer ropes, and a
miniature image of the Mother of God, glued by some miracle
to the inside of a small, flat bottle with a narrow neck. Beside
her were two plaited candles and a lectern with a tiny icon on

157

it. And on her halo I read an inscription: "Rejoice, O unwedded Bride!" It was a wonderful miniature. To this day, having survived all my wanderings as a refugee, this small flat bottle—the old monk's small miracle—stands on my Parisian mantelpiece.

I also went to say goodbye to the Cathedral of Saint Vladimir. In front of the icon of Saint Irina, I saw a little old woman, all in black, on her knees. Her shoes were old and worn, the toes turned inward, toward each other, in a way that seemed timid and endearing. She was weeping. And while the little old woman wept, the magnificent Byzantine Empress, entwined in pearls and framed in gold, gazed sternly down at her.

We left Kiev late at night. Cannons were booming somewhere close by.

The crush at the station was unimaginable. Troop trains were occupying nearly all the lines. We didn't know whether they were just arriving or just departing. They probably didn't even know themselves.

Everyone looked bewildered, resentful, and tired.

With some difficulty we made our way to our allocated carriage. It was third class, which seemed to mean three tiers of sleeping boards. Our cases were thrown in after us.

The train stood at the station for a long time. Official and unofficial departure times had all long come and gone. We were on the second track and there were trains full of soldiers on either side of us. We could hear yells and shots. Through the gaps between cars we could see people rushing about in panic.

Sometimes people would come to our car with the latest news.

"We're all going to be thrown out. The train's being requisitioned for troops."

"Anyway, you can only go about seven miles. Then there's a junction controlled by the Bolsheviks."

"A train that came under fire has just pulled in. With dead and wounded on board."

Dead. Wounded. How accustomed we had grown to these words. No one felt any particular alarm or distress. No one said, "How awful!" or "What a tragedy!"

Our way of life had changed, and, in accord with this new way of life, we just thought, "Remove the dead and bandage the wounded."

The words were a part of our everyday language. And we ourselves could well become "dead" or "wounded," perhaps at this next junction, perhaps soon after it.[64]

Someone's teapot had been stolen. And this occasioned as much (if not more) interest and discussion as the question of the Bolshevik-controlled junction—or the possibility of our train crew now being so frightened that we might not even leave the station at all.

All of a sudden a cardboard box fell on someone's head. This was a good sign. A newly attached locomotive had sent a jolt through the carriages.

We were off.

We stopped many times. At dark stations or in the middle of nowhere, where there was more yelling and shooting and dancing pinpoints of light.

Soldiers with bayonets appeared in the doorways.

"Officers! To the end of the car!"

There were no officers in our car.

I remember seeing people running beside the track, past our windows. Breathless soldiers stormed into the car and stabbed under the benches with their bayonets.

And nobody knew what was going on, and nobody asked. Everyone sat quietly with their eyes closed, as if they were dozing, as if to show that they did not consider any of this to be in the least out of the ordinary.

We arrived in Odessa at night, to an unexpected welcome— we were locked inside the railway station and told we would not be allowed out until morning.

And that was that.

We arranged our things on the floor and sat down on top of them. It all felt very cosy. We were not being searched and we were not being shot at—what more could we want?

Hovering near me just before dawn, I saw a shadowy figure, a yellow vanity case in a delicate hand.

"Armand Duclos?"

"Yes."

He too had been on our train. He sat down beside me and started talking. In his vanity case he was carrying some exceptionally important documents. He had already been offered a million dollars, but nothing would induce him to part with them.

"I think you *should* part with them."

"I can't."

"Why not?"

"I really don't know. But it's exhausting me terribly—never being able to let go of this vanity case."

I dozed off. When I awoke, Armand was no longer there. By my feet lay his treasure, abandoned.

In the morning the station doors were unlocked and we were free to go out into the city. When the porters were piling our luggage into cabs, Armand's vanity case, which had no lock, fell open—and out tumbled a bottle of *Rue de la Paix*[65] and a nail file. And nothing more.

Time passed without any of us so much as glimpsing Armand. In the end we placed an advertisement in the paper: "Can the clairvoyant Armand Duclos please divine the location of his vanity case!"

Followed by a name and address.

So began our days in Odessa.

The same faces appeared once again. And once again people came out with all the same nonsense.

People we thought had returned to Moscow proved to be here in Odessa. Those who should have been in Odessa had long since returned to Moscow.

And nobody knew anything for certain about anyone.

The man in charge of Odessa was the young, grey-eyed General Grishin-Almazov—and no one knew anything for certain about him either.[66] Even he himself seemed a little unsure how he had come to be the city's military governor. He was, I suppose, a minor Napoleon—and his personality, like Napoleon's, mattered less than the historical forces at play around him.

Grishin-Almazov was energetic, cheerful, and strong. He flaunted his buoyant energy; he wanted everyone to know about it. He loved literature and theatre and there were rumours that he had once been an actor.

One day he even called on me and very kindly offered me accommodation at the Hotel London. And so I got a wonderful room—number sixteen. Vladimir Burtsev had stayed there before me and so there were piles of *The Common Cause* in every corner.[67]

Grishin-Almazov liked pomp and ceremony. When he visited me in the hotel, he always left a whole entourage in the corridor and two guards at the main entrance.

He was kind and considerate, easy to be with. He often spoke as if he had stepped straight from the pages of Yushkevich's *Leon Drey*.[68]

"It's very cold today," he would say. "I emphasize the word: *very.*"

"Are you comfortable in this room? I emphasize the word: *you.*"

"Do you have books for reading? I emphasize the word: *for.*"

He encouraged the hotel commandant—a bearded colonel who used to walk around all day long with two wonderful white spitzes—to take special care of me.

Grishin-Almazov was, in short, extremely courteous.

These were difficult months for him.

"The omens bode ill"—it was not for nothing that this was a catch-phrase of the time.

As the Bolsheviks drew nearer, people were little by little being robbed of all they owned; criminal gangs had taken over the abandoned quarries that formed entire catacombs under the city. Grishin-Almazov once tried to negotiate with one of the ringleaders—the notorious "Mishka the Japanese."[69] This evidently achieved little—from then on Grishin was unable to drive around town at anything less than full speed, since he had been promised "a bullet at a bend in the road."

Nevertheless, people did creep out of their unheated flats in the evenings. They went to clubs and theatres to entertain one another with terrifying rumours. When it was time to go back home, they would gather in groups and get themselves an escort—usually about half a dozen students, armed with whatever they could lay their hands on. Rings would be tucked away inside cheeks, watches hidden in shoes. This was of little help.

"So the scoundrel cocks his ear, then homes in on the ticking. I tell him, 'That's the sound of my heart, I'm frightened.' But why would they believe an honest man?"

The brigands would stop cab drivers, unharness their horses, and lead them down into their catacombs.

But we were not easily deterred. All night long, the theatres, clubs and restaurants remained crowded with people. Fabulous sums were lost at cards.

In the morning, stupefied by wine, gambling, and cigar smoke, bankers and sugar manufacturers would emerge from these clubs and blink their puffy eyelids at the sun. Shadowy figures from Moldavanka[70] would be hanging about in doorways, sifting the piles of nutshells and sausage skins for scraps and leftovers. Their eyes hungry and sullen, they would stand and watch as the revellers walked away.[71]

13

The horses of Phoebus are racing downhill.

So our days in Odessa went by. And then they started to fly faster and faster—so fast that they overtook one another.

Clubs, cabarets, little theatres, all came and went.

Some middle-aged gentlemen called round without introduction to ask me to "lend my name" to some kind of "salon." A profoundly artistic salon. Including card games and a hot dinner.

"And what will *my* role be?"

"You will be the hostess and you will receive a monthly fee."

"But I know nothing about card games and nothing about hot dinners. I think you've got a bit muddled."

They shuffled about a little, then increased their offer.

It was clear that we did not understand one another.

In the end they managed to find some popular chanteuse. And everything went like clockwork. That is, they would be closed down, pay a bribe, reopen, be closed down again, pay another bribe, etc.

"Do your police take bribes?" I asked Grishin-Almazov.

"How can you ask such a thing! The money goes exclusively to charitable works. I emphasize the word: *goes*," he replied buoyantly.

At first we refugees found life in Odessa most entertaining.

"Hardly a city at all—more like one long laugh!"

One Odessa actress kept phoning me. She wanted my songs. She had a grand piano—so I really must go to her apartment.

"All right. I'll come round tomorrow, about five o'clock."

A sigh.

"Could you possibly, perhaps, come at six? It's just that at five we always drink tea…"

"Are you quite sure an hour will be long enough for your tea?"

Sometimes we would all get together in the evenings and read aloud from the newspapers. The writers liked to pile it on thick, and their articles contained many small gems:

"The ballerina danced beautifully, which is more than can be said of the scenery."

"During the climatic scene of Ostrovsky's *The Storm*, with Roshchina-Insarova playing the title role…"

"The artiste performed Ernst's *Elegy* quite wonderfully and his violin wept, though he was only wearing a rather ordinary jacket."

"A steamer drove straight up the pier."

"On Monday night Raya Lipshits, the merchant's daughter, broke one of her legs underneath her bicycle."

But life in Odessa soon began to pall. A joke is not so funny when you're living inside it. It begins to seem more like a tragedy.

But there was one ray of light. Our much-loved editor Fyodor Blagov[72] arrived in Odessa and started gathering around him the former staff of the *Russian Word*. The *Russian Word* was to come out in Odessa. There were a number of us who were keen to write for it, and things quickly began to fall into place.

Around the beginning of spring, the poet Maximilian Voloshin[73] appeared in the city. He was in the grip of a poetic frenzy. Wherever I went, I would glimpse his picturesque silhouette: dense, square beard, tight curls crowned with a round beret, a light cloak, knickerbockers, and gaiters. He was doing the rounds of government institutions and people with the right connections, constantly reciting his poems. There was more to this than was at first apparent. The poems served as keys. To help those who were in trouble Voloshin needed to pass through certain doors—and his poems opened these doors. He'd walk into some office and, while people were still wondering whether or not to announce his presence to their superiors, he would begin to recite. His meditations on the False Dmitry[74] and other Russian tragedies were dense and powerful; lines evoking the fateful burden of history alternated with soaring flights of prophecy. An ecstatic crowd of young typists would gather around him, ooh-ing and aah-ing, letting out little nasal squeals of horrified delight. Next you would hear the clatter of typewriter keys—Voloshin had begun to dictate some of his longer poems. Someone in a position of authority would poke his head around the door, his curiosity piqued, and then lead the poet into his office. Soon the dense, even hum of bardic declamation would start up again, audible even through the closed door.

On one occasion I too received a visit of this nature.

Voloshin recited two long poems and then said that we must do something at once on behalf of the poetess Kuzmina-Karavayeva, who had been arrested (in Feodosya I think), because of some denunciation and was in danger of being shot.[75]

"You're friends with Grishin-Almazov, you must speak to him straightaway."

I knew Kuzmina-Karavayeva well enough to understand at once that any such denunciation must be a lie.

"And in the meantime," said Voloshin, "I'll go and speak to the Metropolitan.[76] Karavayeva's a graduate of the theological academy. The Metropolitan will do all he can for her."

I called Grishin-Almazov.

"Are you sure?" he responded. "Word of honour?"

"Yes."

"Then I'll give the order tomorrow. All right?"

"No, not tomorrow," I said. "Today. And it's got to be a telegram. I'm very concerned—we might be too late already!"

"Very well. I will send a telegram. I emphasize the words: *I will.*"

Kuzmina-Karavayeva was released.

In Novorossiisk, in Yekaterinodar, in Rostov-on-Don—at all the remaining staging posts of our journey—I would again encounter the light cloak, the gaiters, and the round beret crowning the tight curls. On each occasion I heard sonorous verse being declaimed to the accompaniment of little squeals from women with flushed, excited faces. Wherever he went, Voloshin was using the hum—or boom—of his verse to rescue someone whose life was endangered.

★

My old friend M appeared in Odessa. Bearing a dispatch from Admiral Kolchak in Vladivostok,[77] he had made his way across the whole of Siberia, through areas controlled by the Bolsheviks; the dispatch—written not on paper but on thin cloth—had been sewn into his greatcoat lining. His hosts, a family we both knew, told him I was in Odessa and telephoned me straightaway to tell me to come round. Our meeting was joyful, but strange. M's hosts were all huddled together in one corner of the room so as not to be in our way. Overcome with emotion, an old family nanny was peering through a crack in the door. Everyone went quiet, waiting with baited breath, imagining the scene they were about to witness: a meeting between two friends each of whom had thought that the other had died. Many tears would be shed... What times we were living through...

I went in.

"Michel! My dear! I'm so glad to see you..."

"Not as glad as I am! Things haven't been easy. Look at all my grey hairs!"

"Nonsense. I can't see a single one. But as for me! Just take a look at my left temple. Please don't make out you can't see them!"

"Not one. Literally, not even one."

"No. Come over here—the light's better. Now what do you call this? What's this if it isn't a grey hair?"

"I can't see even a hint of grey. But as for me! Look—in the light!"

"No. You're being mean and obstinate!"

"No, it's me who's gone grey. You're just wanting an argument."

"Some things never change. A true gentleman. Outshining us nobodies in every way!"

The hosts tiptoed reverently out of the room.

After these first moments of shared joy, M told me many interesting things.

M had, in the past, been anything but a military man—though he had served his country during the war. After the revolution, he had returned to his estate. When his hometown was besieged by the Bolsheviks, he had been chosen, as he put it, "to be the town dictator."

"You won't believe me, of course, but I have risked my life by carrying in my greatcoat lining decrees bearing my own signature."

He showed me these decrees. He was telling the truth.

"The Bolsheviks brought up their artillery and began shelling us. We had to run," he continued. "So there I was, riding through a field of rye. And then I saw two cornflowers right next to each other. There were none anywhere else, just these two. Like two blue eyes. And, would you believe it, I forgot where I was. I didn't even hear the guns any longer. I stopped my horse, got down, and picked the cornflowers. All around me people were running, shouting, falling to the ground. But somehow I wasn't even in the least scared. Why was that? Was it bravery?"

He stopped to think.

"And then?"

"Next it was the Volga. It's absurd! I was in command of a fleet. We didn't fight at all badly. Remember what a fortune-teller said to me around five years ago? How not long before my death I'd be an officer in the navy? And everyone made jokes about a big stout man like me wearing a hat with little ribbons. Well, the fortune-teller was right. Now I'm on my way to Paris and then—via America and Vladivostok—back to Admiral Kolchak. I'll return his admiral's cutlass to him, the one he threw into the water. The sailors fished it out and said I must take it back to him, with their compliments."[78]

He said he'd seen Olyonushka in Rostov. She was acting in a theatre there and living very happily with her husband, who looked like a schoolboy in military uniform. Olyonushka had become a strict vegetarian—she would cook some sort of twigs for herself and steal pieces of meat from her husband's plate.

"Why not just put some meat on your plate to begin with, Olyonushka?" M had asked.

Olyonushka's little husband had gone red in the face with agitation: "Oh no, no! Don't say such things. You'll make her angry. She has her convictions."

M was preparing for a long journey. He was in a hurry. It was important to establish more reliable communications with Kolchak and, in particular, to pass on to him various decisions taken by the authorities in Odessa. M was the first messenger to have got through from Kolchak.

He was in good spirits. He believed ardently in Kolchak and the White cause. "I will gladly, and with no thought for myself, carry out this mission that has been entrusted to me. I feel at peace with myself. Only one thing troubles me—my black opal ring. The opal has cracked—cracked in the shape of a cross. What do you think that means?"

I did not say, but there was no doubting this omen. Exactly a month later, M died.

He had very much wanted to get me out of Odessa. "The omens bode ill!"—as people kept saying.

M was leaving on a torpedo boat and he promised to secure me the necessary permissions. But the weather was vile, there were ferocious storms out at sea, and I refused to go with him.

Countless friendly voices were telling M that I would be all right, that he had nothing to worry about:

"No, if Odessa has to be evacuated, we certainly won't forget Nadezhda Alexandrovna. Surely you understand that!"

"She'll be first to board the steamer, I give you my word!"

"As if any of us could leave Odessa without first making sure she can leave too! How absurd can you get!"

(Things did indeed get absurd, but not in the way these people meant.)

I was awoken early in the morning. It was very cold. There were blue shadows on M's pale cheeks.

When someone wakes you early on a blind winter's morning, it's always for a farewell, or a funeral, or on account of some misfortune, or some terrible news. And in the dim, sunless light your body trembles; every drop of blood in your body trembles.

There were blue shadows on M's cheeks.

"Well, farewell. I'm going now. Make the sign of the cross over me."

"God be with you."

"This time it probably won't be for long. Not long at all."

But in that gloomy dawn, that ghostly image of my future, I had no hope at all of any sweet and simple joys. I repeated quietly, "God be with you. But as for whether we'll see each other again—who knows? We know nothing at all—every time we part, it's forever."

And that was the last we saw of each other.

A year later, the Russian consul in Paris gave me the ring with the black opal.

All M's other belongings had gone. After M's death, some opportunist staying in the same hotel had gone into his room and taken everything. He had taken luggage, clothes, linen, rings, a cigarette case, a watch, even little bottles of scent, but he hadn't dared touch the black opal. He must have sensed something about it.

That opal had an interesting history.

At one time—around the beginning of the war—I had had something of a passion for gemstones. I had studied them and collected legends about them.[79] And an old man by the name of Konoplyov used to come round, bringing precious stones from the Urals, and sometimes even from India. He was someone I felt at ease with—a sweet old man with only one eye. He would spread a piece of black velvet on the table, under the lamp, and with long thin tweezers he called "scoopers" he would reach into the box and take out little shining lights—blue, green and red. He would lay them out on the velvet, examine them, and tell stories about them. Sometimes a stone would misbehave, refusing to yield to the scoopers. It would struggle like a live fledgling, giving off sparks of fear.

"There's a stubborn one for you," the old man would grumble. "Balas ruby, orange—a hot orange, see? And here's a sapphire. Look at how it flowers. Blue, green, like the eye on a peacock's tail. What matters in a sapphire is not whether it's light or dark, but at what point it turns lilac, at what point it flowers. You need to understand this."

You could spend long hours sitting with the tweezers and turning over the cold little lights. I would remember legends: "If you show an emerald to a snake, tears will flow from its eyes. The emerald is the colour of the Garden of Eden. Bitterly does the snake remember its sin."

"Amethyst is a chaste and humble stone. Its touch is cleansing. The ancients used to drink from amethyst cups, lest wine intoxicate them. Of the High Priest's twelve stones, none was more important than the amethyst. And the Pope blesses Books of Prayer with an amethyst."

"Ruby is the stone of those who are in love. It intoxicates without touch."

"Alexandrite—our astonishing stone from the Urals—was first found during the reign of Alexander II. Prophetically, it was named after him. Its shifting colours foretold the tsar's fate—blossoming days and a bloody sunset."[80]

"And the diamond, a clear jasper, symbolizes the life of Christ."

I loved stones. And what wonderful freaks there were among them: a light blue amethyst, a yellow sapphire, another sapphire that was pale blue except for a bright yellow spot of sunlight. Konoplyov called this a "flaw"—but if you ask me, that sapphire had a hot little heart.

Sometimes he would bring a piece of grey rock containing a whole litter of little emeralds. Like children lined up by height—getting smaller and smaller, wan, blind as puppies. They had been hurt; they had been dug up too early. To come to maturity, they would have needed to stay deep in the hot ore for many more millennia.

During this time when I was so in love with stones, the artist Alexander Yakovlev had come round with a few opals.[81] They were strange, dark opals. Some other artist had brought them from Ceylon and asked Yakovlev to sell them for him.

"Opals bring bad luck," I had said. "I'm not sure I want them. But let me have a word with Konoplyov."

Konoplyov said, "If you have doubts, you really mustn't buy them. But let me show you some stones myself, some quite wonderful stones. And I can let you have them for almost nothing. Here, look. A whole necklace."

He unfolded a chamois cloth and, one after another, took out twelve enormous and unbelievably beautiful opals. Pale moonlit mist. And in the moonlight, crimson and green lights flashing: "Stop... Go... Stop... Go..." The shifting colours both enticed and confused...

"You can have them for nothing," Konoplyov repeated with a smile.

I was held by the play of the moonlight. You could stare at it and see only a quiet mist. A flash of light—and then, beside it, a second flash that swelled up into a flame. It would engulf the first; then both would vanish.

"For nothing. But there's something I must tell you. I sold these stones, just as you see them, to Mrs. Martens, the wife of the professor. She liked them very much and bought them. But then, only the next morning, her servant came round with the stones; Mrs. Martens wanted me to take them back. Her husband, Professor Martens, had passed away in the night, quite unexpectedly. So, it's up to you. If this story doesn't put you off, please take them, but I won't try to persuade you."[82]

I didn't take Konoplyov's opals, but I decided to have one of the black ones from Ceylon. That evening I looked at it for a long time. It was beautiful. It had two lights—green and deep blue. And the flame leaping out from the opal was so powerful that it seemed to have a life of its own. It shivered and shimmered not inside the stone but in the air just above it.

I bought one opal. M bought another just like it.

And that's when it all began.

I can't say that the opal brought me any specific misfortune. It's the pale, milky opals that bring death, sickness, sorrow, and separation. This one simply snatched up my life and embraced it with its black flame—until my soul began to dance like a witch on a bonfire. Howls, screeches, sparks, a fiery whirlwind. My whole way of life consumed, burned to ashes. I felt strange, savage, elated.

I kept the stone for about two years and then gave it back to Yakovlev, asking him, if he could, to return it to whoever had brought it to him from Ceylon. I thought that, like Mephistopheles, it needed to retrace its steps, to go back the same way it had come—and the sooner the better. If it tried to go any other way, it would get lost and end up in my hands again. Which was the last thing I wanted.

As for Yakovlev, I know he kept one stone for himself. I don't know if he kept it for long, but I know that he too was snatched away by a blue-green wave, which spun him round and hurled him into faraway slant-eyed Asia.

And the stone M bought did something similar to his own quiet and peaceful life. His life had been so tranquil: a soft armchair, an ivory paper knife between the rough pages of a book by his favourite poet, languid hands with nails polished like precious stones, a grand piano, a portrait of Oscar Wilde in a tortoiseshell frame, Kuzmin's poems copied out in a minuscule script...[83]

And then—the languid hands dropped the uncut book. War, revolution, an absurd marriage, being chosen as the "dictator of his home town," putting his signature to monstrous decrees, guerrilla warfare on the Volga, Admiral Kolchak, a long and terrible journey across Siberia. Odessa. Paris. Death. A deep cross-shaped fissure cutting through the black stone. The end.

New refugees kept appearing in Odessa: from Moscow, Petersburg, and Kiev.

It was easiest to obtain a travel pass if you were an actor or singer. The amount of artistic talent in Russia proved truly remarkable—opera and theatre companies began to head south in droves.

"We got out with no trouble at all," you would hear some Petersburg hairdresser say, smiling serenely. "I was the leading man, my wife was the ingénue, aunty Fima was the coquette, Mama was in charge of the box office and we had eleven prompters. We all got through. Of course, the proletariat was a little puzzled by the number of prompters, but we explained that no element of the dramatic art is more important. Without a prompter a play can't run at all. And prompters get worn out sitting so still in their booths—and so this crucial element of the art has to be repeatedly replaced by fresh elements."

There was an opera company made up entirely of noble fathers.

And a ballet company that was all elderly nannies and headmistresses.

Every new arrival adamantly asserted that the Bolshevik regime was falling apart and that, to be honest, it was hardly even worth unpacking one's bags. But unpack them they did…

There was a general air of excitement, though you couldn't quite call it high spirits.

"The Entente! The Triple Entente!"

We looked out to sea, hoping to glimpse British or French "pennants."[84]

Money started slowly disappearing. Shopkeepers would give change in their own special notes, which they would later sometimes fail to recognize.

Everything was getting more expensive by the day. Once, a salesman pointed with tragic solemnity at a piece of cheese he was wrapping for me and said, "Keep an eye on it—it's growing more expensive by the minute!"

"Well, wrap it up quickly," I said. "Maybe the paper will slow it down."

And then, all of a sudden, we lost Grishin-Almazov. He left Odessa incognito, without a word to anyone. There were urgent matters he needed to discuss with Kolchak. It was not long before we heard the tragic news. He was intercepted by the Bolsheviks while crossing the Caspian Sea. Seeing an approaching ship with a red flag, the grey-eyed governor of

Odessa threw several cases of documents into the water, leaned over the side, and put a bullet through his forehead. He died the death of a hero.

A hero, Grishin-Almazov. I emphasize the word: *hero*!

His death evoked little response in Odessa. I noticed only that the hotel commandant's greetings became more perfunctory and his fluffy dog stopped wagging its tail at me. One day the commandant knocked on my door. Sounding preoccupied, he informed me apologetically that he had found me a room in the International, since the whole of the London was being requisitioned for use as a military headquarters.

I was very sorry to leave my dear room number sixteen where at six o'clock every evening the radiator would warm up a little, where the mirror above the mantelpiece had sometimes reflected the faces of people I loved—the dry, aristocratic face of Ivan Bunin, the pale cameo silhouette of his wife, the piratical Alexey Tolstoy and his lyrical wife Natasha Krandievskaya, and Sergey Gorny, and Lolo, and Nilus and Pankratov.[85]

So there I was, another stage of my journey now over. There were now many behind me—though still many ahead...

And around us we began to glimpse a kind of man we hadn't seen before—coat collar turned up, constantly looking over his shoulder, quick to slip behind the nearest gate.

"They're sneaking in already. Yes, I assure you, we are being infiltrated. We saw a face we'd seen before—a commissar from Moscow. He pretended not to know us and made himself scarce."

"It doesn't matter... The Entente... they'll ship in reinforcements... It'll be all right."

And then, all of a sudden, a familiar phrase. It had caught up with us. It might be out of breath, but there it was: "The o-mens bo-ode ill!"

Yet again!

14

The first issue of *Our Word* came out. The general mood of the paper was combative and buoyant.

My feuilleton "The Last Breakfast" struck completely the wrong note. In it I wrote about the nightlife of the wealthy, the ominous silence all around, the rustles and whispers in the underground world that "they" were already infiltrating—and a prisoner's last breakfast before his execution.[86]

This was not what people wanted.

"Why all this doom and gloom? Why the ominous prophesies? Now of all times—with the Entente... with fresh troops being shipped in... with the French..." And so on and so forth.

"Are you blind? Just look at all the activity in the harbour!"

"...the pennants!"

"...the Triple Entente!"

"...the soldiers from France!"

I must have been very mistaken indeed.

A plucky group of writers and actors decided to open a "cellar" on some rooftop or other. À la Stray Dog of course. All they needed was some money and the right name. The way everyone was talking about the French, I suggested they call it "L'Entente de ma Tante."

The International, I heard people saying, was also going to be requisitioned and turned into a military headquarters. If so, I would once again be homeless. I recalled with horror my first days in Odessa—an icy room in a private apartment where snow blew straight into the bathroom through a broken window. I used to stand at the washbasin while the snow fell onto my head. The owner used to walk to the bathroom in an overcoat with the collar turned up and wearing a sheep-skin hat. His wife somehow managed to wash with her hands tucked in a muff. Perhaps their hats and muffs really did keep the two of them nice and warm, it's hard to say. I just shiv-ered and sneezed and tried to warm up by doing exercises from every gymnastic regime then in existence. This was not an experience I wanted to have to go through again. Even though it was spring, and even though spring can't but lead to summer—which meant that there was no real need to be worrying about the cold—the thought of another difficult search for somewhere to live was upsetting. It was exhausting merely to think about it. Better not to think about anything at all. Not least because I was unable to imagine myself living a settled life in Odessa. While I was still in my room in the London, visitors often used to say to me, "What a wonderful view you're going to have in spring!"

And I had always replied, "I'm not sure. I can't see myself here in the spring. The omens bode ill..."

One bright sunny day I was walking along the street when I saw something unprecedented—black soldiers marching along from the quay, leading heavily laden donkeys. As they approached, I could see the gleaming whites of the soldiers' eyes. This, evidently, was the French Army. The enthusiasm of the city's inhabitants was muted:

"A fine lot they've sent us. Is this the best they could do?"

The negroes grinned, baring their fierce teeth, and shouted out something that sounded like "Habdallah Amdallah"[87]— there was no knowing whether they were swearing at us or greeting us.

But then, what did it matter? We would learn soon enough.

The donkeys were gaily swishing their tails. This was a more cheerful omen.

"So? What do you think to Odessa? Ri-ight?"

A strangely familiar voice.

"Gooskin!"

"Ri-ight? It's hardly a city—more like one great tangerine. But how come you aren't sitting in a café? That's where literally all the whipped cream of society rises."

Gooskin. But I hardly recognized him. All elegantly turned out in subtle shades of dove grey: jacket, tie, hat, socks, gloves. A perfect dandy.

"Oh Gooskin! It seems I'm about to be homeless. I'm in despair."

"Despair!" said Gooskin. "Well, despair no more. Gooskin will find you someplace. You've probably been telling yourself, 'That Gooskin, he's just—pff!'"

"I assure you I've never thought you were 'just—pff!'"

"But the fact is, Gooskin, Gooskin is… Do you want some carpets?"

"What?" For a moment I felt quite scared.

"Carpets. These here Moroccaneers have brought all sorts of junk with them. Absolutely wonderful things, and they're dirty cheap. So cheap they're literally going for a singsong. To give you an idea, I can quote you an exact price: a wonderful carpet, the very latest antique quality, eight and a half foot in length by five and a half foot... no, by five foot six in width... Well, for a carpet like that you'll be paying... what's comparatively a very modest price."

"Thank you Gooskin. Now no one can possibly swindle me. I know exactly what I should pay."

"Ach, Madame Teffi, what a shame you changed your mind back then about going on tour with Gooskin. Not long ago I was touring with this singer. Sobinov—rather a louse, you know. As a matter of fact, I once took a shot at him."

"You tried to shoot Sobinov? Why?"

"Well, I took aim at him, which comes to more or less the same thing. Yes, I took aim at Sobinov, but somehow nothing much came of it. You see, I'd brought this louse of a singer to Nikolaev. I'd rented a hall, sold tickets, got him an audience, everything! And you know what? The scoundrel didn't hit a single high note. Wherever there should have been a high note, what *he* did—and God knows where he got the idea from!— what *he* did was take out his handkerchief and blow his nose as if blowing one's nose on stage were the most natural thing in the world. The audience had paid good money—and there they were, waiting for their high notes, but that scoundrel just kept blowing away. Anyone would have thought he was on his way to Siberia. And then he went to the cashier and demanded his fee. I got angry then, I couldn't have been more like a lion. When I'm angry, my rages are terrible. I said, 'Excuse me, but what about your high notes?' Yes, those were my exact words. He was silent for a moment. Then he said, 'If I hit high notes in Nikolaev, what notes am I supposed to hit in Odessa? Or London, or Paris, or even America for that matter? Or are you going to tell me Nikolaev is as much of a city as America?' Well, what could I say to that? There was no mention of high notes in the contract. So I said nothing at all, although I did say, 'Well, you probably don't even possess any high notes.' And he said, 'Actually I have a great many high notes, but I prefer not to let *you* call the tune. Today you want a high "la" in an aria—tomorrow, in the very same aria, you'll be wanting a high "si." And all for the same price. Well, you go and find yourself some boy to sing for you. This is a small town and it really doesn't need any high notes,' he said, 'especially with all this revolution and brotherly butchery round about.' Well, what could I say to that?"

"Not much."

"But how about *you* giving a public reading now? I'd advertise it, in great big letters, on every post and pillar and on every wall. Ri-ight? Yes, in great big letters: An Upstanding Program…"

"Outstanding, I think you mean."

"Out where?"

"Outstanding. The program."

"All right then—outstanding. I'm not one to argue. Why would I rock the boat over a few split hairs? And we could add: An Outstounding Triumph."

"Astounding, I think you mean."

"You ladies and your delicate nerves! So now you don't want your 'Out' after all. Well, neither do I. After all, everyone writes 'upstanding'—why would I want to stand out!"

Suddenly he stopped, looked around and asked in a whisper, "Perhaps you need some foreign currency?"

"No. What for?"

"For Constantinople."

"But I'm not leaving Odessa."

"Aren't you?"

He looked at me doubtfully.

"Are you sure? Well, if that's what you say…"

It seemed he did not believe me.

"What makes you think I'm going to Constantinople? Who put that idea into your head?"

Gooskin's reply was enigmatic: "Perhaps I have ideas in my head anyway."

I was at a loss. I just stared at the dove-grey Gooskin, at the impatient tails of the donkeys, at the fiercely grinning negroes. Was it those dark faces that had turned Gooskin's thoughts to Constantinople?

Strange…

15

The days began to fly faster still, as if fleeing in fright.

How many more days were there? Not many. Three? Four? Perhaps six? I don't remember.

But one morning I was woken by voices, stamping feet, and slamming doors.

I got up.

I was met by a strange sight. Everyone scurrying about, dragging trunks, suitcases, bundles, and cardboard boxes down the corridor. Doors left wide open. Scraps of paper everywhere, and pieces of string.

Were all of these people being thrown out? Well, I'd find out soon enough.

The lobby was a great heap of baggage—baggage of every kind. People were bustling about, exchanging anxious whispers, pressing money on one another, talking about passes and travel permits. And all in a state of great alarm. Flushed, eyes on stalks, arms spread, hats pushed to the back of their heads.

Clearly the military headquarters was about to arrive: Did this mean I was going to be thrown out too?

Just in case, I went back, took my dresses from the wardrobe and my linen from the chest of drawers, quickly stuffed everything into my trunk, and set off toward the editorial office.

There they were sure to know everything.

But what I saw out on the street was still more unexpected. Once again the black soldiers were driving the donkeys along, only this time the donkeys were going back down toward the sea, their tails to the city. The soldiers were beating them with sticks, and they were going at a fast trot.

What could all this mean?

Out of a laundry, with an armful of wet washing, runs a French soldier. At his heels are two shrieking washerwomen: "No! Stop! You're not getting away with this! No! Might not even be yours!"

Steam billows out through the open door. Inside the laundry I see French soldiers snatching clothes from the hands of washerwomen. Everyone screaming and shouting. And a solitary gentleman in a bowler hat.

What on earth is going on? Has war now been declared against washerwomen?

As I remember it, Odessa washerwomen truly were the scourge of God. What didn't these women try to get away with? I remember one who refused to return half a dozen of my own handkerchiefs.

"You'll be compensated," she said haughtily.

"In what way?"

"I'm not charging you for the laundering of those handkerchiefs!"

At another laundry I saw more hand-to-hand combat.

"Madame Teffi!"

I turned round.

It was a man I barely knew—from *Our Word*, I think. He'd been running and he was out of breath.

"A fine state of affairs, isn't it? They've unleashed a real panic. And here you are—strolling around as if you haven't a care in the world. Don't tell me you've done all your packing already!"

"Packing? Where for?"

"Where for? Constantinople."

Why was everyone so eager to send me to Constantinople?

But he'd already run on ahead, waving his arms about and wiping his forehead.

What on earth had happened?

I had had visitors the day before—and not one of them had said a word about Constantinople. Was the whole of Odessa being evacuated? But why so suddenly?

The editorial office was in chaos.

"What's happened?"

"What do you mean, 'What's happened?'? The French have abandoned us, that's what's happened. We've got no choice—we have to run."

Constantinople. Now I understood.

We had rolled our way down the map, all the way from the north. We had thought we'd just stay a little while in Kiev, then go back home. I'd even joked with my fellow writers. I'd said, "See! Our tongues really have led us to Kiev!"[88]

We'd been forced all the way down the map. Now there was only the sea. We would have to swim for it. But where to?[89]

All kinds of schemes were being concocted.

Our Word was going to charter a large schooner, take all the staff, along with the rotary press and supplies of printing paper, and head under full sail for Novorossiisk.

But no one really believed even the words coming out of their own mouths.

"What about you?" they asked. "Where are you going?"

"Nowhere at all. I'm staying in Odessa."

"But they'll string you up."

"That will be tiresome. But what else can I do?"

"Find some way to wangle yourself a pass—so they'll let you on board some steamer or other. And get on with it—don't waste time!"

I had absolutely no ability to "wangle" things for myself.[90]

Sitting on a windowsill in one of the editors' rooms was Alexander Kugel.[91] He looked pale and unkempt and was evidently thinking aloud: "Where's there to go? If *they* are already here… If no one can protect us… They seem to have the might. What if they have right on their side too?"

I went up to him, but he went on talking to himself, not even seeing me.

Still, it seemed most people really were leaving Odessa. And I couldn't just stay there all on my own. I had to find a way to get out.

Only a month earlier, kind people had been exclaiming—with tears of rapture "of which they were not ashamed"—that should Odessa be evacuated they would see to it that I was first to board one of the ships. This was the moment to remind them about their promises.

I telephoned A, the lawyer. His daughter answered, "Papa's not here."

"Are you leaving?"

"N-no, nothing's at all clear. I don't know."

I rang B.

His landlady answered. "They've left. All of them."

"Where to?"

"To the ship. They got their passes long ago, from the French."

"Oh! Really! Long ago..."

They too had made promises, and with tears in their eyes.

I wanted to have a word with one or two of my literary friends, but much of the city had been cordoned off by soldiers. Why? No one knew. No one knew anything at all.

"Why are the French leaving?"

"There's been a secret telegram from France. France is having a revolution too. Now they've gone Communist, their troops can't go on fighting our Bolsheviks."

Revolution in France? What nonsense![92]

"They're not really leaving," said someone else. "They're only pretending to leave. To fool the Bolsheviks."

A lady I knew darted out of a hairdresser's.

"It's outrageous! I've been waiting for the last three hours. All the hairdressers are jam-packed... Have you had your curls done already?"

"No," I replied in bewilderment.

"What's got into you? The Bolsheviks are coming and we have to leave. Are you telling me you're going to leave without having your hair done first? Zinaida Petrovna's no fool. She said:

'I realized yesterday that things were getting serious, so I went and had a Marcel wave and a manicure straightaway!' Now the hairdressers are all jam-packed. Well, I'm off…"

I was passing the home of the lawyer I'd phoned earlier, so I decided to call in and see if he could tell me anything.

His daughter opened the door.

"Papa's still out. He'll be back in a couple of hours."

Their entire hall was heaped with clothes, linen, hats, and shoes. There were open trunks and suitcases, still only half full.

"Are you leaving?"

"I think so…"

"Where are you going?"

"Constantinople, I think. Although we don't have any passes—Papa's trying to arrange for some now. Very likely, we won't go at all."

The phone rang.

"Yes!" she shouted into the receiver. "Yes, yes. Together. Are the cabins next to each other? Wonderful! Papa's coming to pick me up at seven."

To spare the girl the embarrassment of realizing I would have overheard, I quietly opened the door and slipped out.

Out on the street I had another encounter.

It was a woman I knew, a native of Odessa. She was very excited, even elated.

"Darling!" she exclaimed. "You won't believe it! It's strong as hide. Quick—before it's all gone."

"What? Where?"

"Crêpe de chine. Wonderful quality! I've got myself a dress length. But what are you looking so surprised about? It's an opportunity we can't afford to miss. They're selling it off cheap—otherwise it will all get confiscated by the Bolsheviks. Don't just stand there! What are you waiting for?"

"Thank you, but I'm not quite in the mood."

"Well, the shopkeeper's not going to stand around waiting for your mood to change. And believe me—we may not know what the future holds in store, but we can be sure there'll be no getting by without crêpe de chine."

I called on some other friends, the Ns.

They didn't know anything. They didn't even know that the French troops were leaving. Nevertheless they too had seen troubling signs.

"Our friend Hammerbeak has moved in now. He's taken over the living room. Listen!"

I listened.

The living room was at the far end of the corridor. I could hear the sound of a very unpleasant and rusty voice, singing:

> Madame Lou-lou…
> I love you-ou…

I understood. It was the voice of "Hammerbeak," a very suspicious character indeed, who in the past used to scurry down the corridor with his face turned to the wall. One of the Ns' visitors had recognized him and even told them his Party alias. Hammerbeak was a Bolshevik from Moscow.

He used to call on the Ns' landlady, so he could eavesdrop and spy on everyone. At the same time he had whispered sweet nothings to her and flirted with her, since she wasn't so very old and went about all day in a dress with a plunging neckline. The flesh this revealed was always generously dusted with a coating of flour-like powder. Her eyes bulged out from beneath their plump lids and she had a nose like an awl. In a word—love's young dream.

Late in the evening, when she was done with the prose of denunciations, she would let out little dove-like coos: "Oh, oh! And where is my love? Where is my true joy?"

"Your true joy is right here beside you!" the rusty voice would reply.

And now her "true joy" was no longer in hiding. Her true joy had moved in the day before, with its basket of things, and had bellowed into the kitchen, "Annushka! Clean my breeches!"

The Bolsheviks were no longer in hiding.

The omens did indeed bode ill.

The Ns were not preparing to go anywhere. It was reassuring to know that at least some people were staying put.

I went back to my hotel.

The doormen had all disappeared. Almost all the rooms were empty, their doors wide open.

I'd only just got back when there was a knock at my door.

In flew K, someone I knew from Moscow.

"Ah, I came round a while ago. You don't happen to have any money, do you? The banks are all closed and we've got no money for the journey. My wife's at her wit's end."

"Where are you going?"

"Vladivostok. We're leaving tonight on the *Shilka*. What about you?"

"I'm not going anywhere."

"You're joking! You're mad! Staying behind in a city that's going to be handed over to gangsters! They say the Moldavanka's already sharpening its knives. They're just waiting for the last of the French troops to leave—then they'll take over the whole of Odessa."

"But what can I do?"

"We were quite certain you'd already arranged something. Come with us to Vladivostok. We've got a pass for the *Shilka*. We can take you with us."

"Thank you. I'm very grateful."

"Then be at the harbour at eight sharp, with all your luggage. Don't forget—eight sharp!"

"Yes, of course. And give Leila a kiss from me."

Now that something had been arranged, I realized just how much I wanted to leave. Now that I could gather my thoughts, I felt frightened. I could see what life would be like for me if I stayed. It wasn't death itself that I was afraid of. I was afraid of maddened faces, of lanterns being shone in my eyes, of blind mindless rage. I was afraid of cold, of hunger, of darkness, of rifle butts banging on parquet floors. I was afraid of screams, of weeping, of gunshots, of the deaths of others. I was tired of it all. I wanted no more of it. I had had enough.

16

I opened my window.

I could hear shooting on one of the side streets.

I packed my things, then went downstairs.

The lobby had quietened down. There were still a few suitcases against the walls, but people were no longer bustling about. Even the hotel staff had disappeared. There was just a messenger boy, hanging about by the front door.

"Who's doing the shooting?" I asked him.

"They're just scaring the shpeculators away."

"What speculators?"

"Currency shpeculators. The streets are full of 'em—just look round the corner. They sell foreign currency to the people who're leaving. That's why they're shooting at 'em."

The boy seemed to think this a good thing.

I went outside and glanced round the corner. A little way off, there were indeed many small groups of people, talking and waving their arms about.

A shot would ring out. The groups would slowly break up, then quickly re-form.

The boy stopped me. "No, not that way," he said, "you

might get shot. And you can't go left neither—that way's roped off."

"Why?"

"'cos of the looters—to keep them from the International and the London. Them bourgeois and foreigners make rich pickings. The hotels is always first to get looted."

This was not a comforting thought.

"Are there many people still here in the hotel?"

"Nope. Hardly anyone. All gone."

To save time in the evening, when I'd have my luggage with me, I decided to go down to the harbour and see where the *Shilka* was moored.

The road down to the sea was still open.

The harbour seemed empty.

Further out, at anchor, lay the big ships: the *Kherson*, the *Caucasus*, the various ships from other countries.

Among the barges moored to the quay I found the *Shilka*. It looked rather small. Had it really come all the way from Vladivostok? Across the Indian Ocean?

There wasn't a soul on board, nor was there any smoke coming out of its funnel…

Well, I thought, there's still plenty of time before eight o'clock.

After memorizing the location, I went back to the hotel.

I tried to telephone my friends, but the line was dead.

I tracked down the young messenger boy, and together we pulled my luggage down the stairs.

"Do you think I'll be able to find a cab?"

"A cab? Well, er… If you want a cab, you must flag one down by the quay. You won't find no cabs round here."

We agreed that he would go down to the quay and order a cab to pick me up around seven. It was better to get there early. I didn't want to make my friends anxious.

I went back up to my room.

There was something hopeless about these empty corridors, these gaping doors, these floors strewn with scraps of paper and pieces of string that no one was sweeping up.

A whirlwind had passed through the hotel, leaving only dust and litter…

I sat down in a chair by the window, wanting to gather my thoughts, to look quietly inside myself and think things over.

My eye was caught by my little cypress-wood cross, tied to the headboard of the bed. It was from the Solovetsky monastery, which I had visited a few years before this.[93] I was always forgetting it, then remembering it at the last moment and taking it with me. And it had become a kind of symbol for me… though that's not something I want to talk about.

I untied my cross. A simple cross, carved from wood, it was the kind one places on the breast of the deceased. My thoughts went back to the Solovki islands, to the melancholy, sudden cries of the seagulls and the eternal wind—the cold, salty wind gnawing away at the scrawny branches of the pine trees. And the novices' gaunt faces, pale locks of hair poking out from beneath shabby skullcaps. Severe northern faces. Like icons.

An elderly monk at a tiny church deep in the forest. On the church walls were all seven of the archangels. Michael with a sword; Raphael with a censer; Barachiel the gardener of Paradise, with roses in his hands;[94] Gabriel, the angel of the Annunciation, with a stem of lilies; Jehudiel the avenger, with his whips; Selatiel, the angel of prayer, hands crossed over his chest; and Uriel, the mournful angel of death, holding a candle the wrong way up, its flame pointing down.

"Your saints are all angels, father?"

The little old man blinked, not understanding, not hearing. "Where? Where?"

Then the lines of his wrinkled face radiated out into a smile.

"Holy angels, my dear, holy angels!"

In the little monastery shop were crosses, prayer ropes, woven prayer belts.[95]

A gaunt, weathered-looking old woman, with round hawk-like eyes and an air of foreboding, was rummaging through the belts.

"Death, father, give us everything we need for death. Last rites for all t' family, we be nine. We Orthodox must prepare, Father. It be war and more war. Then, who knows?"

There was indeed no knowing. I chose a small cross made of cypress wood...

Ever since then I had kept it with me, hanging it at the head of my bed. During black and sleepless nights I had buried a great deal beneath this small cross. [96]

There was a knock at the door.

Without waiting for an answer, in rushed P—a minor public figure. His hair was dishevelled, his beard all askew, as if from the wind, and one eye slightly swollen.

"Oh, the struggle it's been to get here!" he cried out. He seemed confused; he was looking straight past me. "Shooting on one side, and all cordoned off on the other... I only just managed to slip through."

"How very good of you to think of me at a time like this."

"How could I not think of you? You were the first person who came to mind! You're sure to be able to help. You know everyone, everyone who matters—you're famous. We're in a terrible situation—we've been let down badly. S promised to get us all onto a steamer for Constantinople. He swore the French would let us on board and told us to go and collect our passes at eleven o'clock this morning. So along we go. And then there we sit, waiting like idiots in front of the locked doors of the French consulate—until finally, at three o'clock, a secretary comes into the courtyard and professes total astonishment at our presence. Monsieur S, apparently, had found it necessary to depart at eight o'clock this morning and had left no further instructions. Well, what do you make of that? Now you're our only hope."

"But what can *I* do?"

"What do you think? Make some arrangements for us. Have a word with people on the *Caucasus* and explain our situation to them. After all, they'll all know who *you* are."

"First, I don't even have a pass for myself. K has promised to take me with his family on the *Shilka*. If it weren't for him, I'd be staying here in Odessa—"

"I don't believe it! You, whom the whole of Russia... Bligken & Robinson named one of their caramels after you. 'Teffi' caramels. I've eaten them myself. And that you, of all people—"

"My caramels are neither here nor there. If it weren't for K, I'd be—"

"In that case we'll go on the *Shilka* with you," P resolved. "You must get us on board. After all, we're hardly nobodies. Russia, at this historical moment, owes us something.

Listen—I'm going to go and look into one or two other possi-bilities. If they don't work out, then you must get us onto the *Shilka*. It's your civic duty. History will be your judge. Give me your hand—I place my trust in you."

I could hardly believe my ears.

He threw open the door, banged his forehead on the lintel, and rushed out. But a second later the door flew open again.

"I assume you have foreign currency with you?"

"No, none at all."

"Dear oh dear oh dear! How on earth? How can you be so improvident? Really, madame, it's as if you've been living on the moon, entirely unaware of the historical moment and failing to consider your options."

He thought for a moment, then added severely, "What if we do end up having to go abroad? Where am I going to get hold of foreign currency now?"

And with that he left, evidently disappointed with me.

It was getting dark—time to go down to the harbour.

My young friend was waiting for me downstairs. He had arranged for a horse-drawn cab to come and pick me up at seven, for an unimaginably steep price.

The boy suggested I have some supper.

"Cook's still here—and two waiters. They'll put something together for you."

But I didn't feel like eating.

I went outside and listened. People seemed to be shooting haphazardly, in one quarter and then in another, just for the hell of it, to send us on our way, like a peasant boy tossing a stick after a gentleman's carriage.

Everyone was on guard. Everywhere was a groundswell of tension—ripples and echoes from a storm that was raging more fiercely elsewhere.

The boy was standing by the entrance and beckoning to me. The promised cab had arrived.

We drive down to the waterfront.

Silence…

We locate the *Shilka*.

The boat is deserted. Not a single light. The entire shore is deserted.

What's going on? I get down from the cab and walk closer.

"Hello there! *Shilka*!"

A figure appears on deck. A Chinaman!

"Hey! Is there anyone on board? Is the *Shilka* sailing tonight? Hey! Yes or no?"

The man disappears below deck.

"Wait! Chinaman!"

From somewhere behind us comes a shot. It's very close.

"Oy!" shouts the cabbie. "Look, lady, you can do as you please, but I'm getting out of here. I'll unload your luggage for you, but I'm not hanging around."

"Oh, just wait a few minutes, my dear!" I beg. "I'll pay you. Any moment now my companions will be here. We've arranged to meet here."

"I don't care what you pay me—I'm not waiting any longer. Can't you hear? There's shooting. Or someone will cut through the traces and steal my horse. I'll unload your luggage for you—and then you can do as you like. If you want to, you can sit here all night."

I stand there a little longer. Not a soul. I call out again: "Chinaman!" It gets darker.

Another shot. Pebbles grating, close by.

The cab driver resolutely descends from his box and takes down a suitcase.

What will I do all by myself on the waterfront? With no lights and no sign of any crew, the *Shilka* clearly isn't going anywhere tonight. But what about the Ks? Have they gone to collect me at the International—or sent me a message there?

The cab driver agrees to take me back for twice the original price. If I have to pay to come down to the harbour again, I may not have enough money.

The hotel is now dark. Only on the ground floor, in the lobby and restaurant, are there still a few lights.

"Has anyone come and asked for me? Or sent me a message?"

No one has come for me, and there are no messages. Just silence, peace and silence.

I feel hungry now, but I'm frightened of spending my money.

I stay below in the lobby. I don't want to walk alone down the empty corridors. I find some little book—Ibsen, I think—and sit as close as I can to a lamp. This feels comforting.

My future was a matter of complete indifference to me. I felt neither anxiety nor fear. In any case there was nothing I could do. In my mind I retraced my strange journey from Moscow, always south, always further south, and always without any deliberate choice. In the form of Gooskin, the hand of fate had appeared. It had pushed me on my way.

"You'll only be away for a month. You'll do a few evenings. The money will be yours. And before you know it, you'll be peacefully back home again. Ri-ight?"

And then there I was, rolling down the map. Fate had pushed me on, forcing me wherever it chose, right to the very edge of the sea. Now, if it so wished, it could force me right into the sea—or it could push me along the coast. In the end, wasn't it all the same?

A waiter came over. All that remained of his uniform was his starched shirt and black tie. His tails had been replaced by a frayed little jacket.

"The chef wants you to eat something," he said.

"Well, if that's what the chef wants, we must do as he says."

"In spite of everything, dinner has been prepared. There's soup, lamb, and stewed fruit."

"That'll be perfect."

He put some cutlery on my small table, then brought me some soup. As he was serving me he kept looking around, listening, and glancing out of the window. Then he disappeared.

I waited and waited. In the end I decided to do a little reconnaissance. I glanced into the dining room.

"Where's the waiter who was serving me?"

"Your waiter?" said a voice from a dark corner. "He's run away. There's shooting in the streets. The Moldavanka will be here soon. Your waiter's a capitalist toady and he's run away."

I went back.

A tall young lady was now dashing about the lobby—from window to door, from door to stairs. Seeing me standing there, she came straight over.

"Are you in room number six? My brother and I are on the same floor, but at the other end of the corridor. Listen—this is the plan we've come up with. We're going to lock all the doors into the corridor but leave the communicating doors open. If they start by breaking into your room, you can escape through the other rooms and lock each door behind you as you go. And if they start with our room, we'll do the same. We'll join you in your room."

"Do you really think they'll break in?"

"Of course they will."

And then, yet again, the all too familiar words: "The Moldavanka's already armed. They're just waiting for the last soldiers to leave before they attack the hotels—the International and the London. They think this is a refuge for bourgeoisie and capitalists."

"Maybe we'd be better off somewhere else?"

"Where? It's nighttime. There's shooting on the streets. Can't you hear? And what about your things? And who's going to take you in at this time of night? No, we've thought it all through. We're staying here. Is this your luggage?"

"Yes, it is."

"I wouldn't leave it here if I were you."

She looked round behind her, then whispered, "The hotel staff, the ones who're still here, are in cahoots with the gangsters. The decent ones have all left. Well then, my brother and I are going upstairs now. We'll start locking the doors."

She ran off.

How sick of all this I now felt. It was all so boring! It was enough to make you think fondly of those early days, of that "springtime" of the revolution when your teeth would be chattering from fear, when you froze every time you heard a passing truck—would it stop at the gate or would it drive on by?—when your heart would lurch nauseatingly at the sound of rifle butts thudding against the door.

Now we were only too used to it all. Everything had become boring, boring to the point of revulsion. It was all just coarse, dirty, and stupid.

But what had happened to K and his wife? Why hadn't he come round, or at least sent me a message? Perhaps the *Shilka* was going to sail in the morning and I'd be hearing from them any moment…

"Nadezhda Alexandrovna!"

It was V, the engineer. He was breathing heavily and the corners of his mouth were turned down. He looked as though he were about to start crying.

"What's happened?" I asked in surprise. "What are you doing here?"

"I've been betrayed. I was promised a pass for the *Korkovado*. I waited all day—and nothing. I've been abandoned by everyone… abandoned like a d-d-dog."

He blew his nose and wiped his eyes.

"I can't be on my own any longer. I wanted to find you. Why haven't you left?"

"I'm waiting for the Ks. We were supposed to meet in the harbour at eight and board the *Shilka* together. Maybe they'll soon be here? What do you think?"

"The Ks? You're waiting for the Ks? They've already gone!"

"Gone? Where to? How do you know?"

"I ran into them earlier this evening. They were on their way to the *Caucasus*, with all their luggage. They're going to Constantinople."

"That's impossible! And they didn't give you a message for me?"

"No, not a word. They were very agitated and they seemed in a hurry. She was wearing your fur stole. Remember? She was feeling cold and you said she could borrow it. Yes, they're on their way to Constantinople."

I was stunned into silence. And then for some reason, I don't know why, the whole story suddenly struck me as terribly funny.

"Why are you laughing?" asked V, clearly alarmed. "They lied to you. They changed their plans and didn't even bother to let you know."

"That's what's so funny."

V clutched his head.

"I'm in the deepest despair—and all she can do is laugh! What's going to happen to my little girl? My little Lelusya, my darling little Lelusya!"

"But your little girl's safe in her village. She's out of harm's way. What are you getting so upset about?"

"I'm so lonely, so terribly lonely! Like a d-d-d-o…"

"Please stop talking about that dog—you'll just set yourself off again."

"Oh please, please come with me on the *Shilka*! I've got two passes—one for myself and one for my wife. We can say you're my wife. Please! I can't be on my own any longer. I'll go mad."

"Are you telling me the *Shilka* is sailing tonight?"

"Yes, around eleven. That's what I've been told."

"All right. We'll go together."

"Oh I'm so glad! Is this your soup? I'll have it myself. Heavens! We might end up starving to death! Now I'll go and get a cab. My cases are here—I've been carrying them around with me all day. You stay where you are! I won't be a moment!"

This time it seemed I really was going to get away. V's suitcases were here in the lobby. Even if he forgot about me, he wouldn't forget his cases.

I decided to go upstairs and speak to the young lady who'd been sharing her plans with me. I needed to tell her I'd soon be leaving.

I went upstairs and walked down the dark corridor, scuffing up scraps of paper and getting tangled in pieces of string, knocking on doors and calling out, "It's me! I'm leaving!"

There was no reply. Either they didn't believe it was really me or else they'd left the hotel and found somewhere else to hide out, leaving me to confront Odessa's brigands alone.

I went back downstairs.

V was already waiting for me, afraid that I'd somehow disappeared. He was terrified of being left on his own.

"Well, let's go."

We drove along the dark streets to the harbour.

We heard the odd shot somewhere nearby; in the distance, though, the gunfire sounded more serious.

We got down to the sea. There she was—the *Shilka*. There were lights moving about the deck. Did this mean there were people on board?

We drove closer.

The harbour was full of people, trunks, bundles, and suitcases. Gangplanks had been put in place. Up on the bridge I could see the white cap of a naval officer.

"Quick! Quick!" said V, hurrying me along. "Before all the places are taken. Don't fall behind! I'm afraid of being on my own!"

How lucky I was that V had suddenly developed this particular neurosis. Otherwise, I'd never have left Odessa.

"Come on! Come on!"[97]

17

A strange ship.

> No sound of a captain,
> No sign of a sailor...[98]

And no sign of electricity either—everything was in darkness.

The subdued sound of the passengers' voices as they moved slowly up the gangplank. The *Shilka* was evidently not carrying cargo—her waterline was far above the water and the gangplank was at a steep angle.

No sense of commotion, no hysteria. Everyone was quietly alert. Exchanging businesslike whispers. Only now and again did I hear a louder voice:

"Is General M present?"

"Present."

"Warrant Officer R? We need the warrant officer."

"Present!"

And again only the murmuring of the passengers. A warm, dark night. The very faintest of drizzles. Along with everyone else, I slowly made my way up to the deck. There wasn't even anyone checking our passes.

"Let's see if we can get to the cabins," said V. "The weather looks like it will turn nasty."

But it was impossible to get through—there were already too many people.

"I wonder how we'll manage to get underway?" I ventured. "There's not a sound from the engines."

"Maybe they'll get them working soon. We most certainly can't stay where we are! Listen! Can you hear the gunfire? That's Ataman Grigoriev[99]—I've heard he's almost taken the freight station. He and his men will probably be here before morning."

The steamer was getting more and more densely packed. It was already difficult to move about the deck.

"Wait here," said V. "I'll see if I can get through the crowd."

I went over to the side and looked out at the sea.

The sea, our new road into the unknown, was quiet, dark and calm. There was a smell of wet rope. Lights were glittering out in the bay, where large, serious, and important ships full of important and well-informed persons were exchanging mysterious signals. They were preparing themselves for a long journey, out into open seas, toward peaceful shores.

"We're done for," murmured someone beside me. "If they can't find a tug to pull us out into the roadstead, it'll be the end of us. Time to say our prayers."

"Ba-ba-boom!" replied the freight station.

"Look! The whole sky's lit up."

"I hear the looting's already started."

"Oh my God! Oh my God!"

And then someone began softly singing. A beautiful female voice. I looked down. Perched on a suitcase, one leg swung over the other, was a smartly dressed young lady. She was pensively singing a gypsy romance:

> Where'er the scent of spring may lead me,
> One dream still holds my heart in sway...

The young woman was singing!

"How can you?" someone asked in astonishment. "At a time like this?"

"I've had enough of all this. I might as well sing as do anything else."

"I can see you haven't known much suffering yet."

"I'd say I've known my share. Our house in the country was burned down, my brother disappeared without a trace... We only just managed to get away ourselves."

"So you're a landowner, are you?"

"Me? I'm still a student."

Turning her face toward the quiet sea, she went back to her romance:

> Where'er the scent of spring may lead me,
> One dream still holds my heart in sway...

She was sitting on a suitcase, one leg over the other, and gently swinging her foot. On it was a bright summer shoe. She was in a world of her own.

Beside me someone was chewing on some bread, letting out sounds that might have been sighs or might have been hiccups. And a small pot-bellied gentleman was timidly asking, "Excuse me, are you Madame Teffi? Excuse me, I'm Berkin. I've seen you in the city a few times. Perhaps you could advise me. I don't know whether to stay on board or go back into Odessa."

And then, in a whisper: "I have a considerable sum of money on me. Can you guarantee that no Bolsheviks have managed to get on board?"

"How would I know? All I can say is—I'm staying on board myself."

"True, but maybe you're not risking anything. While I, as I've already told you, am risking a great deal… Please excuse my shivering. I'm wearing a jersey—all this shivering, please excuse me, is because I'm afraid… So, you're advising me to stay on board? Please, I'm begging you, I'll do whatever you say!"

"But how can I take on such a responsibility?"

"But I'm begging you!"

I looked at him. His entire face was quivering; the corners of his mouth were turned down. Was this man crying?

"I think you should stay on board. It's safer. Besides, how are you going to get back into Odessa now? It's dark, the streets are deserted—you'll be robbed."

"Oh, you're so right! I feel better already—you've calmed me down."

V came back.

"The cabins and corridors are all full. The only space I could find was in a bathroom. It'll be us and two other men. You're being given the bench, one of the other men gets the bath—and the second will be sharing the floor with me. Our things have already been piled into the hold."

O, an engineer, came over to us with some news: Not one of the ship's crew was on board. They had all made off into the city, evidently wishing to yield the ship to the Bolsheviks. The engine had been dismantled and many parts had gone missing. Either this was sabotage—the parts had been taken away or destroyed to prevent our departure—or else the engine was under repair. Several Chinese had been discovered hiding down in the hold. At first they pretended not to know or understand anything at all, but when threatened with a revolver they revealed where some of these engine parts had been hidden. Then there had been a search for engineers and mechanics among the passengers. O and a few others had stepped forward and got down to work. They were hoping to reassemble the engine, but this would be difficult and they would have to fashion some of the parts themselves. They needed a particular kind of bearing. If they succeeded with the engine, we were saved; if not, we were in trouble.

Next there was a search for potential ship's officers. There turned out to be several passengers with naval experience, and Captain Ryabinin was put in command.

Most of the passengers, however, knew nothing about any of this and weren't even asking any questions. Instead, they were settling in—putting their children to bed and rearranging their luggage so they could sit more comfortably. O went down to the engine room.

I set off to have a look around. Here and there I glimpsed a familiar face: Professor Myakotin, Fyodor Volkenstein, Ksyunin, Titov... Ilyashenko, the deputy minister of justice, later to be murdered by the Bolsheviks.[100]

On the stairs, on the floors of corridors, on top of bundles of rope and around the base of the ship's funnel, on benches and below benches—wherever I looked, I saw people. Some were sitting, some lying down.

"Ladies and gentlemen! Look!" someone called out joyfully. "Look! We're moving!"

"We're off! We're off!"

Very gently, the shore was spinning away from us; the lights on the ships moored out in the roadstead were also moving.

"We're underway!"

But there was no sound from the engine, nor was there any smoke from the funnel.

"It's a tug! We're being pulled out by a tug!"

"Well, thank God! At least we'll be a bit further out. The further from this accursed shore the better."

The tugboat *Roma* was taking us out into the roadstead.

What next?

There we were, out in the roadstead just like the "grown-up" ships.

Shuttling about between these ships were little rowing boats.

One little boat tied up to our *Shilka*. A grim-looking Odessan climbed the ladder, tracked down some acquaintances, who were placidly chewing on dates, and swore to them that they were certain to perish. His acquaintances spat out their half-eaten dates and gave themselves over to stormy despair, while the man from Odessa, with the air of having performed an onerous duty, strode briskly back to the ladder and climbed down into his little boat.

My new friend "Excuse-me-I'm-Berkin" suddenly jumped up and decided he too needed to go in a rowing boat and visit another steamer.

"What do you want to do that for?"

"Well, I can see what it's like on their ship and I can tell them what it's like on ours."

The owners of the little boats were demanding outlandish sums, yet there were quite a number of people who, like Berkin, felt compelled to go see what it was like and tell what it was like.

"Excuse-me-I'm-Berkin" visited two other steamers.

"Well, I had plenty to tell them!"

"Like what?"

"I said we'd been informed by radio that the Bolsheviks are coming from Sebastopol. By sea."

"What radio? Our radio receiver isn't working."

"It's working just perfectly."

"But I've just been speaking to the junior officer in charge of the radio."

"And you believe him? You'd be better off believing what *I* say."

"And how do *you* know about our radio?"

The man was a brazen liar.

The rowing boats went on shuttling about. People were spending unbelievable sums to go and scare one another. How could they skimp in the service of such a lofty cause?

Berkin went three times.

"That's my last trip. I can't allow myself any more. The boat owners are a shameless lot—profiteering out of human misery."

Toward morning the rumourmongers finally quietened down.

Our officers had three concerns: to get the *Shilka* underway, to obtain coal for the furnace, and to get food for the passengers.

The Chinese men, threatened once more with a revolver, had revealed stores of rice and tinned food. But these would not be enough.

It turned out that there was a cargo boat moored close by, delivering provisions from Sebastopol. We asked it for help. It refused, sternly informing us that the provisions were for Odessa.

"But the city's in the hands of the Bolsheviks!"

"Makes no difference to us," came the answer.

At this, the *Shilka* grew indignant. She opened hostilities, dispatching two lifeboats with machine guns.

They managed to seize some provisions, but the offended steamship complained to the *Jean Barthes*. The French ship then bellowed menacingly at the *Shilka*, "Brigands! Bolsheviks! Explain yourselves! This instant, or else…"

With dignity and feeling, the *Shilka* replied that she had hungry women and children on board, and that the French had always been renowned for their chivalry.

The *Jean Barthes* calmed down and immediately dispatched a lifeboat carrying chocolate, flour, and condensed milk.

O came up from the engine room and announced that the *Shilka* was now able to move under her own steam, but only in reverse.

Many of the passengers took fright—to them, "in reverse" meant going back to Odessa.

Myakotin, Titov, and Volkenstein—members of the same political party, I forget which—kept coming up on deck to hold meetings beneath the ship's funnel. They would whisper animatedly, falling pointedly silent whenever anyone came near them. Ksyunin, meanwhile, stayed down in the hold, starting up a newspaper he intended to publish with the help of his typewriter.

18

The tug towed us over to a coal freighter. Then came an announcement addressed to everyone on board—"to everyone, I repeat *everyone*, without exception: You must load the coal onto the *Shilka* yourselves. There are no workers on the freighter and we have no crew. If you want this ship to move, you must all get to work."

"Everyone? Surely not *everyone!*"

"Yes," came the reply. "Everyone."

This was followed by a most curious scene.

Wanting to show that they knew all this was a joke, elegant young men in smart suits smiled nervously. Any moment now, of course, it would become obvious that elegantly dressed young men cannot be forced to hump coal. That would be simply too absurd! Ridiculous!

"All right—everyone line up on deck!" called out a commanding voice. "Every man present, except the old and infirm."

The elegant young men were dumbstruck. They looked around in confusion. This joke was going on too long.

"Well? What are you waiting for?" someone shouted at one of them. "Didn't you hear the order? Get up on deck."

Up on deck, perhaps, their elegance would be more apparent. It would be obvious that they were the wrong men for the job.

The deck quickly began to fill with rows of passengers.

"You are about to be given a basket. Place this basket on your back."

The elegant young men smiled and shrugged their shoulders, as if playing along with some absurd joke that, in due course, they could enjoy telling people about.

But then an argument broke out on the gangway.

"Excuse me," someone was shouting, "but on what grounds are you refusing? You're a strong, healthy man."

"Will you please stop this! Leave me alone!"

Out onto the deck came a thickset gentleman of about forty, his eyes flickering with rage.

"Will you please stop this at once?"

"Only when you tell me on what grounds you are refusing to carry out your share of the work now required from each man on board!"

"On what grounds?" bellowed the thickset gentleman. "I'm refusing on the grounds that I'm a landowner and a nobleman. I have never worked, I never shall work and you won't see me working today. Get that into your heads once and for all!"

A ripple of indignation passed through the crowd.

"Excuse me, but if we refuse to work, this boat will never get out to sea!"

"My husband's a landowner too," came a squeaky voice.

"We'll fall into the hands of the Bolsheviks!"

"What's that got to do with me?" the gentleman cried out indignantly. "Hire someone! Do whatever is necessary! We've been living in a capitalist society and I fully intend to adhere to capitalist principles. If you prefer all this socialist nonsense and labour for everyone, then what are you doing on this ship? Go ashore and join your Bolshevik comrades. Understand?"

This caused confusion and division.

"Well, up to a point..."

"But on the other hand, we can hardly just wait here for the Bolsheviks..."

"And if we've all got to work, why shouldn't he?"

"Lynch him!" snorted an old lady who had just appeared on the deck.

"Come on now," said a good-natured merchant from Nizhny Novgorod. "Please, sir, try and see reason."

"Jump to it!" came the voice of authority. "No dawdling!"

We could see the white cap of a naval officer.

"Make your way down to the coal carrier. With your baskets."

One of the elegant young men ran up to the officer and began whispering in his ear, glancing now and again at the gentleman with the principles.

The officer shook his head and calmly replied, "To hell with him!"

Loading began.

Moving up and down the gangways were long processions of blackened, soot-covered porters. The remaining passengers all emerged from the hold, and from cabins and corridors, to watch this unprecedented spectacle: models of male elegance, in patent leather shoes and silk socks, supporting heavy baskets of coal with their yellow-gloved hands.

Very soon the young men were spitting and swearing, entering into their new role.

"Come on, lads! No dawdling!"

"Heave-ho!" answered the nearest "lad"—the balding, pot-bellied, stick-legged "Excuse-Me-I'm-Berkin."

"What are you all staring at?" shouted another "lad," an actor and public reciter as long and thin as a fishing rod. "They ought to set you lot to work too. That'll teach you to stare!"

"Yes, they know how to stare all right," said the merchant from Nizhny Novgorod. "But when it comes to real work..."

"Yes," replied a snub-nosed student. "They don't want to work. But they won't be hanging about like that when it's time for dinner... Parasites!"

Someone began to sing one of the silly little songs of the time:

> Boiled or roasted,
> grilled or fried,
> even a chicken
> wants to stay alive.

Someone else interrupted with:

> Gorge on pineapple!
> Chomp on grouse!
> Your days are numbered,
> bourgeois louse![101]

Which was followed by:

> Sweet little apple,
>
> stay where you belong.
>
> Don't let the Cheka
>
> silence your song![102]

Singing along and swearing with gusto, the young men were now working as though their lives depended on it.

"Ah!" I thought, "Yevreinov's 'Theatre for Itself'! They play at being coalmen—and once they know the role, they get carried away. You can even see which character types they've chosen."[103]

Coming up the gangway was pot-bellied "Excuse-Me-I'm-Berkin." Moving jerkily and tripping over himself, his round body precariously balanced on its stick legs, he was like an ungainly spider. But the look on his face was that of a Volga rebel—the look of Stenka Razin himself:[104]

> Swing free, my strong arm—
>
> strong wing of the storm!
>
> Fly swift, my bright scythe—
>
> swift as bee to the hive![105]

and so on...

He was carrying a heavy basket which, without the inspiration afforded by his role, he would never have been able to lift at all.

Next came some kind of intellectual, with a long forelock.

Trudging gloomily along, a bitter and obstinate smile on his lips, he must have been imagining himself as a barge hauler—pulling on his rope while he nurtured in his breast the flame of the people's wrath: I may be pulling on this rope now...

> But the day will soon dawn
> When our people awake![106]

Behind him was some kind of scarecrow in white gaiters and a Tyrolean hat with a feather. He was staggering along, wiping away the black streaks on his cheeks with a fine suede glove and repeating, with a peasant accent: "Well, my dear brethren, seems we'll be pulling on these 'ere straps till the end of our days!"

O emerged from the engine room. He was wearing a worker's smock and was covered in soot.

"I think I've fixed it. I think I've fixed it. Now we've got a chance."

He said something about a winch, and about some bearings, then slipped back into the engine room.

And then we heard a terrible groan, a howl, a grinding shriek, as if hundreds of goats and thousands of piglets had escaped from a torture chamber where they were being skinned alive. This had come from our funnel, now belching out black smoke. The funnel was breathing and bellowing; it was alive. The steamer shuddered. There was a squeal from the tiller chain—and the boat quietly began to turn.

"But we're going backwards!"

"We're moving! Without the tug!"

"Open se-e-e-a!"

Fyodor Volkenstein was standing beside me, watching a large steamer as it headed out. It was moving swiftly and freely.

"That's the *Caucasus*," he whispered, "on its way to Constantinople. It's gone now... It's gone..."

After watching the ship for a long time, he said, "My little boy is on that ship. Will I ever see him again? Maybe only in twenty years' time—and he won't recognize me. Or maybe never."[107]

Now we too were in the open sea. The steamer was shuddering gently, its propeller knocking away, its tiller chain grumbling. Waves were slapping firmly against the starboard side.

Gradually everything was falling into place. Up on the bridge appeared Captain Ryabinin. Short and slim, he looked like a boy cadet. Then the first mate appeared, followed by a few midshipmen and ship's boys. O was in the engine room, along with some mechanics and technical students. The other officers were in the boiler room.

The passengers felt touched by the collective work being carried out by these volunteers. They were especially moved by the self-sacrificing conduct of the officers in the boiler room.

"They've burned holes in their clothes. They'll have nothing to wear when we get back on shore."

A committee was established—to collect money and clothes for those in need.

"We could declare a 'Power to the Poor' week," someone suggested.

But this was rejected out of hand—the phrase had unpleasant associations.

"Why don't we simply requisition linen and clothing?" someone else suggested. "We can organize flying squads."

This met with horror and indignation: "What do you mean?

That's downright insulting! Whatever they need, we'll gladly donate it..."

"All right, then we're all agreed. We'll each donate two hundred roubles, two changes of linen, and one suit to the officers now working in the boiler room."

"Magnificent! Wonderful!"

"But... Excuse me," said an all-too-familiar voice.

It was Excuse-Me-I'm-Berkin.

"Excuse me," the voice went on, "but we really mustn't be too hasty about these donations—the clothes might get spoiled down there in the boiler room, heaven forbid. We shall distribute them on our arrival in Novorossiisk—this will be significantly more convenient for all parties. Isn't that so?"

"Yes!"

"Yes!" said the other passengers. "You're right." And off they all went, a look of relief on their faces.

Subsequently the sum of money to be donated by the grateful passengers kept dwindling. By the time we got to Sebastopol, people were talking about donating only linen and suits.

And by the time we reached Novorossiisk, even this had been forgotten.

19

The ladies too were required to do their share of labour. The fresh fish seized from the cargo boat (the stolen fish for which we had been held to account by the French steamer) had to be gutted and cleaned. And so the ladies were called up on deck.

Boards were laid across trestles to form makeshift tables. Knives and salt were distributed and work got underway.

I managed not to appear on deck until all the places at the tables had been taken. I would have liked to dispense a little advice to the housewives (those who don't know how to work are always generous with their advice), but the sight and smell of the fish entrails forced me to be sensible and go back down again.

On the way I bumped into Mr. Excuse-Me-I'm-Berkin.

"How are you?" he asked cheerfully. Then he lowered his voice and, with an altogether different look on his face, hissed, "Treason! Have you heard?"

He glanced around, then added still more quietly, "The captain's a traitor. He's taking us to Sebastopol to hand us over to the Bolsheviks."

"But that's nonsense! Who told you that?"

"It was a radio message. A passenger happened to overhear. But hush! Don't say a word! Not a word—but do warn your friends."

He looked around once more, pressed a finger to his lips, and made off.

I went back up and found the midshipman in charge of the radio.

"Tell me—is the ship's radio working?"

"No, not yet. I'm hoping we'll get it working by tomorrow."

"And are you certain there are no Bolsheviks in Sebastopol?"

"I'm afraid no one can be certain, since we're unable to receive news. And we haven't yet met any ships coming the other way. But we'll do everything possible to find out in good time. Would you like to have a look at the radio?"

Oh Berkin, Berkin! Dear Excuse-Me-I'm-Berkin! Where, oh where did you get all these mad ideas from?

Meanwhile, dinner was being served downstairs: fish soup and rice with corned beef.

Passengers were forming two long lines, with bowls, plates, and spoons.

I had neither bowl nor spoon, and no idea where to get hold of such items. One kind soul generously gave me the lid from a tin teapot.

"You can use it for the rice."

Good. Now I just needed a spoon. I went into the kitchen. There I found two Chinese men—the cook and his assistant. Neither understood a word I said.

"Do you have a spoon? A spoon? Understand? Spoon?"

"Dututanpun?" the cook replied.

"Yes, yes, a spoon. Give me a spoon!"

"Dututanpun," his assistant repeated placidly—and the two men returned to their work, entirely ignoring me.

"I'll bring it back. Understand? I'll pay for it."

I held out some money.

Suddenly, like a storm cloud out of nowhere, a young woman was bearing down on me. She looked like a pike.

"Bribery!" she shrieked. "Employing money to bribe the ship's staff! Attempting to buy privileges beyond the reach of the poor!"

"What's the matter?" I asked in amazement. "All I need is a spoon. If they don't want a tip, they can just give me the spoon—I'm happy either way."

At the word "tip," the girl became apoplectic.

"Here on this ship we have no nobility, no tips, and no money. Everyone has to work and everyone receives the same rations. I saw you trying to employ money in order to obtain privileges. I'm ready to bear witness to all I have seen and heard. I shall go to the captain and tell him everything."

She spun round and flew out of the kitchen.

Not only was I a depraved criminal but I was also, for all my depravity, still in need of a spoon.

Gloomily, I started back up again. I met one of our senior officers.

"Goodness me!" he said jovially. "Have you finished your dinner already?"

I gave a despairing shrug and said, "I have neither bowl nor spoon. I am, moreover, being reported to the captain."

"What on earth for?" said the astonished officer. "Go to your cabin and I'll have your dinner sent to you straightaway."

And ten minutes later I was regally installed on our bathroom bench. I was sitting cross-legged, with a plate of rice and corned beef on my knees. Sticking up out of the rice were a fork and a spoon. How high fate had raised me!

Late in the evening, after I'd lain down on my refugee's sealskin coat, someone flung open the cabin door. Silhouetted against the murky light of the corridor was the pike-maiden.

"Are you asleep?"

"Not yet."

"You've got a guitar in your luggage, haven't you?"

"Yes. Why?"

Sleepy as I was, I felt frightened. What if she went and reported me to the captain for carrying musical instruments "while the people are starving."

"No," I said to myself. "They can throw all my clothing overboard if they like—but I'm not going to let them have my guitar."

"Please be so kind as to hand over your guitar," the pike-maiden pronounced icily. "It's required in the hospital bay, where we have a sickly element."

This was the first time I'd heard of the sick being healed with guitars.

"No," I replied no less icily. "I'm not giving you my guitar. Anyway, it's down in the hold—they're not going to go through every last item of luggage just because of you and your whims."

"So that's your attitude toward your civic duty, is it?" the maiden replied, gasping hysterically. "Well, you haven't heard the last of this!"

How I wished she would go away! Never would I let her get her fishy fins on my beloved guitar, on my singing joy!

The "sickly element" would, no doubt, overtighten the pegs and then begin to strum away:

> I shall go to the bank of the strea-ea-eam,
> To the bank of the swift flo-o-o-wing river...

How horrible!

I so love her, my "seven-stringed friend."[108]

Ever since I was a little girl I have known the power of strings.

I remember first hearing Zabel's "Solo for Harp" during a ballet at the Mariinsky Theatre.[109] It affected me so deeply that, when we got back home, I went alone into the living room and wrapped my arms around a stiff sofa cushion. On it was a dog, embroidered in beads. I wept, pressing my face against its beaded paws until it hurt; I knew no way to speak of the ineffable bliss, the exquisite anguish that, for the first time in my life on earth, those strings had awoken in me.

The sound of strings was one of the first musical joys known to mankind. Still earlier, of course, came the pipe, the shepherds' pipe. But in the first prayers, in the first places of worship there was always the solemn, exalted song of the strings.

Egyptian women and Assyrian priestesses, with small harps that they held in their hands...

The Book of Psalms. David's instructions to the choirmaster: "With stringed instruments, upon an eight-string lyre. A psalm of David."[110]

Then lyres and lutes and—at last—the guitar. The strings of the guitar sounded all through the fifteenth, sixteenth, and seventeenth centuries, making them sing, making them weep.

Through their songs the minstrels, *minnesingers*, and wandering poet-musicians spread love charms and the sorcery of the grimoires. And so, through strings, all the poetry of medieval life found its way into people's hearts.

In the depths of the Middle Ages, when silent recluses concealed their true thoughts like secret lamps in the dark cells of the monasteries, when their agonized search for some great principle of reason in life was meeting no reward but the fires of the Inquisition—in those dark days the joys of this earth were known only in song, in songs spread by singer-poets with guitars in their hands.

In Russia, only the gypsies understood the guitar's true beauty. The Russians themselves treated her as if she were a mere balalaika. They strummed drearily away or picked out the harmonies as they sang: "I shall go to the banks of the strea-ea-eam..."

Gypsies never strum. They know how to make guitar strings speak, how to make them burst out in fiery cries of emotion, how to silence a stormy chord in an instant with a gentle but commanding hand.

Everyone has their own way of touching a string—and the string, in turn, responds differently to each person. The string too has its moods and does not always give the same response even to a touch it knows well. "It's the humidity," people say, or "It's the dryness."

Maybe. But then are not our own moods affected by our milieu—by the humidity or dryness around us?

My old, yellowed guitar with its slender and resonant soundboard—just think how many sounds it has accumulated over the years, how many vibrations from fingers that have touched it in song! A guitar like this will sing of its own accord—you need only reach out to it. Within it there is always a string attuned to some string deep within you, to some string that will respond with a strangely physical sensation of melancholy and passion deep in your chest, in what was understood by the ancients to be the home of the soul.

No, I could not yield my guitar to the pike-maiden for the entertainment of some "sickly element."

20

That morning Smolyaninov came to see me. He was in charge of various administrative tasks on our ship. In his previous life he may have worked for *The New Age*,[111] though I don't know for sure.

"I have to tell you," he said, "that some of the passengers are unhappy that you didn't join in yesterday when they were gutting fish. They're saying you're work-shy and that you're being granted unfair privileges. You must find a way to show that you are willing to work."

"All right, I'm quite willing to show my willingness."

"But I really don't know what to suggest. I can hardly make you scrub the deck."

Ah! Scrubbing the deck! My childhood dream!

As a child I had once seen a sailor hosing the deck with a large hose while another sailor scrubbed away with a stiff, long-handled brush with bristles cut at an angle. I had thought at the time that nothing in the world could be jollier. Since then, I've learned about many things that are jollier, but that stiff, oddly-shaped brush, those rapid, powerful splashes as the water hit the white planks, and the sailors' brisk efficiency (the one doing the scrubbing kept repeating "Hup! Hup!") had all stayed in my memory—a wonderful, joyous picture.

There I had stood, a little girl with blue eyes and blonde pigtails, watching this sailors' game with reverence and envy, upset that fate would never allow me this joy.

But kind fate had taken pity on that poor little girl. It had tormented her for a long time, but it never forgot her wish. It staged a war and a revolution. It turned the whole world upside down, and now, at last, it had found an opportunity to thrust a long-handled brush into the girl's hands and send her up on deck.

At last! Thank you, dear fate!

"Tell me," I said to Smolyaninov. "Do they have a brush with angled bristles? And will they be using a hose?"

"What!" said Smolyaninov. "Do you mean it? You're really willing to scrub the deck?"

"Of course I mean it! Only don't, for heaven's sake, change your mind. Come on, let's go…"

"You must at least change your clothes!"

But I had nothing to change into.

For the main part, the *Shilka's* passengers wore whatever they could most easily do without. We all knew that it would be impossible to buy anything when we next went ashore, so we were saving our everyday clothes for later. We were wearing only items for which we foresaw no immediate need: colourful shawls, ball gowns, satin slippers…

I was wearing a pair of silver shoes. Certainly not the kind of shoes I'd be wearing next time I had to wander about searching for a room.

We went up on deck.

Smolyaninov went off for a moment. A cadet came over with a brush and a hose. Jolly streams of water splashed onto my silver shoes.

"Just for a few minutes," whispered Smolyaninov. "For appearances' sake."

"Hup! Hup!" I repeated.

The cadet looked at me with fear and compassion.

"Please allow me to relieve you!"

"Hup-hup!" I replied. "We must all do our share. I imagine you've been humping coal; now I must scrub the deck. Yes, sir. We must all do our share, young man. I'm working and I'm proud of the contribution I'm making."

"But you'll wear yourself out!" said somebody else. "Please allow me!"

"They're jealous, the sly devils!" I thought, remembering my childhood dream. "They want to have a go too! Well, why wouldn't they?"

"Nadezhda Alexandrovna! You truly have worn yourself out," said Smolyaninov. "The next shift will now take over."

He then added, under his breath, "Your scrubbing is abominable."

Abominable? And there I was, thinking I was just like that sailor from my distant childhood.

"And also, you look far too happy," Smolyaninov went on. "People might think this is some kind of game."

I had no choice but to relinquish my brush.

Offended, I set off down below. As I passed three ladies I didn't know, I heard one of them say my name.

"Yes, I've heard she's here on our boat."

"You don't say!"

"I'm telling you, she's here on this boat. Not like the rest of us, of course. She's got a cabin to herself, a separate table, and she doesn't want to do any work."

I shook my head sadly.

"You're being terribly unfair!" I said reproachfully. "She's just been scrubbing the deck. I saw her with my own eyes."

"They got her to scrub the deck!" exclaimed one of the ladies. "That's going too far!"

"And you saw her?"

"Yes, I did."

"Well? What's she like?"

"Long and lanky. A bit like a gypsy. In red boots."

"Goodness me!"

"And nobody's breathed a word to us!"

"That must be very hard work, mustn't it?"

"Yes," I said. "A lot harder than just stroking a fish with a knife."

"So why's she doing it?"

"She wants to set an example."

"And to think that nobody's breathed a word to us!"

"Do you know when she'll be scrubbing next? We'd like to watch."

"I'm not sure. I've heard she's put her name down to work in the boiler room tomorrow, but that may just be a rumour."

"Now that really is going too far!" said one of the ladies, with concern.

"It's all right," said one of her companions reassuringly. "A writer needs to experience many things. It's not for nothing that Maxim Gorky worked as a baker when he was young."

"But that," said the other lady, "was before he became a writer."

"Well, he must have known he'd become a writer. Why else would he have gone to work in a bakery?"

Late that evening, when I was sitting alone in our bathroom-cabin, there was a quiet knock at the door.

"May I?"

"You may."

In came a man in uniform. I had never seen him before. He looked around the cabin.

"You're alone? Perfect."

And, turning round, he called out, "Come in, gentlemen, we'll be on our own."

In came a few other men. Among them was O the engineer.

"Well?" asked O. "What is it we've come here to discuss?"

"A very serious matter indeed," whispered the man in uniform. "We're being deceived. They say we're going to Sebastopol, but really we're heading for Romania, where the captain will hand us over to the Bolsheviks."

"Why on earth would there be Bolsheviks in Romania? You're talking nonsense."

"By the time you know for sure that I'm not, it will be too late. I can only tell you that the *Shilka* is at this very moment heading toward Romania. There's only one thing we can do: Go to the captain tonight and confront him. Then we must hand over the command to Lieutenant F. He's a man we can trust. I know him well, and what's more, he's related to a very well-known public figure. So, we must act straightaway. Please make your decision."

Everyone fell silent.

"Gentlemen," I began, "none of this is substantiated and it is all extremely unclear. Why don't we just wait till tomorrow? We could simply go to the captain and ask him why we're no longer heading for Sebastopol. Confronting him in his cabin at night would be outright mutiny."

"So that's where you stand, is it?" said the ringleader—and fell ominously silent.

There we were in the half-dark little cabin, whispering together like inveterate conspirators. Clattering above our heads was the tiller chain—our traitorous little captain steering the boat toward Romania. All straight out of an adventure novel.

"You're right," said O the engineer. "Best to wait till tomorrow."

And the ringleader unexpectedly agreed: "Yes, maybe. Perhaps that will be best of all."

In the morning O told me that he had been to see the captain. And the captain had gladly given him a very simple explanation: He had changed course in order to avoid some minefields.

How surprised the poor man would have been had we burst into his cabin in the middle of the night, clenching daggers between our teeth.

Later I saw Lieutenant F. A tall, melancholy neurotic, he seemed not to have known about the plan to proclaim him the ship's dictator. Or maybe he *had* known... When we reached Sebastopol, he left the ship.

21

L ife on board was settling into a routine.

Those first days of heroics, when Colonel S had stood on the deck, rolled up his sleeves, and kneaded dough for flatbreads, a gold bracelet jingling on his handsome white wrist, while a famous statistician sat beside him and calculated in a loud voice the total weight of the bread to be baked, in proportion to the number of working souls on board, and then half-souls and quarter-souls—those first days of heroic amateurism were long gone.

Now our rations were being supervised by the cook, Chinese Misha.

Misha was a consumptive, an old man with the face of a startled old maid. When he had no work to do and felt like a rest, he would squat down and puff on a special pipe that allowed the smoke to be drawn through a bowl of water. A kind of hookah.

Another Chinese, a rather foolish young man by the name of Akyn, said that until only recently Misha had been fit and healthy, but that he had once got so very angry and carried on swearing so long and so loudly that he had "torn his throat."

And there was a third Chinese man—a general servant and laundry hand.

I began to take an interest in the Chinese language.

"Akyn, how do you say 'old man' in Chinese?"

"Tasolomanika," Akyn replied.

"And 'glass'?"

"Tasagalasika."

Chinese sounded surprisingly similar to Russian.

"And how do you say 'captain'?"

"Tasakapitana."

Hm… The words seemed to be almost the same.

"And 'ship'?"

"Tasashipa."

Astonishing!

"And 'hat'?"

"Tasahata."

We were joined by a midshipman I knew.

"I'm learning Chinese. It sounds remarkably like Russian."

The midshipman began to laugh.

"Yes, I overheard. He thinks you're getting him to learn Russian. What he's been saying to you is his idea of Russian. You're a fool, Akyn!"

"Tusafulaka!" Akyn readily agreed.

The days passed monotonously by.

We ate rice with corned beef. We drank disgusting water from the desalinator.

We didn't talk about the past, we didn't think about the future. We knew that, in all probability, we would indeed reach

Novorossiisk, but who and what we would meet there we did not know.

The *Shilka* was supposed to be going all the way to Vladivostok. I very much hoped it would. I could meet up there with my friend M, then return to Moscow by way of Siberia. There was no reason for me to remain in Novorossiisk. And what would I find to do there?

In the meantime I used to wander about the deck at night. I would stand for a while on the moonlit side, then cross over to where it was dark.

I had grown accustomed to the steamer's various sounds. Lying on my narrow bench in our bathroom-cabin, I would listen to the clatter of the tiller chain and the stamping of the cadets' feet as they swept the deck.

The passengers had shaken down, each finding his or her place like potatoes in a sack. An old dignitary who looked like a fat Tatar had attached himself to a young woman from Kiev, a plump little teacher.

"So, do you continue to maintain," the dignitary would say, his voice as deep and booming as that of any general, "do you really continue to maintain that curd dumplings are tastier than cold *botvinya* soup?"[112]

And he would shake his head reproachfully.

"Ay, ay, ay! Can you really not see that curd cheese is something truly vile?"

"No, curd dumplings are delicious," the teacher would reply, pouting her lips. "You just want to tease me. That's the kind of man you are."

What she meant by this was unclear. But the dignitary liked

it anyway and looked at the teacher with pleasure. She was as round as a cherry; she had tight pigtails and wore a dirty raspberry-pink ribbon around her neck.

O the engineer had taken on the role of chief mechanic and was spending most of his time in the engine room.

V, who had got me out of Odessa, had sunk into melancholy. He ate double portions of rice to which he would add slices of stone-hard salami bought long ago in Sebastopol. After eating all this with gusto and with tears in his eyes, he would say, "I'm afraid we'll end up starving to death."

There was a young woman who had been a maid to a count. She would emerge from the hold in the evening, wrapped in a precious Manila shawl, and stand sadly by the ship's rail. Resting her chin on her fist, she would quietly sing:

> Shine, oh shine, my wondrous star,
> O star of love, O star of dawn...

Once, we happened to anchor for a few hours alongside a coal freighter. The freighter was black all over, all smoke and soot. She was called the *Violetta*.

One of her sailors, himself as black as a lamp wick, kept staring at this count's maid wrapped in a shawl. He would move away from the side of the ship, then reappear. He couldn't take his eyes off her.

"Looks like our Traviata has made a conquest!" the passengers joked.

But the proud maid did not deign even to glance at the soot-covered sailor.

Shine, O shine, my wondrous sta-ar…

But when the *Violetta* weighed anchor, the sailor suddenly leant over the side of the freighter and shouted, "Anyuta! Is that you?"

The maid was dumbfounded. She looked up. She turned white.

"Lord have mercy! I don't believe it… Your Excellency! It's the count, our count… Heavens! Who'd have thought it?"

And turning to face us, she said, as if in a trance, "No one had any idea what had become of him. I did my best, I took care of his belongings for a long time, but in the end everything was looted anyway." As she spoke, she kept twisting the ends of the precious shawl in her hands. "Everything went, everything was looted."

How long had we been at sea? Eight days? Ten days? One person said eleven. Surely not!

In the afternoon, when my cabin-bathroom was unoccupied, I would lie on the narrow bench and think about how very little there was—only a thin layer of wood and metal—between me and the cold blue abyss. There were fish swimming about not far below; jellyfish were coiling and uncoiling their long arms and a crab was waving his claws. The crab had hooked itself to a deep underwater cliff and was staring after the bottom of our ship as it glided by: Maybe someone would come tumbling down for its breakfast. Wasn't there sure to be at least one person who had reached the end of their tether? And still further down were rocks, seaweed, and some whiskered monster slowly moving its tentacles, waiting.

They say the ocean carries the bodies of the drowned to the shores of South America. Not far from these shores lies the deepest spot in the world—and there, some two miles down, can be found crowds of the dead: fishermen, friends and foes, soldiers and sailors, grandfathers and grandchildren—a whole standing army of the dead. The strong salt water preserves them well, and they sway there gently year upon year. An alien element neither accepts nor changes these children of earth.

I close my eyes and gaze into the transparent green water far beneath me… A merry shoal of tiny fish is swimming by. A school of tiny fish. Evidently they are being led by some wise fish, some fish sage and prophet. With what touching obedience the entire shoal responds to his slightest movement. If he moves to the right, they all move to the right too. If he turns back, so do they all. And there are a large number of these fish. Probably about sixty of them. Circling, darting this way and that way, wheeling about… Oh little fish, little fish, can you trust this leader of yours? Are you sure your foremost philosopher-fish is not simply a fool?

Soon we would be in Novorossiisk.

No one was particularly happy about this. It was, rather, a source of anxiety.

Those with family in Novorossiisk were no happier than anyone else. Would their family still be there? What might have happened to them was anyone's guess.

The *Shilka*'s radio was now more or less functioning, but we had been unable to make contact with anyone. We were sailing into the unknown. It might be good; it might be evil.

The days dragged by, long and dreary.

> What do I care where we hit land?
> Cape joy, grief cliff, or bird island—
> all the same when you feel so tired
> you can't even lift your eyelids.

> My bright porthole may show me
> purple birds or gardens of gold,
> sun-kissed palms of the tropics,
> pale blue ice of the poles...

> What do I care for palace or park?
> Cape joy, grief cliff, or bird island—

How strange it was several years later to hear these ragged lines—now smartened up and set to music—being sung from the stage of the Salle Gaveau...[113]

As if I'd thrown the lines out to sea in a sealed bottle—and the waves had carried this bottle away to distant, happier shores. Someone had found the bottle and opened it. There had been a public announcement. People had come together and my SOS had been read aloud to everyone... To everyone, I repeat *everyone*, everyone without exception...

> No sight can bring joy to your heart
> when you can't even lift your eyelids.

22

Early one morning I was woken by the bellow of the ship's horn.

What was going on up above me?

I went up on deck and was met by a sight the like of which I had never seen. A pearl-grey fog, thick and motionless, gripped hold of me and cut me off from the entire world. I took a few steps—and could no longer find the ladder I had just climbed. I stretched out my arms—and lost sight of my own fingers.

Meanwhile, the horn continued to bellow in alarm, and the whole ship was shivering, shuddering.

Had we come to a stop or were we still moving?

Somewhere nearby, as if they too were muffled by the fog, I could hear indistinct voices. Otherwise everything was unusually quiet, like a dream—a cloudy dream.

I didn't know if I was alone on deck or if there were people around me. Maybe everyone on board had gathered here, near this bellowing horn, and I was only imagining that I was alone.

I took a few steps forward and stumbled against some kind of barrier. I held out my arms and touched... the ship's rail. I was standing beside the rail. Beyond it lay the pearly void.

And then, right in front of my face, the fog quivered and floated away—like so many bits of muslin curtain in a theatre, being whisked off in different directions. As if in some strange dream—so close I could have touched them—appeared crimson fezes, black faces, the whites of eyes, teeth bared in a fierce grin. I recoiled in shock. Whatever these Africans saw through the gap in the fog must have seemed no less like a dream. They rushed to the rail, waving their arms about and shouting something like "Guzel Kare! Kare guzel!"[114]

More and more crimson fezes. More and more waving arms. More white teeth. More whites of eyes...

And then suddenly this little "window into Africa" turned dim and murky. In an instant, it was lost in the fog.

"Goddamit!" said a nearby voice. "That was a near miss."

The foghorn was still bellowing, the whole ship quietly shivering.

We were approaching Sebastopol. Timidly.

We waved a piece of rag at a boat coming toward us; we had a little talk, asked a lot of questions, and didn't believe what we were told. We met a second boat and had another little talk. But in the end we had no choice. We needed to take on coal, and so we entered the harbour anyway.

Everything turned out all right. Sebastopol was still held by the Whites.

Half of our passengers left, to remain in Sebastopol.

The rest of us just went ashore for a walk. We wandered about the streets. Important items of news were passed on excitedly: "We found four pairs of suede shoes in a cobbler's. Three enormous pairs and one that's absolutely tiny."

The ladies rushed to try them on. Me too, of course. There truly were three pairs that were quite gigantic and one that was tiny.

"Where in the world have you seen feet like this?" I asked.

"But what quality! And what style—style to make any foot smile!"

"But one pair's enormous and I'll never get into the other pair. What do you expect me to do with them?"

"Why not buy two pairs? That'll be perfect. One big pair and one small pair—they'll average out."

A born salesman.

Sebastopol seemed dusty, dismal, and shabby.

After a while, we all returned to the *Shilka*. We knew that the coal was being loaded as quickly as possible and that we would set sail again the moment we could.

The ship seemed empty. But just before sailing, we took on new passengers—passengers very different from ourselves.

There was an entire unit of young men who had been guarding Crimean palaces and who were now on their way to join the Caucasus Volunteer Army. They were handsome and smart and they chatted away merrily, casually coming out with the odd word of French and singing French songs with perfect accents. They settled down on deck.

And then there was an infantry detachment that had already seen its share of action. Rattling their mess tins and bayonets, the men rolled into the hold like a grey wave of dusty felt.

The two units did not mix and appeared not to notice each other.

The young men up on deck called out in merry voices:

"*Où es-tu, mon vieux?*"[115]

"Coco, where's Vova?"

"Who's spilled my eau de cologne?"

Or they sang, "Rataplan-plan-plan!"[116]

The weary grey men from down in the hold would come up to the galley for freshly boiled water. Clinking their tin mugs, tightening the torn straps on their clothes, clomping their great boots or flapping loose soles, they would make their way past the gilded youths without looking at them.

But these poor gilded youths had few days of merriment left to them. Little joy awaited them in the Caucasus. Many were to meet their death with courage and grace. For many, "Rataplan" was their last song.

One of them had a remarkably beautiful voice. He sang late into the night. Someone said he was the nephew of Smirnov the baritone.

Late in the evening a swell got up.

I stood alone on deck for a long time.

Scraps of song, merry conversation and laughter drifted up from the saloon.

The grey dusty men in the hold had long fallen silent. They were not merry. They had been through too much to be merry. They slept soundly and simply, like peasants at harvest time who know they must sleep if they are to get through the heavy labour of the coming day.

The *Shilka* creaked and swayed. A black wave crashed dully against her side, then bounced back. It shattered the rhythm of the song; it was alien to the small, cheerful light shining out from the saloon into the dark night. The wave had its own deep and awful life; it had its own power and will, about which we knew nothing. Not seeing or understanding us, not knowing us at all, it could lift us, drag us, hurl us about. It was elemental; it could destroy.

A large star blazed like a bonfire. Like a small moon, it cast a path of broken gold across the sea.

"That's Sirius," said a voice close by.

A young boy—a stoker.

White against his sooty face, his eyes were gazing intently into the sky. His shirt was caked brown with dirt. Through its open collar I could see a bronze cross on a grimy string.

"That's Sirius."

"You know the stars?" I asked.

He faltered.

"A little. I'm a sailor... A stoker... When you're at sea, you often have to look up into the sky."

"From the boiler room?"

He looked around.

"Yes. I'm one of the stokers. Don't you believe me?"

I looked at him. What reason was there not to believe him? Broken black fingernails, that bronze cross...

"Of course, I believe you."

Black waves with white fin-like crests were rolling along beside us, lazily vicious, thumping and slapping the hull. Sirius's golden path faded away. It began to drizzle.

I moved back from the rail.

"Nadezhda Alexandrovna!" the stoker said quietly.

I stopped.

"How do you know who I am?"

He looked around again and said, still more quietly, "I visited you in your apartment on Basseinaya Street. A student friend of mine, Sebastyanov, introduced me to you. Do you remember? We talked about stones, about a yellow sapphire…"

"Yes, yes… It's coming back to me now…"

"Nobody on board knows who I am. Not even in the boiler room. This is my third time at sea, my third voyage. My people are all dead. My father's gone into hiding. He told me I must never forget, not even for one minute, that I am a stoker. Only then will I be able to survive and carry out the task I've been entrusted with. This is my third voyage and I have to return to Odessa."

"But the Bolsheviks will soon be well entrenched there."

"And that's why I have to go back there. I started speaking to you because I was certain you'd recognize me. I trust you. I even suspect you're just pretending you didn't recognize me, so as not to alarm me. Is my disguise really that good?"

"It's remarkable. Even now I feel certain that you really are a stoker and that what you've just said is only a joke."

He smiled.

"Thank you."

He bent down, quickly kissed my hand, and darted toward the ladder.

A small spot of soot was left on the back of my hand.

Yes. Petersburg. Evenings. Languid, high-strung ladies, sophisticated young men. A table adorned with white lilac. A conversation about a yellow sapphire...

A slender boy who spoke with a slight lisp... What was it he'd said about a yellow sapphire?

How many more journeys would he make, with his bronze cross on its grimy string? One? Two? And then he would rest his weary shoulders against the stone wall of a black cellar and close his eyes...

Only a small dark spot of coal soot on the back of my hand. Nothing more...

23

Another night. A dark, still night.

Far off, in a half circle, the lights of the shore.

A very still night indeed.

I stand there a long time, listening into the silence. I keep thinking I can hear the sound of a church bell from the dark shore. Maybe I really can… I don't know how far we are from the shore. All I can see are the lights.

"Yes," says someone nearby, "it's a church bell. The sound carries well over water."

"That's right," says someone else. "It's the night before Easter."

Holy Saturday.

We have all lost our sense of time. We have no idea where we are either in time or in space.

Holy Saturday.

This distant ringing that has come to us over the waves of the sea is solemn, dense, and hushed to the point of mystery. As if it has been searching for us, lost as we are in the sea and the night, and has found us, and has united us with this church on the earth, now bathed in light, in singing, in praise of the resurrection.

This sound I have known all my life, this solemn sound of the Holy Eve, takes hold of my soul and leads it far away, past the screams and the bloodshed, to the simple, sweet days of my childhood.

My little sister Lena… She was always by my side—we grew up together. A round rosy cheek, and a round grey eye, were always there at my shoulder.

When we argued, she would hit me with her tiny fist, soft as a rubber ball. Then, horrified by her own wild violence, she would weep as she repeated again and again: "I could kill you!"

She was a crybaby. When I wanted to draw her portrait (when I was five, art was something for which I felt a real love—a love that my elders eventually managed to kill), I always began by drawing a round open mouth and filling it in with black. Only after that would I add her eyes, nose, and cheeks. These, as I saw it, were mere extras, of no significance—what mattered was this open mouth that so perfectly captured the very essence of my model's physical and spiritual being.

Lena liked to draw too. She always did what I did. When I was sick and had to take medicine, she too had to have a few drops in a glass of water.

"Well, Lenushka, feeling better now?"

"Yes, thank God, I seem to be a little better," she would say with a sigh.

Lena, like me, liked to draw, but she set about it very differently. She often drew Nanny, and she always began, very carefully, by drawing four parallel lines.

"What's that?"

"It's the wrinkles on Nanny's forehead."

Two or three more quick strokes—and there was Nanny, now complete. But getting those first wrinkles right was difficult and Lena would huff and puff and spoil sheet after sheet of paper.

Lena was indeed a crybaby.

I remember one terrible, shameful incident.

I had already been going to the *gymnasium*[117] for a whole year when Lena started there too. She was in the junior preparatory class.

And then one day our whole class was lined up on the stairs waiting to go down into the entrance hall. The little ones from the preparatory class had gone down already.

And then I saw a little figure with a clipped tuft of hair on its forehead, dragging a heavy bag of books, fearfully trying to edge its way along beside the wall but not daring to go past us.

Lena!

Our class mistress went up to her:

"What is your surname? Which class are you in?"

Lena looked up at her with an expression of animal terror, and her lower lip began to tremble. Without answering, she hunched her shoulders, snatched up her bag, and, her tuft of hair shaking as she burst into loud sobs, rushed down the stairs—a small bundle of misery.

"What a funny little girl!" said our mistress, and began to laugh.

This was more than I could bear. I closed my eyes and hid behind a friend's back. The shame of it! What if the class mistress found out that she was my sister? A sister who, instead of saying straightforwardly and with dignity, "I'm from the junior preparatory class" and then bobbing a curtsy, simply began to howl. The shame of it!

…The sound of Easter. Now I can hear the bell quite clearly…

I remember how, in our old house—in the half-dark of the hall, where the chandeliers' crystal drops used to tremble and tinkle of their own accord—Lena and I would stand side by side, looking out into the night and listening to the bells. We were a little scared—because we were alone, because the bells sounded unusually solemn, and because Christ would soon be risen.

"But why," asked Lena, "why isn't it angels ringing the bells?"

In the half dark I could see a little grey eye—shining and frightened.

"Angels only come," I replied, "when it's your last hour." And I felt scared by my own words…

Why now? Why, on this Easter Eve, has my sister come thousands of miles, to this dark sea? Why does she stand beside me as a little girl—the little girl she was when I loved her most of all.

I don't know.

Only three years later will I find out that on this very night, thousands of miles away in Arkhangelsk, my Lena was dying.[118]

We sailed into Novorossiisk.

What an enormous port!

Jetty after jetty, one after another.

Cranes towered everywhere, like the necks of gigantic black waterbirds. And endless sheds, depots, warehouses…

And people, crowds of people, all over the waterfront and the landing stages.

At first I thought they were passengers waiting for a steamer.

But, after walking about a little, I soon saw that they weren't waiting there—they were living there. They had rigged up tents out of baskets and pieces of cloth, hung up their ragged things—and there they now lived.

There were old women roasting scraps of food on braziers.

And there were half-naked children playing with mutton bones and bits of broken bottles. Swarthy children with tousled black hair.

In front of each tent stood a pole, and tied to this pole was a cluster or garland of garlic.

These people were Armenian refugees. They had been in Novorossiisk for a long time and had no idea where they would be sent next. There had been an outbreak of typhus in the city and many of them were sick. Children were dying of fever. The clusters of garlic were there to ward off infection. Ghosts, vampires, werewolves, and a variety of diseases all strongly dislike the smell of garlic. As do I myself; I entirely understand these ghosts, vampires and werewolves.

These refugees were leading a strange life.

They had been driven here from one place, and they would soon be driven on to some other place. And though all they owned in the world might be a few rags and a frying pan, they seemed to be finding their lives quite tolerable. I sensed neither despondency nor even impatience.

They bickered, laughed, wandered through the camp to visit one another, and smacked their children. Some were even selling dried fish and pressed mutton.

A boy was blowing on a clay whistle and two little girls were dancing, their arms around each other.

No one grumbled, worried, or asked too many questions. They accepted their present life as something quite normal.

I saw one woman in a torn dress made from silk—not long ago she must have been rich. She was showing her neighbour how she'd stretched a shawl over a rope. She was very pleased with herself. And if the shawl had been a quarter—yes, just one quarter—as long again (she demonstrated several times with her palm how much more material she needed), then she could have completed their tent.

She was just that quarter of a shawl away from total comfort.

It's true, everything is relative. Her neighbour could not help feeling envy—she herself had only a garland of garlic with which to protect her home from vampires, disease, and prying eyes.

I went on into the city, where passengers from the *Shilka* were already wandering about in unshepherded flocks, looking for people they knew and finding out about rooms, prices and—most important of all—the Bolsheviks.

It was here that we first heard about the "Greens."

The Greens were new, and a little hard to understand. Where had this new colour come from? Had it emerged from the Whites or the Reds?[119]

"They're over there," people would say, gesturing toward the tall white mountains to the right of the harbour. "Beyond Gelendzhik."[120]

"They live and let live…"

What kind of lives were they living there? Why were they hiding, and who from?

"Even White officers are going over to them."

Dismal grey groups of passengers from the *Shilka* hung about at street corners and crossroads, talking dismal nonsense.

"Well, gentlemen," said a deep businesslike voice, "it's clear as daylight. We must go to Trebizond."[121]

"*Trebizond?*"

"Yes, gentlemen, Trebizond. Apparently butter is very cheap there."

"Don't be so stupid. The Bolsheviks will be gone within a week, two at most, and it'll be quicker to get back home from here in Novorossiisk."

But the butter lover was intransigent.

"Excellent," he said. "Let's say they *will* be gone in two weeks. But isn't it better to find a way to enjoy those two weeks? And we'll find it hard to do that here in Novorossiisk."

"What with the journey, what with this and that, we'll barely have time to spread your cheap butter over a slice of bread before we have to make our way back here again."

"Well, what do *you* think we should do?"

Other groups were talking about the typhus epidemic. Apparently the whole city was in a state of terror. People were dropping like flies.

The pharmacies were selling all kinds of patented remedies, ointments, liquids, and even amulets, to ward off infection.

People said we should tie the ends of our sleeves tightly around our wrists to prevent anything from crawling up our arms.

The general mood of the city was indeed dismal.

24

Yes, Novorossiisk seemed very dismal indeed.

We wandered around for a long time, asking about apartments. Everywhere was full; every last room—every last little corner—was jam-packed.

I met a woman I knew from the *Shilka*—a former lady-in-waiting.

"Relatively speaking," she said, "we really haven't done at all badly for ourselves. We've found a room and the landlady's put several more mattresses down on the floor. There'll be eleven of us altogether, but as far as living space is concerned two are just little children, so really they don't count at all. Of course they'll probably cry, these little ones, but all the same it won't be any worse, actually, than being on the *Shilka*, and moreover there isn't the slightest danger of feeling seasick."

This lady-in-waiting feared seasickness more than anything in the world. But in that respect the *Shilka* had done us proud—there had been only one episode of pitching and rolling and it had not been severe, even though I myself was one of the passengers. Until my voyage on the *Shilka*, every ship I had ever set foot on had, almost at once, begun pitching and rolling—no matter what the atmospheric conditions beforehand.

What seas had not tossed me about! The Baltic, the Caspian, the Sea of Azov, the Black and the White Seas, the Mediterranean, the Sea of Marmara, the Adriatic… And not only seas! Even Lake Geneva, when I was doing the half-hour trip from Saint-Gingolph to Montreux, had turned so rough that all the passengers had felt sick.

My power to conjure up storms had never particularly troubled me. I enjoyed storms at sea and suffered little ill effect from them. But in the Middle Ages I would certainly have been burned at the stake.

I remember the sufferings of a landowner from Orlov who had refused to believe in my powers.

I was travelling from Sebastopol to Yalta and this landowner gallantly offered to accompany me. I thanked him warmly but felt it my duty to caution him: "It will be a rough trip."

The landowner didn't believe me—the sea was like a mirror and there was not a cloud in the sky.

"Wait and see!" I said darkly, but he just shrugged his shoulders. The weather was divine and, anyway, he was a heroic sailor. He understood, of course, that *I* would need looking after, but he had no concerns about himself.

"Well, so much the better."

We boarded the steamer.

Everyone was thrilled that the weather was so divine, but the captain said unexpectedly, "Let's have breakfast as soon as we can. Once we're past the lighthouse, it might turn a little choppy."

I gave the landowner a pointed look.

"Doesn't matter," he said, "I have no concerns about myself. And as for you—well, don't worry, I'll be keeping an eye on you."

During breakfast this landowner of mine talked unstoppably, advising everyone about the right way to sit, the right way to lie, the importance of sucking a lemon, of chewing on the rind along with a little salt, of trying to arch your spine while pressing your head back against your chair, and heaven knows what else.

I felt surprised that a man with so strong a connection to his land should also be so impressively *au fait* with matters maritime.

The other passengers listened attentively and respectfully. They asked for still more advice. The landowner's answers were prompt, sensible, and detailed. I did of course, for all my surprise, listen carefully. It would have been wrong for me to ignore the advice of so experienced a man.

What he emphasized most of all was the importance, unless it was very rough indeed, of staying on deck. And so, straight after breakfast, up on deck I went. My landowner followed.

The captain proved right. No sooner had we rounded the lighthouse than the ship adopted the gait of a camel, dipping its nose and then raising first its right side, then its left side, high into the air.

I was chatting merrily away, holding the ship's rail. I was looking at the horizon and the distant flashes of lightning between the blue-grey clouds. I was enjoying the moist salty air.

But then two or three of my questions went unanswered. I turned around to find nobody there. My landowner had disappeared. What could have happened? The few passengers who had come up with me after breakfast had also disappeared. At this point I realized I was feeling very dizzy indeed.

I needed to lie down.

Walking was rather difficult, but somehow, holding onto the railings with both hands, I negotiated the stairs. I then found that all the places in the ladies' saloon had been taken. Everyone was lying down.

I found an empty corner and somehow managed to settle myself there, my head on someone's suitcase.

But where was my landowner? It was specifically to look after me that he had come along. The least he could do was to bring me a lemon or find me a pillow.

I lay there, feeling puzzled, mulling over his advice and instructions.

As well as the large saloon, there were six little cabins that opened onto it. These cabins were, of course, also all occupied, so I decided to stay where I was and try to sleep.

Suddenly the saloon door swung open and in rushed my landowner.

Hatless. Dishevelled. Eyes darting from side to side.

"Are you looking for me?" I called out. "I'm over here!"

But he didn't hear me. He flung open the door of one of the little cabins and thrust his head inside. There was a wild shriek, then something like the bleat of a crazed goat—and the door slammed shut.

"He's looking for me!" I thought. I tried to catch his eye.

But he didn't see me. He rushed to the next cabin and again flung open the door and thrust his head inside. Again there was a crazed bleat and a wild shriek. This time I even made out a word: "Outrageous!"

He leaped back again and the door slammed shut. "He must think I'm in one of those cabins," I said to myself.

"Nikolay Petrovich! I'm over here!"

But he was already at the third cabin. He thrust his head inside, bleated something incomprehensible—and was met by wild shrieks of feminine outrage.

"What on earth's got into him?" I wondered. "Why does he keep bleating like a goat? Why doesn't he just knock and ask?"

Then he thrust his head into the fourth cabin, nearer to where I was lying, and was immediately propelled back out again. Looking like death, he stopped, shouted, "For the love of God, where the hell is it?"—and rushed toward the fifth door.

At this point I understood. I hid my face in my scarf and pretended to be asleep.

By now the other women were getting indignant: "This is outrageous! Opening the doors of ladies' cabins and—!"

"That gentleman's travelling with you, isn't he?" asked one woman.

"No, he most certainly isn't," I replied, sounding shocked and offended. "I've never even set eyes on him before now."

I doubt she believed me, but she must have understood that I had no choice: I could hardly admit to having such a companion.

After equally brief visits to the fifth and sixth cabins, he shot out into the corridor, to the accompaniment of yet more furious shrieks.

When we reached Yalta, I found him by the gangway.

"At last!" he said in an unnaturally bright voice. "I was waiting for you all day long. It's been wonderful up on deck! Open horizons, the incomparable might of the sea! The beauty of it all, the elemental power! No, no words are enough. I spent the whole time on deck—it's been an almost mystical experience for me. But such things, of course, are not for everyone. The captain and I were the only people who managed to stay on our feet. The first mate's got good sea legs but—though I'm sorry to say this—even he lost his nerve. And the passengers were all flat on their backs. Yes, a truly lovely, bracing trip."

"I got myself a private cabin," I said, trying not to look at him.

"Yes, somehow I knew things would be complicated with you," he muttered, trying not to look at me.

25

How it warms the soul to discover—amid naked rock, amid eternal snow, beside a cold, dead glacier—a tiny velvety flower, an edelweiss. In this realm of icy death it alone is alive. It says, "Don't believe in the horror that surrounds us both. Look—I'm alive."

How it warms the soul when, on an unfamiliar street in an alien city, when you are tired and homeless, an unknown woman comes up to you and says, with a delightfully Odessan accent, "Hello! Well, what do you say to my new dress?"

There I was—wandering around Novorossiisk, unable to find shelter—when an unknown lady comes up to me and, in the way of women all over the world, asks, "Well, what do you say to my new dress?"

Noticing my obvious bewilderment, she adds, "I saw you in Kiev. I'm Serafima Semyonovna."

Reassured by this, I look at the dress. It's made from what looks like remarkably nasty muslin.

"It's an excellent dress," I say. "Very nice."

"But can you guess what it's made of? And do you realize how impossible it is to find *any* kind of material here? You can't

266

even get hold of calico—not for love nor money. Well, what you see here is medical gauze that was being sold to make bandages."

I don't feel so very surprised. In Petersburg we had made underwear from tracing paper. We soaked it in something or other and ended up with something not far from batiste.

"Of course, this gauze may not be all that strong," she says, "and it does tend to snag, but it's cheap, and it comes nice and wide. But you won't find any now—it's all been snapped up. The only gauze left is the kind with iodoform. It's a pretty colour, but it smells rather nasty."

I express my sympathy.

"You know," the woman continues, "my niece bought some dressings at the pharmacy—very nice they were too, edged with blue—and she used them as trimmings on a dress just like this one. She sewed some strips along the hem and it really does look very nice indeed. And it's good hygiene too—thoroughly sterilized."

O sweet and eternal femininity! Edelweiss, living flower on the icy rock of a glacier! Nothing can break you. I remember how, as the machine guns rattled away, officials told people living in central Moscow to go down into their cellars. And there, while people wept or gritted their teeth, another such edelweiss, another Serafima Semyonovna, had heated her curlers over a small tin in which—since there was no methylated spirit anywhere—she was burning some foul-smelling anti-parasite solution.

And there had been another in Kiev, rushing out—under machine-gun fire—to buy herself some lace for a blouse. And yet another in Odessa, sitting in a hairdresser's while panicked crowds besieged the ships.

I remember her wise words: "Well yes, everyone's running

for it now. But really! How can you run anywhere without a proper hairdo?"

No doubt, during Pompeii's last minutes, there had been edelweisses hurrying to fit in a quick pedicure.

Calmed by these thoughts, I ask this unknown Serafima Semyonovna if she knows of a room anywhere.

"I do know of one, and it's really not at all bad, but you won't feel comfortable there."

"Heavens—what's comfort got to do with it? I'm hardly in a position to pick and choose!"

"No, I really do advise you to wait a little. There are two typhus patients living there. If they die, there's a chance the room will be disinfected. You'd be better off waiting."

I remember searching for a room in Odessa. Here—typhus; there—it had been that terrible Spanish influenza. I had been given a letter of introduction to an engineer who was going to let me have a room in his apartment. On reaching Odessa, I had gone straight to this address. I had rung the bell repeatedly. Finally someone opened the door a crack and asked in a whisper what I wanted. I passed him the letter and explained why I'd come. The door opened a little wider and I saw the miserable, exhausted face of an elderly man. It was the engineer.

"I can't let you come in," he said, still in a whisper. "I have got a room, but I must tell you that five days ago I buried my wife and two sons. My third son is dying now. My last son. I'm on my own with him here. I don't even dare to give you my hand—I may already have the flu myself. You really mustn't come in."

Yes, there it had been Spanish influenza; here it was typhus. Serafima Semyonovna launches into the details with gusto:

"One young lady goes to church for a friend's funeral. Some woman asks her, 'Why are you in such deep mourning?' She replies, 'I'm not in mourning, I'm just wearing a black dress.' But the woman points at her skirt and says, 'Then why do you have a grey band sewn onto your hem?' The young lady looks down—and sees her dress is crawling with lice. Well, what do you think happens next? She passes out. They start trying to bring her round, but then they see the telltale signs. Typhus rash—all over her body."

Cheered by these tales, I go back to look for the *Shilka*, which has been moved to a distant pier. There are no other ships there. Silent and naked, she stands high in the water, her long gangways now almost vertical.

A quick look is enough to convince me that I won't be able to get back on board. There aren't even any footholds on the gangway, which is little more than two narrow planks. I try to take a few steps but my feet slide back down—and beneath me lies a sheer drop into deep water.

Losing heart, I sit down on an iron bollard and try to summon up pleasant thoughts.

Say what you will, I think, I've really not done at all badly for myself. It's a lovely day, there's a splendid view, no one's threatening me or driving me away. I'm sitting like a lady on a comfortable bollard, and if I tire of sitting I can stand up for a little while or go for a walk. I can do as I please and no one will dare to stop me.

High up above me, someone is leaning over the ship's rail. A man with a shaved head is looking down at me.

"Why don't you come on board?" he shouts.

"How?" I shout back.

"Up the planks!"

"I'm too frightened!"

"Oh!"

The man steps back from the rail. A moment later he is gaily stepping sideways down the planks.

It's an officer from the engine room.

"So you're frightened? Take my hand."

This time it's even worse. The planks spring up and down. If you take a step with your left foot, the right-hand plank jumps up almost to your knee. A step with your right foot—and up jumps the left plank.

"Tomorrow they're going to put up a rope," the officer says reassuringly. "Then there'll be something to hold on to."

"But I can hardly wait till tomorrow," I reply. "Go and get me a stick. Maybe that'll help."

Obediently, the officer runs off down the pier. He returns with a long stick.

"Good," I say. "Now sit here on this bollard and sing me a circus song."

"I don't know any circus songs. How about the 'Tango Argentina'?"

"All right—let's try."

"In far-awa-a-a-y sultry Argenti-i-ina!" the officer begins. "But how does it go after that?"

"For heaven's sake, don't stop! Keep singing and keep to the beat!"

I grip the stick with both hands and, making sure it stays horizontal, step onto the planks.

"Where the ski-i-i-es are so-o-o cra-a-a-zy and blu-u-u-e!" sings the officer.

Good grief! What a ridiculous voice. The last thing I need is to start laughing.

Now: Don't look down. Look straight ahead. Look at the planks. Walk straight. Keep to one plank. Keep humming.

"And the w-i-i-i-men are pretty as pictures!"

Hurrah! I've done it. Now I need only lift up one leg, step over the side and...

And then my feet slip backwards. I let go of the stick and close my eyes. But there is someone above me. Firm hands grip my shoulders. I lean forward, seize hold of the ship's rail, and step on board.

When I told him I hadn't yet found a room, the diminutive captain suggested that I stay on board as a guest. I could have a small cabin at a very cheap price and eat, along with the crew, "from the common pot." And in time, no doubt, it would become clear where the *Shilka* was going next. If it truly was Vladivostok, then I was welcome to stay on board.

This was just what I needed. I thanked the kind captain with all my heart.

So began our strange, dreary life on a steamer moored to a long, white, empty pier.

No one knew when we would set sail, or what our destination would be.

The captain stayed in his cabin with his wife and child.

The first mate made boots for his wife and his sister-in law Nadya, an enchanting curly-haired young woman, who darted up and down the ladders in a muslin dress and ballet shoes, disturbing the peace of mind of the ship's young men.

Midshipman S strummed on his guitar.

Engineer O was eternally tinkering with one thing or another in the engine room.

V, who had enabled me to get out of Odessa, was also staying for the time being on the *Shilka*. All day long he would wander around the city, hoping to happen upon friends and acquaintances. He would come back with some smoked sausage, have a bite to eat, let out a sigh, and say yet again how frightened he was of starving to death.

The Chinese cook prepared our dinner. The Chinese laundryman washed our linen. Akyn cleaned my cabin.

The sun would go down in the evenings, quietly marking off the lacklustre days with glowing red sunsets. Waves would slap gently against the hull; cables would sigh and chains rattle. White in the distance stood the high mountains, cutting us off from the world.

It was all very dismal.

26

Then came the northeasterly.

Back in Odessa I had heard many stories about it.

A colleague from the *Russian Word* had returned from Novorossiisk all bandaged up and covered in plasters. He'd been caught by a northeasterly. He'd been quietly walking along—and then the wind had knocked him off his feet and rolled him along the street until he managed to catch hold of a lamppost.

I'd also heard of steamers being ripped from their moorings and blown out to sea. Only one had been left in the bay—a cunning American who had got up full steam and headed into the wind. By making straight toward the shore, he had managed to stay in one place.

While I didn't exactly believe all these stories, I was, nevertheless, eager to see what this northeasterly was really like.

People said it could only count in threes. It blew for three days, or six days, or nine days, and so on.

And then my wish was granted.

Our *Shilka* began shrieking, screeching and groaning. Not one of her bolts, chains, or cables was silent. The rigging whistled; every bit of metal clanged.

I set off into town with the secret hope that I too would be knocked off my feet and rolled along the street, like my colleague from the *Russian Word*.

I got as far as the market without incident and was buying a few little bits and pieces when, suddenly, splinters were flying, a dark cloud of dust was soaring into the air, and the awning above the stalls gave a great clap. Something crashed to the ground—and then something pink and frothy closed me off from the rest of the world.

I desperately tried to shake myself free. The world opened up again and the pink thing—my own skirt, which had billowed up over my head—wrapped itself around my legs.

Embarrassed, I looked around. Everyone was screwing up their eyes, rubbing them, shielding their faces with their bent arms. My first introduction to the northeasterly appeared to have passed unnoticed. There was just one woman some way away, a bagel seller, who was still watching me, and shaking with laughter.

The northeasterly continued to rage for twelve days. Every kind of howl in the world—anguished, spiteful, sorrowing, savage—could be heard from the ship's rigging. Sailors were swept off decks and traders blown away from the market; the streets were emptied of people. Not a boat was left in the roadstead, not a cart on the shore.

Yellow columns of dust roamed about the town as they pleased,[122] rolling stones down the road, whirling debris of every kind through the air.

One day the waves brought us the bloated corpse of a cow.

Evidently it was not uncommon for the wind to hurl cattle into the sea.

The cadets tried to push the cow away with long boat hooks, but it kept coming back. It floated about for a long time, a monstrous, swollen balloon, now moving away a little, now bobbing up right beside us.

Those of us still left on the *Shilka* wandered about dejectedly.

To your left, if you went up on deck, you saw a silent city, all dust and debris, exhausted by anxiety, fear, and typhus. And to your right lay the boundless sea, the waves hurriedly and mindlessly buffeting one another, mounting one another and then dropping back down, crushed by other, newer waves that spat at them in foaming fury.

Agitated gulls were swooping about, bitterly flinging what sounded like last words—hopeless, fragmentary last words—at one another.

Grey sky.

It was all very dismal.

At night, the thudding and crashing overhead made it impossible to sleep. If you left your airless cabin and went up on deck, the wind would spin you round, seize hold of you, slam the door behind you, then drag you away into the darkness, where it whistled and howled as it harried a frightened crowd of waves, driving them off, driving them away...

Away from these shores of despair. But where? Where to?

Soon we too might be driven away by the raging elements, but where would we go? Where in the wide world?

And so you would return to your cabin.

And lie on your hard wooden bunk and listen to the

midshipman strumming his out-of-tune guitar and to the violent coughing of the old Chinese cook—the man who had once "got so angry his heart broke."[123]

I was wandering about the city, hoping to find something out. I came upon what had once been the editorial office of what had once been the Novorossiisk newspaper. But nobody there knew anything. Or rather, everybody there knew a great deal, each knowing the exact opposite of what everyone else knew.

On one thing, however, they were all agreed: Odessa was now in the hands of the Bolsheviks.

Once, as I was walking about the town, I saw Batkin, the famous "sailor."[124] He turned out to be a young dandy of a student, always strolling about the city with a crowd of admiring young ladies. He would tell them the story of how he had almost been shot by a firing squad. Only thanks to his extraordinary eloquence had he got away with his life. But he told all this without much conviction or flair and didn't seem particularly bothered about whether or not his story was believed. The only dramatic moment was when he was facing death with the name of his beloved on his lips. At this point the young ladies would all lower their eyes as one.

Looking at this sleek, well-groomed student, I remembered the fiery sailor who used to come out on stage at the Mariinsky Theatre, stand in front of a large Saint Andrew's flag,[125] and passionately exhort the audience never to give up the fight. Correspondents from the *Evening Stock Exchange*[126] would then clap and cheer from the royal box.

This sailor might have been a phoenix, he might have risen from the flames, but he too was soon whirled away by the northeasterly... Only dust and debris... Later, or so I heard, he offered his services to the Bolsheviks. It's not impossible.[127]

Dust and debris.

But I shall not forget the evenings I saw him standing in front of the Saint Andrew's flag.

I continued to wander about the city.

I began to come across new groups of refugees. Among them were people I had already met elsewhere.

In their faces I saw something new. What struck me, what stayed in my mind, was the way these people's eyes were constantly darting about. Shifting about in embarrassment, in confusion, and even—momentarily—taking on a look of insolence. As if they needed just a few more seconds before they could settle into this insolence, before they could feel secure in it.

I understood later that these were people who, like poor Alexandr Kugel, were troubled by a sense of uncertainty: On whose side were might and right now?

These people were waiting to see which way the wind was blowing. They wanted to establish themselves *here* while keeping in with the authorities back *there*.

I happened to meet the senior official who, in Kiev, had declared he would not rest until he had slain seven Bolsheviks on the grave of his executed brother "so that their blood seeps through the earth, so that it seeps down to my brother's tortured body!"

He was not looking especially militant. Shoulders hunched, he was constantly turning this way and that way, looking around furtively, glancing slyly out of the corners of his eyes.

His whole manner with me was rather strained. He did not so much as mention his seven Bolsheviks and he made no great display of feeling. He seemed more like a man trying to make his way across a swamp, struggling to keep his footing on a narrow log.

"But what about your family?" I asked. "Where are they?"

"At the moment they're in Kiev. Still, we'll be seeing each other soon."

"Soon? But how are you going to get back to Kiev?"

For some reason he looked around him. The same new look of furtive resentment.

"Soon there'll probably be all kinds of opportunities. But this isn't really the moment to be talking about them."

Opportunities did indeed soon arise for him. And he remains an esteemed and successful figure, working in Moscow...

My memories of those first days in Novorossiisk still lie behind a curtain of grey dust. They are still being whirled about by a stifling whirlwind—just as scraps of this and splinters of that, just as debris and rubbish of every kind, just as people themselves were whirled this way and that way, left and right, over the mountains or into the sea. Soulless and mindless, with the cruelty of an elemental force, this whirlwind determined our fate.

27

This whirlwind did indeed determine all our fates—tossing us to the right, tossing us to the left.

A fourteen-year-old boy, the son of a sailor executed by the Reds, made his way back north in search of his relatives. He was unable to find even one of them. And then, within a few years, he had joined the Communist Party. As for the family he had been trying to find, they had all emigrated. When they spoke of their son, it was with shame and bitterness.

An actor who sang popular Bolshevik songs and ditties happened to get left behind in some town or other after a Bolshevik withdrawal. He refashioned his songs till they sounded appropriately anti-Bolshevik and then remained White forever more.

Eminent artistes ended up stranded in the south. Far from their theatres and loved ones, they found life unbearable. Lost and bewildered, they span around for a while in the White whirlwind. Then, breaking free, they were swept north like migrating birds, flying over rivers and burning cities, obedient to the pull of their native roosts.

★

Enterprising little gentlemen began to appear, shuttling between Moscow and the south along paths known to them alone. Bringing things to us in the south and taking things back to Moscow on our behalf... They would politely offer to deliver money to relatives; or they could go and fetch things we had left behind in Moscow or Petersburg.

These little men were strange. It was clearly not merely to be of service to us that they went on these long journeys. But what *was* the reason for their constant shuttling? Who were their masters? Whom were they serving? Whom betraying? No one seemed very bothered by any of these questions. People just said, "So and so is going to Moscow soon. He knows a way through."

But how did he know? Why had he needed to know? These were questions people chose not to ask.

Occasionally someone would say casually, "He's probably a spy."

But their tone of voice was benign and matter of fact. They might just as well have been saying, "He's probably a lawyer."

Or "Probably a tailor."

Spying, it seems, was a profession like any other.

And the little men kept scuttling about, shuttling back and forth, always buying and selling.

The population of Novorossiisk was changing. Gone were the encampments that had made the waterfront so lively and colourful.

The first wave of refugees had receded.

Denikin's White Army was advancing and those who, only a few months before, had been fleeing the Bolsheviks were now pouring back into the towns Denikin had liberated.

News of Denikin's successes was a source of feverish excitement. This excitement concealed both farce and tragedy.

I often came across a man from Kharkov, always arm in arm with a pretty young actress. Gesturing perplexedly, he would say, "Why do they have to keep advancing so quickly? They ought to have a little rest. Don't you agree that soldiers should be allowed to get their wind back? I know they are heroes, but even heroes sometimes need a break."

Then he would add hopelessly, "The way things are going, it won't be long before we all have to go back home."

He had a wife in Kharkov.

But another element in this tragedy was more farcical still. His wife—and I knew this for certain—was no happier than he was; *her* delight in Denikin's victories was equally bleak.

"Your poor darling wife," I once said to him. "She must be overjoyed!"

And then silently, to myself, I went on, "Poor woman! Every time she hears news of a White victory she probably wanders about the house tearing up letters, clearing away telltale cigarette butts, her hand trembling as she writes little notes: 'The Whites are approaching. To be on the safe side, you'd better not come tomorrow...'"

"Yes," I went on aloud, "the poor darling must be well and truly overwhelmed."

I shall never know just what he was thinking, but he replied, "Yes indeed. You know what she's like—such a meek little soul. Sometimes I almost wish she'd love me a little less. Self-denying love like hers always brings suffering. I am, of course, as you know, both faithful and devoted—"

"Yes, yes, of course..."

"These days, marriages like ours are few and far between. We couldn't be more faithful to each other—not if we were Bobchinsky and Dobchinsky themselves."[128]

What happened when husband and wife were reunited, I do not know. Maybe Bobchinsky succeeded in tidying away the evidence. Maybe Dobchinsky was able to lie his way out of trouble.

Two actresses unexpectedly paid me a visit. They had been sent by an impresario from Yekaterinodar who wanted to put on two evenings of my plays. The actors—and they were a good company—would perform the plays, and I was to give a short reading myself. The terms were not bad. I agreed.

The actresses also gave me a letter from Olyonushka. She too was in Yekaterinodar. She was writing to tell me that her husband had died of typhus and that she was planning to come and see me.

Poor Olyonushka. It was hard to imagine Olyonushka as a widow, in mourning.

Then came a telegram: "Arriving tomorrow."

The *Shilka* was taking on coal. The large coal barge—already nearly empty—was moored alongside.

I was sitting on deck, keeping an eye on the gangway, waiting.

All of a sudden our cadets began laughing and shouting, "Bravo! Bravo!"

I turned around. Walking along the narrow band of planking around the edge of the barge, above the gaping black abyss of the almost empty hold, was a young lady. Using a little travel case as a balancing aid, she was walking with a spring in her step, almost skipping along.

"Olyonushka!"

I had pictured her wearing a long black veil, with a handkerchief in her hand. But the woman I saw before me had a bright, rosy face and a plaid cap perched on the back of her head.

"Olyonushka! I thought you'd be in mourning…"

"No," she replied, giving me a firm kiss on the cheek. "Vova and I made a vow. We each promised that should the other die, we would do all we could not to be sad. Instead of grieving, we'd go out and enjoy ourselves. We'd go to the cinema. That's what we promised each other."

Then she told me the complicated story of her marriage.

When she got to Rostov, Vova had been expecting her. He had booked her a room, the one next to his, but they didn't tell anyone else in the hotel that they knew each other. They got married, but in secret, continuing to pretend to everyone that they were complete strangers.

"But why?"

"I was worried about Dima in Kiev," Olyonushka said awkwardly. "I was afraid he'd shoot himself if he heard I'd married. Or that he'd suffer most dreadfully. And I can't bear people to suffer."

Olyonushka kept a little picture of Vova on her bedside table. This was a source of constant surprise to the chambermaid.

"Your brother looks just like that young officer who's staying here!"

"Does he really?" Olyonushka would respond with no less surprise. "I must remember to look out for him."

She and Vova had had little money, but they had been quietly happy together. Vova's work often took him away. Even though he was only nineteen, he was already a captain and was being sent on important missions. Before he set off, Olyonushka would bless him with a tiny pearl-embroidered icon of the Mother of God. He would then take the icon away with him, as well as a little plush dog she gave him "so he wouldn't feel lonely."

After one of his missions Vova came back looking tired and sad.

"When I was at the station," he said, "a big shaggy dog came up to me. It kept looking at me, begging me to stroke it. It looked so wretched and dirty. And for some reason I kept thinking, 'If you give in, if you stroke this dog, you'll catch typhus.' But it kept looking at me. It kept begging to be petted. Now I'm probably going to die."

From that day on Vova was very subdued. And it seemed to him that whenever he entered a room, some kind of strange, transparent, gelatinous figure would be standing by the wall. Then it would bend down and vanish.

Vova was called to Yekaterinodar again. He set off, then disappeared. The days passed: He should have been back in Rostov long ago. And Olyonushka kept hearing the most terrifying rumours about Yekaterinodar. Apparently people were collapsing in the street, struck down by typhus as if by lightning. And then they died without even once regaining consciousness.

Olyonushka took two days' leave from the Renaissance (as her little theatre was called) and went off in search of her husband. She went round all the big hotels and hospitals in Yekaterinodar, but he was nowhere to be found. There was no record of Vova anywhere.

She went back home.

And then she received a message that her husband was indeed badly ill—in a hospital in Yekaterinodar.

Olyonushka asked for leave once again. She found the right hospital. There she was told that her husband had been picked up unconscious in the street and that he'd had a fever for a long time—the most severe form of typhus. He had died without ever coming back to himself and had already been buried. In his delirium he had kept repeating just two words: "Olyonushka, renaissance." Eventually it had occurred to one of his fellow patients that he might be asking the hospital staff to contact the theatre in Rostov.

"The poor boy," the doctor said to Olyonushka. "He never stopped calling for you. He was calling for you with all his heart, and none of us understood."

The widow was given "the possessions of the deceased"—a little plush dog and a tiny pearl-embroidered icon of the Mother of God.

And then Olyonushka had to go straight back to Rostov. She had to take part that evening in some idiotic Bat-style cabaret.

And that was the story of Olyonushka's marriage.

Just like the Polish children's song:

> Little bear
> jumped on the chair
> and blinked.

A good song
and not too long...

Our lives were indeed at the mercy of a whirlwind. It tossed us to the left; it tossed us to the right.

28

My evenings in Yekaterinodar were coming up soon.

I have no idea why the thought of any kind of public appearance fills me with such dread. I can't explain this at all. Maybe it is beyond the understanding of anyone except the psychoanalyst Sigmund Freud.

I certainly can't say that the public has ever treated me badly. When I've had to read at charity events I have always been given an undeservedly warm welcome. A warm welcome and an equally generous and enthusiastic ovation. What more could I ask for? This should be enough to make anyone happy.

Far from it.

I wake up with a jolt in the middle of the night: "Heavens! What is it? Something is about to happen. Something awful, quite unbearably vile... Yes, of course. I'm giving a reading at a dentists' benefit night."

And the lies I tell in my attempts to escape such horrors!

Usually it starts with a telephone call: "There's something very important I need to talk to you about. Just for a few minutes. When may I come and see you?"

Here we go.

"If you would be so kind," I say (and even I myself feel surprised how flat my voice sounds), "perhaps you could just give me some idea now of what this is about."

This, alas, is something the speaker rarely agrees to. For some reason, these ladies have an unshakeable faith in the invincibility of their personal charm.

"But these things are so difficult to talk about over the telephone!" the lady trills. "Please allow me just five minutes. I promise I won't take up any more of your time."

I make up my mind to unmask her there and then: "Does it, by any chance, have something to do with an entertainment you're putting on?"

Now she has no way out. I need only say, "And when will this evening be?"

And, no matter what she says, the date turns out to be "utterly impossible for me, I regret to say."

Now and again, however, I am given a date in the distant future—a whole month or even a month and a half away. And I frivolously say to myself that it really isn't worth getting worked up about something so very distant. By then, after all, our whole solar system may have undergone some dramatic transformation. Or the lady may simply forget about me. Or the evening will be postponed. Anything can happen.

"With pleasure," I reply. "What a wonderful cause. You can count on me."

Then one fine morning I open the newspaper and see my own name. Yes, there it is, plain as day, in a list of writers and actors who are to perform in three days' time in the main hall of the Assembly of the Nobility—a benefit evening, let's say, for students who have been expelled from the Gurevich Gymnasium.[129]

What can I do? Fall sick? Slit my wrists? Catch the plague?

I remember one quite awful occasion. Now it seems like a bad dream. Yes, people have told me of exactly this kind of thing happening to them in dreams. "There I am in the Mariinsky Theatre," an old professor of chemistry once told me, "and I'm going to have to sing. I go on stage—and all of a sudden, I remember I simply cannot sing. No, not for the life of me. And to make matters worse, I'm wearing only my nightshirt. But the audience is waiting, the orchestra is already playing the overture, and the tsar himself is sitting in the royal box. Dear God, the things one dreams!"

The story I'm about to tell you is very similar. Both nightmarish and funny.

While you're sleeping, while you're there inside the story, it's a nightmare. Afterward, when you're back outside it again, it's funny.

A young man had called round. He wanted me to take part in a debate about the fashionable topic of the silent cinema: the "Great Mute," as we called it then.

Leonid Andreyev was going to speak. As were Arabazhin, Volynsky, Meyerhold, and several others. I no longer remember who—but they were all important figures.[130]

I was, of course, appalled.

Going onstage with a book and reading a story you've written is one thing. And it's really not so very difficult. But speaking—in public—is another matter. It's completely beyond me. I've never spoken in public and I don't ever want to.

The young man tried to win me over. If I really wasn't up to speaking, I could just write down a few words beforehand and read them out.

"But I know nothing about the cinema. It's not something I ever even think about."

"Then start now!"

"I don't know how to. I've got nothing to think."

A great deal was being written about the "Great Mute," but it had all passed me by. I had no idea where to begin, whose opinions I could rely on, and whose I should challenge.

But then the young man said something marvellously soothing: "The debate isn't for another six weeks. You've got more than enough time to find out everything you need to know, and then you can just read from your notes."

It all sounded so nice and easy—and, more important still, the debate was a whole six weeks away.

I agreed, of course—and the young man, elated, went on his way.

The days passed. No one bothered me; no one so much as mentioned the debate to me. I forgot all about it.

Then one dull evening when I had nothing to do and didn't feel like seeing anyone, I went to the Liteiny Theatre. I went partly out of boredom and partly for professional reasons. Several of my plays were in repertoire, and I needed to go along now and again to keep an eye on things. The actors often got so carried away (they were all young, bright and talented) and would do so much "embellishment" (their term for adding words of their own) that by the tenth or twelfth performance some passages had moved so far from the original that even a play's author might fail to recognize it as their own creation. And an author who left the actors to their own devices for a while and then went along to the twentieth or thirtieth performance might feel genuine puzzlement: What *was* this jolly nonsense? None of it made any sense, yet it all seemed vaguely familiar.

I still vividly remember a very talented actor in my play *Diamond Dust*.[131] He was playing the enamoured artist. Instead of saying to his beloved, "I'll follow you like a black slave," I heard him clearly and distinctly pronounce, "I'll follow you like a black sleigh."

I thought I'd misheard, or that the actor had simply come out with the wrong word. I went backstage and asked: Had I simply imagined this black sleigh?

"No, it's something I thought up myself."

"But why?" I asked in bewilderment.

"Because it's funnier like that."

I was at a loss what to say.

But there are worse things than black sleighs.

Once, after not seeing one of my plays for a long time, I went to the theatre and heard the actors spout such a load of nonsense that I took fright. I rushed backstage. The actors greeted me with cheery pride.

"So! Do you like what we've done with your play? Works well, doesn't it? The audience just loves it!"

"It's absolutely enchanting, of course," I replied. "But I must, I regret to say, ask you to return to my humble text. I don't feel comfortable putting my name to someone else's work."

They seemed surprised.

And so, there I was, on my way to the Liteiny Theatre. It was an evening I shall not forget.

It was nearly ten o'clock and the performance had evidently begun some time ago. I had free entry, so I went to the back of the hall and found a seat.

There were a lot of people, but... what was this play? And why were the house lights on?

Up onstage is a table covered with green cloth. Behind the table, sitting in the middle, is Meyerhold—I recognize him instantly. Arabazhin is standing up; he's saying something. Volynsky's there too. And sitting at the end of the table is some young man. Meyerhold screws up his eyes and stares at me; evidently he recognizes me. He beckons to the young man (whose face seems strangely familiar) and says something, pointing toward me... The young man nods and makes his way offstage.

What's happening? I suppose he just wants to be courteous and offer me a seat further forward... But what's going on? What are they all doing here?

In the meantime the young man has entered the auditorium through a side door and is purposefully making his way toward me.

He stops beside me.

"Would you rather speak now," he asks, "or after the interval?"

"I... erm, no, not right now... I don't understand..." I stammer in total bewilderment.

"All right then, after the interval," says the young man in a matter-of-fact tone. "In any event, I've been asked to invite you to join us onstage and take your place at the table. Let me show you the way."

"Oh no… no… I can manage. Goodness! What's going on?"

He raises an eyebrow in surprise and returns to the side door.

At this point I start to take in some of what's being said on stage:

"The Great Mute…"

"The role of the Cinema…"

"Whether or not it can be called Art…"

And something begins to dawns on me. Some thought begins to take shape—a shape that, though still vague, is distinctly unpleasant.

I get up quietly and make my way to the exit. Beside it I see an enormous poster: The Cinema—a Debate.

And there in the list of speakers is my own name, plain as day.

I rush back home. There I frighten my poor maid out of her wits, telling her to put the door on the chain and not to open it on any account to anyone. I take the telephone off the hook, get into bed, and hide my head under the pillow. Dinner is ready, but I'm too scared to go and eat it.

I am afraid that if I go to the dining room, it will be easier for "them" to find me.

How fortunate that everything in the world comes to an end.

29

A nd so the day came for me to travel to Yekaterinodar, to take part in the two evenings of my work being put on at the local theatre.

Tired and downcast, I left Novorossiisk at nightfall. The train was overflowing, hordes of soldiers and officers filling every car. Evidently they were on their way north, to the front. But they did not look as if they had been on leave for any length of time; they looked too drawn, too worn out, too haggard. Perhaps they were simply being flung from one front to another. I don't know.

I found myself squashed into a third class car with a broken window and no lighting.

Everywhere I looked—on the benches, on the floor—were figures in brown greatcoats. The car was stifling and full of smoke.

Many of the soldiers fell asleep before the train had even set off.

Standing diagonally across from me, leaning against the side of the car, was a tall, emaciated officer.

"Andreyev!" someone called out. "Come and sit down, we can squash up a bit."

"I can't," the officer replied. "I'm better off standing."

And so he remained all through the night. His head was thrown back and I could see the whites of his half-closed eyes. On his brow, beneath the skewed peak of his cap, a round crimson spot was slowly going black. As if nailed to the mast like the captain of the *Flying Dutchman*, he stood there almost without moving, just rocking a little when the train gave a jolt, his long, thin legs spread wide apart. No one talked much, apart from one officer who was sitting beside the smashed window. This man was telling some endless story, never pausing, and I soon realized he was simply talking to himself and that no one was listening to him.

Then a man sitting near me asked somebody else a question: "Have you heard about Colonel K?"

This colonel was a man I had already heard about. Apparently the Bolsheviks had tortured this colonel's wife and two children to death right in front of him. Ever since, whenever he took any Bolshevik prisoners, he had had them put to death then and there, and always in exactly the same way. He would sit on the porch drinking tea and have the prisoners strung up in front of him, first one, then another, then another.

While he carried on drinking tea.

This was the man my neighbour was asking about.

"Yes, I have," came the reply. "He's insane."

"No, he isn't. For him, what he's doing is entirely normal. You see, after all he's been through, it would be very, very strange if he were to act in a more ordinary way. *That* really would be insane. There's a limit to what the soul can take, to what human reason can endure. And that's as it should be. The way Colonel K behaves is, for him, entirely normal. Understand?"

The other man said nothing. But someone sitting a little further away, on the other side of the aisle, said loudly, "They gouged a boy's eyes out, a ten-year-old boy. They cut them right out. If you've never seen a face like that with gouged-out eyes, you can't imagine how terrible it looks. He lived on like that for another two days, screaming the whole time."

"That's enough... Don't..."

"And the agent—did you hear about him? They tied his hands and stuffed his mouth and nose with earth. He suffocated."

"No, Colonel K is not insane. In his world, in the world he lives in, he's perfectly normal."

It was dark in the car.

The wan light coming in through the broken glass—moonlight, I think, although we could not see the moon itself—picked out the dark silhouettes of the men close to the window. Everyone else—those sitting further from the window or on the floor—formed a single, dense, murky shadow. This shadow muttered, swayed, cried out. Were these men asleep? Or awake but out of their wits?

One voice pronounced clearly, too loudly, and with excessive effort, "I can't go on anymore. Since 1914 they've been torturing me, torturing me, and now... now I'm dead. I'm dead..."

It was the voice of a man who was not alive, a man no longer conscious of himself. It was like the voices of *those who are no more*—at a spiritualist séance or on an old gramophone recording...

Our old, beaten-up carriage was rattling every one of its

bolts, its rusty wheels squealing and screeching as it rolled these semi-corpses along toward torment and death.

Day began to break.

In the half light the rocking heads and pale faces seemed more terrible still.

These men were asleep. Talking in their sleep. And if one of them awoke, he would at once quieten down, straighten his stiff shoulders, and smooth down his greatcoat. Calmly and simply, as if nothing were the matter. He didn't know what his soul had been weeping about as he slept.

But most terrible of all was the man still standing upright before them, greatcoat wide open, his thin, dead head thrown right back, a bullet hole in his forehead.

He was facing us, like a commanding officer preparing to lead his men forward. A man with a bullet hole in his forehead, the captain of the *Flying Dutchman*—the ship of death.[132]

The train reached Yekaterinodar early in the morning. The city was still asleep.

The bright sunny day, the dusty streets, and the creaking horse-drawn cab quickly brought me back to my usual, more spacious state of mind. The previous night had vanished, dying away like a distant moan.

"It's all right," I said to myself encouragingly. "Soon the *Shilka* will be allowed to go east. And then in Vladivostok I'll be with M, a loyal and devoted friend. I'll get my breath back. And by then things will be a bit clearer…"

I began to think about these two evenings of mine; we needed to start rehearsing straightaway.

When I reached the house of the impresario who had invited me, the shutters were still closed. It seemed everyone was still asleep.

I rang the bell—and Olyonushka let me in. She was one of the company.

30

Yekaterinodar was at this time our centre, our White capital. And it really did have the air of a capital.

One glimpsed generals' uniforms; one heard snatches of important conversations:

"I have ordered that…"

"The minister, however…"

"I shall issue a severe reprimand, without delay."

Typewriters. Officials. Ordinary buildings now housing government institutions…

Unexpectedly, I received a letter from Novorossiisk—a request from the ship I had abandoned. I was being asked to go in person to the naval authorities and petition them to allow the *Shilka* to set sail for Vladivostok.

I cannot bear any kind of government institution or bureaucratic formality. Even just going to the post office to pick up an innocent registered letter has an unfortunate effect on me. The businesslike look on the face of the official asking for my signature instantly makes me forget the date, the year, and my own surname. You're allowed to ask about the date, and if you look around you can sometimes spot the year on a wall calendar—but if you have to think about your own surname, the official will refuse to hand you the letter.

But I had no choice. I wanted to do our dear *Shilka* a good turn, and the thought of sailing east was appealing. Until now fate had only driven us straight down the map. Why shouldn't we go sideways for a change?

I asked where the naval authorities were now housed and set off.

I was directed to a tall gentleman with a bright ginger beard. I no longer remember his name, only that he had ginger hair, that he was very courteous, and that his naval authority was considerable.

He didn't ask me the date and he already knew my name, so I was able to babble out the *Shilka's* request quite spiritedly.

He paused for a moment, then surprised me by saying, "Tell me, what makes you so eager to drown? Captain Ryabinin has made this request before. We refused it. The *Shilka* is a small vessel, and Captain Ryabinin has never sailed to Vladivostok. He'll send you to the bottom of the sea."

I defended the *Shilka*. So what if she wasn't so very big? That hadn't stopped her from reaching the Black Sea. And where had she sailed from? Vladivostok!

"We see that as a happy accident unlikely to repeat itself. If she makes the journey again, she's sure to be caught in a typhoon."

It didn't feel right to explain that for me personally this would be the most interesting part of the journey. I only said I was certain that the *Shilka* could cope with any storms or typhoons.

The naval authority laughed. He did not share my confidence.

"It would be the end of the *Shilka*. Your Captain Ryabinin is a brave man, but we cannot permit such madness."

I sent a sad telegram to the *Shilka* and gave up my attempts to intervene.

The rehearsals and the two evenings took up three or four days. Throughout this period I stayed with the impresario.

He was a very sweet man of French descent who had retained only one custom from his forgotten homeland: If roast chicken was being served, he liked to carve it himself, at the table.

Several months previously he had married a young actress from his company. She had quickly fattened up from her new life of plenty and had left the stage. Plump, pink, and sleepy, she flounced about in extravagant muslin frills, called her husband "Papa" and talked like a doll: "Pa-pa! Baby wants watermelon! Pa-pa!"

The house was always full. There were actors, actresses, and critics, and there were always people staying on for one meal or another. It was noisy, convivial, and chaotic. There was little talk of politics. People who had to return to Moscow, and who were free to return, mingled with people who knew they could never return. Not that anyone really knew anything anyway—it seemed easier to leave the understanding and decision-making to those of a more activist disposition. In this little artistic bohemia, people lived purely for their professional pursuits. Probably everyone was simply too frightened to give any real thought to what was going on around them.

More and more people kept appearing. By hook or by crook, new troupes of actors were constantly finding their way through from the north.

An elderly theatre critic arrived. He had sent a telegram saying he was unwell and asking for a room to be made ready for him. Someone booked him into a hotel and two tender-hearted actresses went to the station to meet him.

"Everything's ready," they told him. "We've even ordered you a bath!"

"A bath?" repeated the now frightened critic. "Is my condition really so very serious?"

The actresses were embarrassed.

"No, no, of course not! It's just so you can have a good wash after your dreadful journey."

The critic smiled condescendingly.

"If that's all there is to it, my dears, then I have to say that a bath is not something for which I feel any particular need."

The two people I most remember from this motley crew are the silent cinema star Osip Runich and the comic actor and light opera singer Alexander Koshevsky[133]—a tragic individual who was always imagining himself to be mortally ill. Even as he was piling a third helping onto his plate, he would say despairingly, "Yes, I know my loss of appetite is most suspicious. Undoubtedly an early symptom of meningitis…"

He had an interesting wife, about whom one actress said, "She's from a very interesting family. Apparently Dostoevsky's *Brothers Karamazov* is modelled on her auntie."

Then the day came. They were putting on three of my little skits; the actresses were also going to read some of my short stories, sing a few of my songs, and recite some poems.

The impresario insisted that I read too. I fought long and hard, but in the end I was forced to yield.

Our actresses were getting excited. One after another they were rushing up to me and asking if I would allow them to do my makeup for me before I appeared on stage.

"What are you going to read?" they kept asking.

"I haven't yet made up my mind."

"What? I don't believe it!"

In the evening, with much squealing, shrieking, and shouting, the house's entire population hurried off to the theatre. I decided to go a little later.

I quietly got dressed and went out.

It was a still night; the sky was dark and studded with stars. This made my soul too feel strangely still.

There are moments when threads snap—all the threads that tie what is earthly in the soul to the earth itself. Your nearest and dearest become infinitely distant, barely even a memory. Even the events in your past that once mattered most to you grow dim. All of the huge and important thing we call life fades away and you become that primordial nothing out of which the universe was created.

So it was on that night—the black, empty, round earth and the boundless starry sky. And me.

How long this moment lasted I can't say. I was brought back by the sound of voices: People were walking past, talking loudly about the theatre. And I remembered everything. This, I remembered, was my evening. I was going to have to hurry. I seemed to have wandered a long way—beside me I could see a bright strip of water and some little black walkways.

"Please! For the love of God!" I called out. "Which way is the theatre?"

Someone told me.

I hurried off, clacking my heels on the pavement, so I could hear that I had returned to my ordinary everyday life.

Backstage there is much excitement and bustle.

"Denikin's here![134] It's a full house."

From the wings I can see the front rows. Gold and silver lace, the glint of uniforms—true splendour.

This splendid hall is laughing and applauding. The laughter even spreads backstage.

Then I hear calls of "Author! Author!"

More bustle backstage. "Author! Where's the author?"

"Where's the author?" I repeat like an automaton. "Where's the author? Oh my God! It's my own play! *I'm* the author!"

What would my dear impresario make of all this? What if he knew what a strange creature he has invited to his theatre! A normal author would have been a bundle of nerves all through the day. A normal author would be saying things like, "Feel my hands—they're like ice!" And what do *I* do? I cultivate a state of cosmic non-being—and then, when the audience calls for me, I ask with calm curiosity, "Where's the author?"

Yet he'll be paying me as if I were a proper, sensible author!

"Get on stage!" yells the director.

I quickly put on a carefree smile, take hold of the hands stretched toward me and join the actors on stage to take my bow.

My last bow to a Russian audience on Russian soil.

Farewell, my last bow...

S ummer in Yekaterinodar…

Heat. Dust. Through a murky veil of dust, turmoil, and all the years that have passed I glimpse faces and images.

Professor Novgorodtsev. The pale blue, very Slavic eyes of Venedikt Myakotin. The ever-sentimental Fyodor Volkenstein's thick mane of hair. The faraway, intent gaze of Pyotr Ouspensky, the mystic…[135] And others, "slain servants of the Lord" whom we were already remembering in our prayers.

And there was Prince Y—one of my many Petersburg acquaintances. Always cheerful, feverishly animated—still more so after being shot through the arm.

"The soldiers adore me," he would say. "I know how to treat them. I bash them in the face—just like you bash a tambourine."

What they really loved him for, I think, was his reckless daring and his extraordinary cheerful bravado. They liked to tell the story of how he had once galloped through a village held by the Bolsheviks, whistling loudly, his epaulettes clearly visible on his shoulders.

"But why didn't they shoot at you?"

"They were flabbergasted. They couldn't believe their eyes: a White officer—suddenly riding through their village! They all rushed out to look, eyes popping out of their heads. It was ever so funny!"

I've heard the most astonishing accounts of Prince Y's subsequent adventures. In due course, in some other town in the south, he fell into enemy hands. He was tried—and sentenced to hard labour. Since the Bolsheviks didn't have any proper labour camps at that time, they simply put him in prison. But then they turned out to need a public prosecutor; it was only a small town and everyone with any education had either fled or gone into hiding. And they knew that the prince had completed a degree in law. So they thought for a bit, then appointed him public prosecutor. Prince Y would be escorted to the court to prosecute and to pass sentence, and he would then return for the night to his "hard labour." Many people felt envious: They too would have been glad of free bed and board.

Yekaterinodar, Rostov, Kislovodsk, Novorossiisk...

Yekaterinodar, city of the elite. And in every government establishment—the picturesque beret, cloak, and curls of Maximilian Voloshin, declaiming his poems about Russia and petitioning on behalf of the innocent and endangered.

Rostov, city of traders and profiteers, its restaurant gardens the scene for hysterical drinking bouts that culminated in suicides.

Novorossiisk, city of many colours, ready to spring into Europe. Young men and chic ladies, motoring about in English cars and bathing in the sea. Novorossiisk-les-Bains...

Kislovodsk, which greeted approaching trains with an idyllic picture of green hills, peacefully grazing flocks and—against the backdrop of a scarlet evening sky—a finely etched black swing with a stub of rope.

A gallows.

I remember how haunted I was by that singular picture. I remember leaving the hotel first thing in the morning and setting off toward those green hills, seeking the evil mountain.

Toward it I went, climbing a steep, well-trodden path. Seen from close by, the swing was no longer black. It was grey, like any other piece of ordinary unpainted wood.

I stood right in the centre, beneath its strong crossbeam.

What, in their last moments, had these people seen? Hangings were, as a rule, carried out early in the morning. From this spot, they would have seen their last sun. And this line of hills and mountains.

Down below to the left, the market was already getting underway. Brightly dressed peasant women were taking earthenware from their carts and laying it out on straw, the morning sun glistening wetly on the glazed jugs and bowls. Then, too, there would probably have been this same market. And to the right, farther off among the hills, were flocks of sheep. In tight waves (like the curls of the Shulamite),[136] these flocks were now rolling slowly down the green slope, and shepherds in furs were leaning on long crooks straight out of the Bible. A blessed silence. They, too, would have heard this silence.

It would all have been utterly simple and routine. People would have led someone up here, then stood them exactly where I was now standing myself. One of the shepherds might have looked this way, shielding his eyes with the palm of his hand, and wondered what was going on up above him.

One of those hanged here had been Ksenya G, the famous anarchist.[137] Bold, gay, young, beautiful—always chic, and the companion of Mamont Dalsky.[138] Back in the days of revolutionary fever, many of my friends had gone out carousing in the company of these two and their lively, entertaining fellow-anarchists. And they all, without exception, had struck us as fakes and braggarts. Not one of us had taken them seriously. We had known Mamont's colourful persona too well and too long to believe in the sincerity of his political convictions. It was posturing, hot air, a hired costume, the greasepaint of a tragic villain. Intriguing and irresponsible. On stage Mamont had, throughout his career, played Edmund Kean in the play by Alexandre Dumas; off stage he had played not only Kean but also the "genius" and the "libertine" of the play's title. But Mamont had died (oh, the little ironies of fate!) because of an act of old-fashioned courtesy. Standing on the running board of a tram, he had stepped back to make room for a lady. He had lost his footing and fallen beneath the wheels. And several months later his companion, gay, chic Ksenya G, had stood here, in this very spot, smoking her last cigarette and screwing her eyes up as she looked at her last sun. Then she had flicked away the cigarette butt—and calmly thrown the stiff noose around her neck.

Sunlight playing on the glazed earthenware in the bazaar. Brightly dressed women, milling about by the carts. Farther away—shepherds moving slowly down the steep green slopes, leaning on their staffs. And probably, a faint ringing, as there always is in the mountain silence. And the silence was blessed.

★

People often complain that a writer has botched the last pages of a novel, that the ending is somehow crumpled, too abrupt.

I understand now that a writer involuntarily creates in the image and likeness of fate itself. All endings are hurried, compressed, broken off.

When a man has died, we all like to think that there was a great deal he could still have done.

When a chapter of life has died, we all think that it could have somehow developed and unfolded further, that its conclusion is unnaturally compressed and broken off. The events that conclude such chapters of life seem tangled and skewed, senseless and without definition.

In its own writings, life keeps to the formulae of old-fashioned novels. We learn from the epilogue that "Irina got married and I have heard tell she is happy. Sergey Nikolaevich was able to forget his troubles through service to society."

All too quick and hurried, all somehow beside the point.

Those last days in Novorossiisk before our contrived, unexpectedly far-fetched departure were equally hurried and uninteresting.

"It'll be difficult to return to Petersburg right now," I was told. "Go abroad for a while. Come spring you'll be back in the motherland."

"Spring," "motherland"—what wonderful words...

Spring is the resurrection of life. Come spring I'd be back again.

Our last hours on the quayside, beside the steamer *The Grand Duke Alexander Mikhailovich*.[139]

Hustle, bustle, much whispering. The strange whispering that, along with a constant looking back over the shoulder, had accompanied all our arrivals and departures as we slid down the map, down the huge green map across which, slantwise, was written *The Russian Empire*.

Yes, everyone is whispering; everyone is looking back over their shoulder. Everyone is frightened, constantly frightened, and not until their dying day will they find peace, will they come to their senses. Amen.

The steamer shudders, whipping up white foam with its propeller, spreading black smoke over the shoreline.

And slowly, softly, the land slips away from us.

Don't look at it. You must look ahead, into the wide, free expanse of blue.

But somehow the head turns back. Eyes are opening wide and they keep looking, looking...

And everyone is silent. Except for one woman. From the lower deck comes the sound of long, obstinate wails, interspersed with words of lament.

Where have I heard such wails before? Yes. I remember. During the first year of the war. A grey-haired old woman was being taken down the street in a horse-drawn cab. Her hat had slipped back onto the nape of her neck. Her yellow cheeks were thin and drawn. Her toothless black mouth was hanging open, crying out in a long tearless wail: "A-a-a-a-a!" Probably embarrassed by the disgraceful behaviour of his passenger, the driver was urging his poor horse forward, whipping her on.

Yes, my good man, you didn't think enough about whom you were picking up in your cab. And now you're stuck with this old woman. A terrible, black, tearless wail. A last wail. Over all of Russia, the whole of Russia… No stopping now…

The steamer shudders, spreading black smoke.

With my eyes now open so wide that the cold penetrates deep into them, I keep on looking. And I shall not move away. I've broken my vow, I've looked back. And, like Lot's wife, I am frozen. I have turned into a pillar of salt forever, and I shall forever go on looking, seeing my own land slip softly, slowly away from me.

Appendix: The Last Breakfast

The articles and sketches Teffi wrote during the years 1917–19 are gradually being republished. The most recent edition, *Teffi in the Country of Memories* (Kiev: LP Media, 2011), contains over seventy pieces, though it may well be incomplete. Twenty of these were published in Kiev newspapers, mostly between October 1918 and January 1919, and three were published in Odessa, in early 1919. Teffi clearly drew on some of these articles for *Memories*, and excerpts from them are quoted in the endnotes. "The Last Breakfast" (first published April 2, 1919, in *Our Word*, Odessa), the best piece from these months, and one which Teffi refers to directly in Chapter 14 of *Memories*, is translated here in full.

In times gone by, when Europe was peaceful and life settled, a condemned man would be offered breakfast on the morning of his execution. His last breakfast.

Le dernier déjeuner!

Witnesses to this last breakfast always noted with surprise the heartiness of the man's appetite.

Strange indeed.

If, in normal circumstances, someone is woken at four in the morning and offered breakfast, it is unlikely he'll respond with much interest. But a condemned man, knowing he has no more than two or three hours left to live, will gladly devote half an hour to a plate of roast beef.

Those whose last hours have been counted out and who have been handed the bill may, perhaps, slip into some peculiar state—a state of psychological coma. The soul has died away, died off, but the body's complex and cunning laboratory continues to function of its own accord. The smell of food makes nostrils flare; saliva fills the mouth, digestive juices start to flow, and what we call an appetite arises. The body lives. Surprising though it may seem, the body continues to live. It lives and breakfasts with relish. Nobody, of course, believes that the Bolsheviks might be coming. To believe such a thing would be improper, impolite, a sign of ill breeding and ingratitude. There is no escaping the patriotism of the moment.

Nobody believes such a thing.

Yet every epoch, even every little turning point in an epoch, has a phrase or word—a leitmotif—that captures the general mood. You will hear this word everywhere: in theatres, in cafés, in restaurants, at business meetings, at the card table, and out on the street. Wherever people are talking, whatever they are talking about, you cannot get away from this word.

The word of the moment is "visa."

Remember the day, take note of the day, when you don't hear this word.

In the month of March, 1919, life in Odessa is ruled by the sign of "visa."

"I am getting a visa."

"You will get a visa."

"He has got his visa already."

"We…" etc.

"The Bolsheviks aren't coming, but I'm trying to get hold of a visa."

"For where?"

"Anywhere—it's all the same to me."

This could be accurately translated as: "I, of course, have not been condemned to death, but just to be on the safe side I am petitioning for a pardon anyway."

Or to put it more simply: One fine morning people come and assure you, in the most impassioned of tones, that you have absolutely nothing to worry about, your life is really not in any danger. And your previous sense of peace and calm is lost forever.

"I believe you. I know full well that I'm not in any danger. But why do you have to keep telling me that? Hmm…"

"The Bolsheviks aren't coming. It won't be allowed. Have you got a visa?"

Perhaps this is true—the Bolsheviks won't come, and their coming is simply not possible. But in that corner of your consciousness, in that region of your brain that deals with the intricacies of obtaining foreign passports, the Bolsheviks have already taken over. They have been allowed into the city, they are making themselves at home here, and they are doing as they please with you. And fate offers you a last breakfast. *Le dernier déjeuner*. Clubs and restaurants are packed to bursting. People are guzzling chicken feet at eighty roubles each. People are blowing their "last odd million" in games of *chemin de fer*.

Bellies bulging, lifeless eyes, and a one-way visa to the island of Krakatakata (wherever that may be). And you're not allowed to stop anywhere en route.

Cold dreary days. Apocalyptic evenings.

In the evening people gather together, wearing hats and fur coats. With pale lips, their breath coming in clouds, they repeat, "The Bolsheviks, of course, aren't coming. A visa—must get hold of some kind of visa."

And they throw the last chair into the stove, after taking turns to sit on it for a minute by way of farewell.

This too is a kind of *dernier déjeuner*.

Cold days.

But if one morning the sun happens to leap up into the faded sky—a sky that is exhausted from waiting for spring—what absurd pictures we will see. These pictures are gloomy and sinister; they are not pictures fit for the sun.

The owner of a sugar refinery has walked out of a gaming house. He has been playing cards with abandon—and by morning he has lost two and a half million. By any standards that is quite a sum. But he has promised that by tomorrow he'll come up with some more money, to win back his losses.

The sun hurts the man's eyes, which are weary from his sleepless night. He squints, unable for a moment to take in a curious little scene being acted out right there in front of him.

On the pavement a man is poking about in a hole dug for a tree. Evidently, a former actor—you can tell from the stubble on a face that has now gone some time without a shave. The skin hangs from his cheeks in deep folds, pulling down the corners of his mouth. The actor is wearing only a light summer coat, and over it—like a beggar king—a brownish-black threadbare blanket.

The actor is engaged in a serious task. He is picking through discarded nut shells. Searching for a mistakenly spat-out kernel. Ah! He seems to have found something. He lifts this something up to his face and, slightly squinting, with a quick monkey-like movement of both hands, picks out a fragment of nut. The owner of the sugar refinery, screwing up his tired eyes, watches all this for a few seconds, calmly and without embarrassment, as one might observe a monkey unwrapping a sweet. The actor looks up, also only for an instant. Then he returns to his task. Equally calmly and without embarrassment, like a monkey being watched by some other species of wild animal.

He carries on with his *dernier déjeuner*.

"Hey, sun! Put those beams of yours away. Nothing worth gawping at here!"And what's all this about "psychological comas"? It's nothing of the kind.

People are just carrying on with their lives, living the way they have always lived, as is their human nature.

Translated by Lois Bentall with
Robert and Elizabeth Chandler

ROBERT CHANDLER is a poet and translator best known for his prize-winning translations of Vasily Grossman and Andrey Platonov. He is a co-translator of Teffi's *Subtly Worded* and *Rasputin and Other Ironies*.

ELIZABETH CHANDLER is a co-translator, with Robert Chandler, of Alexander Pushkin's *The Captain's Daughter* and of several titles by Andrey Platonov and Vasily Grossman.

ANNE MARIE JACKSON has translated many Russian works and is the editor and co-translator of Teffi's *Subtly Worded* and *Rasputin and Other Ironies*.

IRINA STEINBERG is a lawyer and translator, and a co-translator of *Subtly Worded* by Teffi.

Translator's Note

Memories was first published, in instalments, between December 1928 and January 1930, in Paris, in the Russian-language newspaper *Vozrozhdenie*. Its first readers were Russian émigrés. Nearly all were from the same cultural world as Teffi and many had been through similar experiences during their last months in Russia. I have provided endnotes, to the best of my ability, to fill in the cultural and political references that Teffi could take for granted in her original readership. What I have not done is to fill in the strictly personal details that Teffi has left vague or purposely obscured. Teffi was uncommonly reticent about her personal life, and I have chosen to respect this. But I whole-heartedly encourage anyone wanting to know more to turn to Edythe Haber's forthcoming biography.

Teffi is now widely read in Russia—new editions of her best-known stories come out almost yearly—but she still receives little scholarly attention. Probably because of her lack of pretence, she remains underestimated. In 1931, in a review of a new collection of Teffi's short stories, the Russian émigré poet Georgy Adamovich wrote, "There are writers who muddy their own water, to make it seem deeper. Teffi could not be more different: the water is entirely transparent, yet the bottom is barely visible." These words are still more apt with regard to *Memories*, an elegant and carefully composed work of art that appears, on first reading, to have been thrown together casually and spontaneously.

In essence, *Memories* is a series of goodbyes: to Moscow, Kiev, Odessa, and Russia itself; to friends—some who died and some who stayed in Soviet Russia; to the Russian theatre; and to Russia's two most important religious centres. Each of these goodbyes is in its distinct emotional register. Teffi's departure from Moscow is solemn; her departure from Odessa is farcical; her final departure on the boat to Constantinople is deeply sad. Teffi avoids repetition, but she makes skilful use of echoes and symmetries. Most poignant of all, perhaps, is the contrast between her account of her last public reading in Soviet Russia—in a "Club of Enlightenment" packed with Red Army soldiers and Cheka officers draped in bullet belts—and her account near the end of the memoir of an evening in a Yekaterinodar theatre where the glittering audience includes the commander-in-chief of the White Army. The former ends with a few well-wishers in the audience—women who appear "infinitely weary" and "hopelessly sad"—calling out to Teffi "Sweetheart! We love you! God grant you get out of here soon!" The evening in Yekaterinodar ends with Teffi joining in excited calls for the author to go out onstage, momentarily forgetting that she is herself the author of the plays just performed. The nature of authorship—the extent to which anyone is in control of their own life and the extent to which an artist does, or does not, have authority over their own creations—is another of Teffi's leitmotifs in *Memories*.

The final chapter is astonishing; shortly before leaving Russia, Teffi imagines saying goodbye to life itself. Standing at dawn beneath the hilltop gallows where an anarchist known as "Ksenya G" was hanged by the Whites, she imagines Ksenya's last minutes. Ksenya was "bold, gay, young, and beautiful." She was "always chic"; she was independent-minded. She has much in common with Teffi herself, and Teffi knows this. This scene may, amongst other things, serve as a source of bleak comfort, a reminder to Teffi that there are still worse fates than losing one's country. Had Teffi chosen to stay, she too might well have been executed.

Like many of the greatest Russian prose writers of the last century—Ivan Bunin, Vladimir Nabokov, Andrey Platonov, and Varlam Shalamov, among others—Teffi began her literary career as a poet. Like these other writers—with the possible exception of Shalamov—she is more truly a poet in her prose than in her verse. She writes precisely, colloquially and with delicate modulations of tone. There are subtle echoes and symmetries not only in the book's overall structure, but also at the level of individual chapters, paragraphs, and even sentences. Irony, tragedy, absurdity, and high spirits interweave, sometimes undercutting one another, sometimes reinforcing one another. Behind every sentence the reader can sense a living voice; the intonation of every phrase can be clearly heard.

All this makes Teffi's prose difficult to translate. It also makes it ideal material for practising the art of translation— my thanks to the several hundred students of all ages who have tried their hand at translating passages from *Memories* in courses and workshops during the last five years at the *London Review* Bookshop, Pushkin House (Bloomsbury), Queen Mary University of London, and the annual literary translation summer school founded by Ros Schwartz and Naomi Segal and now known as "Translate in the City." Many of these students have contributed phrases to the present translation.

Thanks also to the following for their help and suggestions: Alexandra Babushkina, Lois Bentall, Marina Boroditskaya, Ismene Brown, Roger Clarke, Mahaut de Cordon-Prache, Richard Davies, Natalya Duzhina, Darra Goldstein, Colin and Lis Howlett, Alina Israeli, Nathan Jeffers, Sara Jolly, Yelena Karl, Clare Kitson, Sophie Lockey, Elena Malysheva, Irina Mashinski, Melanie Moore, Natasha Perova, Caroline Rees, Peter Scotto, Richard Shaw, Dmitry Shlyonsky, Stanislav Tsalik, and Christine Worobec.

I am especially grateful to Anne Marie Jackson and to Irina Steinberg, but for whose passionate enthusiasm for Teffi this project would not have got off the ground. And also to Edythe Haber, for generously sharing her encyclopedic knowledge of Teffi's life and work; to Michele Berdy, Masha Bloshteyn, Boris Dralyuk, Rose France, and Elena Trubilova for help with translation problems; and to my wife, whose ear for language grows more sensitive with each year.

Thanks also to *The New Yorker* for publishing extracts from *Memories* on their website: http://www.newyorker.com/books/page-turner/stepping-across-ice-teffi-1872-1952

—*Robert Chandler*

Further Reading

OTHER MEMOIRS OF THIS PERIOD

Ivan Bunin, *Cursed Days: Diary of a Revolution*, tr. Thomas Gaitan
 Marullo (Ivan Dee, 1998)
Viktor Shklovsky, *A Sentimental Journey*, tr. Richard Sheldon
 (Dalkey Archive Press, 2004)
Edith Sollohub, *The Russian Countess* (Impress Books, 2011)
Marina Tsvetaeva, *Earthly Signs: Moscow Diaries, 1917–1922*, tr.
 Jamey Gambrell (Yale University Press, 2011)

Edith Sollohub, unlike Bunin, Shklovsky, and Tsvetaeva, was
never a professional writer. Hers, though, is the most interesting of these memoirs. Like Teffi, she writes vividly and with
understanding about all the many people, from all classes, whom
she encountered during her last years in Russia. At times her
narrative attains a real spiritual depth.

OTHER WORKS BY TEFFI IN ENGLISH

Subtly Worded (Pushkin Press, 2014)
Rasputin and Other Ironies (Pushkin Press, 2016)

Stories by Teffi are included both in *Russian Short Stories from Pushkin to Buida* (Penguin Classics, 2005) and in *Russian Magic Tales from Pushkin to Platonov* (Penguin Classics, 2012).

Elizabeth Neatrour's translation of Teffi's play *The Woman Question* (first performed in 1907) is included in Catriona Kelly (ed.), *Anthology of Russian Women's Writing 1777–1992* (Oxford University Press, 1994).

RUSSIAN EDITIONS OF TEFFI

There is not yet any complete edition of Teffi's work. The most useful collected editions are the five-volume *Sobranie sochinenii* published by Terra in 2008 and the seven-volume *Sobranie sochinenii* published by Lakom in 1997–2000; the latter also includes useful notes. There are numerous single-volume selections, mostly oddly similar in their choice of texts. Some of Teffi's finest volumes have yet to be republished; as far as I know, none of the stories in her outstanding *Vechernii Den'* (Prague, 1924) have been reprinted at all.

The volumes on which we have drawn for *Memories* are:

1. *Moya letopis'* (Moscow: Vagrius, 2004)
This contains the complete text of *Vospominaniya* as well as the articles about writers and other important figures that

Teffi hoped, toward the end of her life, to publish as a separate volume titled *Moya letopis'* (My Chronicle).

2. *Teffi v strane vospominanii* (Kiev: LP Media, 2011)
An excellent compilation of articles and sketches written by Teffi between 1917 and 1919. Many were published in journals and newspapers in Kiev and Odessa during Teffi's last months in Russia, the period Teffi describes in *Memories*. Most of these pieces are also included in a smaller but more easily obtainable volume: *Kontrrevolyutsionnaya bukva* (Azbuka, 2006).

Notes

A longer version of "Before a Map of Russia" was published in *Vozrozhdenie* (Oct. 2, 1925). This shorter version was published in the almanac *Na zapade* (New York, 1953). The present translation first appeared in *The Penguin Book of Russian Poetry* (Penguin, 2015), ed. Chandler, Dralyuk, and Mashinski.

INTRODUCTION

1   "Retrospektivnyi vzgliad i udivlenie," *Novyi Satirikon*, no. 6, (Mar), 1918: 13. Rep. in Teffi, *V strane vospominanii. Rasskazy i fel'etony 1917–1919*, ed. S.I. Kniazev & M.A. Rybakov (Kiev: LP Media, 2011), 164.

2   M[ark] A[ldanov], "Teffi. *Passiflora*," *Sovremennye zapiski*, 1923, no. 17: 485.

3   "Nadezhda Teffi," in F.F. Fidler, ed., *Pervye literaturnye shagi: Avtobiografii sovremennykh russkikh pisatelei* (Moscow: I.D. Sytin, 1911), 203.

4   Teffi, "Chuchelo," *Vozrozhdenie*, Jan. 11, 1931 (no. 2049): 2.

5   "Mne snilsia son…," *Sever*, 1901 (no. 35): 1101; Fidler, 204–5.

6   Teffi, "Pokaiannyi den'," *Teatr i iskusstvo*, 1901, no. 51 (Dec. 16): 955; "Novyi god u pisatelei," *Zvezda*, 1901, no. 52 (Dec. 29): 14–16, 18.

7   The play, "Zhenskii vopros," has been translated by Elizabeth Neatrour as "The Woman Question: A Fantastical Farce in One Act," in *An Anthology of Russian Women's Writing, 1777–1992*, ed. Catriona Kelly (Oxford: Oxford University Press, 1994): 174–92.

8   Aldanov.

9   "Znamia svobody," *Vpered*, Mar. 2 (15), 1905. Pub. as "Pchelki" in *Novaia zhizn'*, no. 2 (1905) and in Teffi's collection of poetry, *Sem' ognei* (Spb.: Shipovnik, 1910), 57–58.

10 I. Gukovskii, "Iz vospominanii I.E. Gukovskogo," *Novaia zhizn':
    Pervaia legal'naia S.-D. bol'shevistskaia gazeta, 27 oktiabria—3 dekabria
    1905 goda*, ed. M. Ol'minskii, vyp 1, no. 1–7 (Leningrad: Rabochee
    izd. "Priboi", 1925), x.

11 "18 oktiabria," *Novaia zhizn'*, Oct. 27, 1905 (no. 1): 7.

12 For Teffi's retrospective view of *Novaia zhizn'* and the Bolsheviks, see
    "45 let," *Novoe russkoe slovo*, June 25, 1950 (no. 13939): 2; "'Novaia
    zhizn'"," *NRS*, July 9, 1950 (no. 13953): 2. For an English translation,
    see *Rasputin and Other Ironies* (Pushkin Press, 2016).

13 "Smekh," *Russkoe slovo*, Nov. 18 (Dec. 1), 1910: 2.

14 *Iumoristicheskie rasskazy* (SPb: Shipovnik, 1910).

15 M. Kuzmin, "Zametki o russkoi belletristiki," *Apollon*, no. 9 (Jul.–Aug.,
    1910): 34.

16 N. Lerner, "N. Teffi. 'Dym bez ognia'," *Literat. i popul.-nauchn. prilo-
    zhenie 'Nivy'*, no. 2 (July, 1914): 459.

17 Anastas'ia Chebotarevskaia, "Teffi. 'I stalo tak…'," *Novaia zhizn'*, July,
    1912 (no. 7): 255.

18 I. V[asilev]ski, "'Nichego podobnogo'. Novaia kniga Teffi," *Zhurnal
    zhurnalov*, 1915, no. 10: 20; Ark[adii] Bukhov, "Teffi," *Zhurnal zhurna-
    lov*, 1915, no. 14: 17.

19 "Srednii," *Novyi Satirikon*, Apr. 2, 1917 (no. 13): 6.

20 "Dezertiry!" *Russkoe slovo*, June 15 (28), 1917 (no. 135?): 2; *V strane*, 22.

21 *V strane*, 24–25.

22 "Nemnozhko o Lenine," *Russkoe slovo*, June 23, 1917 (no. 141): 1; *V
    strane*, 47, 48. For an English translation, see *Rasputin and Other Ironies*
    (Pushkin Press, 2016).

23 "Iz mertvogo goroda," *V strane*, 149. Orig. pub. in *Novoe slovo*, Mar.
    8 (21), 1918, no. 34.

24 Ibid., 151.

25 "Peterburg," *V strane*, 171. Orig. pub. in *Kievskaia mysl'*, Oct. 4 (17),
    1918, no. 188.

26 "Letuchaia mysh'," *Rampa i zhizn'*, May 6 (19), 1918 (no. 20): 11.

27 "Khronika," *Teatr i iskusstvo*, Jan. 7, 1918 (no. 1): 5.

28 "Peterburg," 170.

29 "Gorodok (Khronika)," in *Gorodok* (Paris: Izd. N.P. Karbasnikova,
    1927), 5.

30 Ibid., 6.

31 "Ot avtora," *Vospominaniia* (Paris: Vozrozhdenie, 1931, 5. *Memories* was first serialized in the newspaper, *Vozrozhdenie* between 1928 and 1930.

32 M. Tsetlin, "N.A. Teffi. *Vospominaniia*," *Sovremennye zapiski*, 1932, no. 48: 482.

33 "Baba–Yaga," *Novosel'e*, June 1947 (no. 33–34): 29–37. Repr. in Teffi's last book, *Zemnaya raduga* (NY: Chekhov Press, 1952), 264–68. Translated by Robert and Elizabeth Chandler in *Russian Magic Tales from Pushkin to Platonov*, ed. Robert Chandler (Penguin, 2012), 213–17.

34 "Tot svet," "N.A. Teffi v gazete 'Russkie novosti' (1945–1947)," ed. E.G. Domogatskaia, in *Tvorchestvo N.A. Teffi i russkii literaturnyi protsess pervoi poloviny XX veka*, ed. O.N. Mikhailov, D.D. Nikolaev, E.M. Trubilova (Moscow: Nasledie, 1999): 214. Orig. pub. in *Russkie novosti*, Aug. 3, 1945 (no. 12): 4.

MEMORIES

1 The *Russian Word* was a liberal Moscow daily newspaper, eventually closed down by the Bolsheviks. See Introduction, p. x.

2 Arkady Averchenko (1881–1925), a comic writer and playwright, founded two journals, *Satirikon* (1908–1913) and *New Satirikon* (1913–1918), to which Teffi contributed regularly.

3 Fatback (*salo*)—the layer of hard fat under the skin of a pig's back—is considered a delicacy in many parts of eastern Europe. Fatback, onion, and *horilka* (the Ukrainian equivalent of vodka) is a classic Ukrainian dish.

4 Some of these names sound Russian, some Jewish, some German, but none sound Ukrainian. All sound funny. "Koka" is a vulgar form of "krestnaya" (godmother); "Pupin" evokes the Russian word for the belly button; "Fik" and "Shpruk," especially in the plural, sound equally odd.

5 The Bat was a theatre-cabaret in Moscow, founded in 1908 by actors from the Moscow Arts Theatre. It closed in 1920 but later reopened in Paris.

6 Cléo de Mérode (1875–1966) was a French dancer of the Belle Époque. Born to a Belgian family of nobility, she made her professional debut

at the age of eleven. Postcards and playing cards bore pictures of her, and one of her hairstyles became hugely popular.

7   Torquato Tasso (1544–1595) was an Italian poet.

8   Lolo was the nickname of Leonid Munstein (1866–1947), a poet, satirist, critic, and editor. A friend of Teffi, he too emigrated to France via Kiev, Odessa, and Constantinople. The operetta, with music borrowed from Offenbach, was produced in Moscow in August 1918.

9   The Ancient Theatre, co-founded by Nikolay Yevreinov (1879–1953) and Baron Drizen (1868–1935), with the philosophy of "artistic historic reconstruction," played just two seasons, 1907–1908 and 1911–1912. The singer Bella Kaza-Roza (1885–1929) was a friend of Teffi; her repertoire included settings of poems by Teffi.

10 *Silva* (known in English as *The Riviera Girl* or *The Gipsy Princess*), an operetta by the Hungarian composer Emmerich Kalman (1882–1953), was premiered in Vienna in November 1915. It remains popular in Hungary, Austria, and Germany and was made into a successful film in the Soviet Union.

11 Valery Bryusov was one of the founders of Russian Symbolism. Always an influential figure, he joined the Communist Party in 1920. There are several accounts of his abusing his position in the Soviet cultural apparatus to attack more gifted colleagues.

12 This three-headed dragon appears in one of the most famous Russian *byliny* or heroic songs.

13 The Soviet security services were originally called the "Extraordinary Committee" or *Cherezvychainy komitet*, usually shortened to *Cherezvychaika* or *Cheka*. Later acronyms were the OGPU, the NKVD, and the KGB.

14 "Vova" is an affectionate form of the name "Vladimir." The intentionally ludicrous implication is that Fedosya received this shawl and portrait as a gift from Lenin himself.

15 Savely Schleifer (1881–1943). Born in Odessa, Schleifer studied there and in Petersburg. After living in Paris from 1905 to 1907, he returned to Petersburg. He taught there after the revolution but emigrated to Paris in 1927. Arrested by the Nazis soon after the outbreak of World War II, he died in Auschwitz.

16 Lydia Yavorskaya (1871–1921) was a well-known actress.

17 From "The Tryst" (1841) by Mikhail Lermontov.

18 After the October Revolution, Moisey Uritsky (1873–1918) was appointed head of the Petrograd Cheka (i.e. security police). On 17 August 1918 he was assassinated by Leonid Kannegisser, a poet and former military cadet. Soon after this, and after an attempt on Lenin's life, the Bolsheviks initiated the wave of arrests and executions known as the Red Terror. Kannegisser was executed in October 1918. Ironically, Uritsky had been one of the few important Bolsheviks to disagree with Lenin about the need to resort to terror. See Ivan Bunin, *Cursed Days*, ed. Thomas Gaiton Marullo (Phoenix Press, 2000), p. 216, note 9.

19 This conversation is condensed from "Repentant Fate," first published in 1913 and included in the collection *Smoke without Fire* (1914). In the story the actress assures Teffi that she would gladly help Teffi's unfortunate protagonist by giving him money of her own, if only she could. Teffi returns to this theme—the artist as an "imitator of God" —in the last pages of *Memories*.

20 The Russian word *mestechko* (literally "little place") was used for settlements too large to be classed as villages but too small to be classed as cities. From 1791, Jews were generally only permitted to live within "the Pale of Settlement" (a region roughly corresponding to present-day Belarus, western Ukraine, eastern Poland, and the Baltic republics). Even within the Pale, Jews were generally prohibited from living in either large cities or small villages. Most Jews, therefore, lived in shtetls. In April 1917, the Pale of Settlement was abolished.

21 Maximilien de Robespierre (1758–1794) was one of the most important figures of the French Revolution. Accused of being the "soul" of the Reign of Terror, he was arrested and executed in July 1794.

22 The shtetl Teffi and her companions have just reached is Unechka, in Bryansk province. For a few months this unremarkable town assumed great importance, as the frontier station on the main route between Moscow and Kiev. The Cheka was exceptionally active there, not only seizing valuables from those trying to leave Soviet Russia but also guarding against infiltration from the Ukraine, which, from March until December 1918, was under German occupation.

23 Vsevolod Meyerhold (1874–1940) was an influential and innovative theatre director. In an article written after his death, Teffi explains that

the three corners of his "magic triangle" were the actor, the author, and the director and that Meyerhold believed that the author and the actors should communicate with one another via the director (i.e. along the two short sides of the triangle), rather than directly (i.e. along the hypotenuse). Teffi clearly disagreed with all this, observing sarcastically, "The director always sees the author as the enemy of the play. The author's observations only mess things up. The author wrote the play, but it is the director, of course, who best understands just what the author wanted to say" (*Moya letopis'* [Vagrius, 2004], p. 187). As for the young actress, she blends Meyerhold's terminology with the political jargon of the time; Trotsky, Bukharin, and others often spoke of "parallelograms of forces." Teffi knew Nikolay Yevreinov well (see note 9); a theatre director associated with Russian Symbolism, he spent most of his last thirty years in Paris. *Commedia dell'Arte* developed in Italy in the sixteenth century; it emerged from Carnival and is characterized by the use of masks and the central role played by such stock characters as Arlecchino (Harlequin) and Pulcinella (Punch). "Theatre as collective ritual" alludes to the theories of the Symbolist poet Vyacheslav Ivanov (1866–1949). He dreamed of a new type of mass theatre—a "collective action," modelled on ancient religious rituals, Athenian tragedy, and medieval mystery plays.

24   A reference to *zaum*, the "transrational" or "beyond-mind" language advocated by the Futurist poets Alexey Kruchonykh and Velimir Khlebnikov. It was Kruchonykh who coined this word, brilliantly translated by the late Paul Schmidt as "beyonsense."

25   This commissar was, in reality, Fruma Khaikina (1897–1977), who adopted the surname "Rostova," after Natasha Rostova in *War and Peace*. She was head of the local Cheka and a member of the town's "RevKom"—that is, Revolutionary Committee. In late 1918 she married Mykola Shchors (1895–1919), a Ukrainian Red Army commander elevated after his death to almost legendary status. She was notorious for her brutality.

26   One of the banknotes issued by the Provisional Government whose last prime minister, in the summer and early autumn of 1917, had been Alexandr Kerensky. The Soviet government continued to print these notes until 1919, so the general was doing nothing illegal.

27 The poem Olyonushka recites is *"Angelika"* (included in *Passiflora*, 1923). Fedosya dies alone in a ditch and is taken up by angels into the presence of Christ and the Virgin Mary.

28 In Gogol's story "Christmas Eve" (1832), the blacksmith makes the sign of the cross over the devil. This forces the devil to let the blacksmith ride on his back.

29 A song written in 1906, to honour those who had died in the Russo-Japanese war of the previous year. During and after the Civil War the song was sung by both Whites and Reds.

30 The Imperial Petersburg Institute of Technology, founded in 1828.

31 A popular satirical magazine. See note 2.

32 A Polish form of address, once the equivalent of the English "Sir." Since the late nineteenth century, it has been closer to "Mr."

33 "Where is Moscow?" (Yiddish)

34 "What a little scholar he is!" (Yiddish, probably meant ironically)

35 "The crazy head!" (Yiddish, colloquial)

36 George Boreman was the owner of a successful Petersburg chocolate factory, nationalized in 1918.

37 In an article published in Kiev in January 1919, Teffi is more critical of Russian condescension towards the Ukrainian language. Many of the Ukrainian words that Russians find so risible, she points out, are in fact more Slavonic than their Russian equivalents, which are often borrowings from French or German. She continues, "I cannot understand why they are so irritated by the free existence of the Ukrainian language. [...] What has happened? Is it really so terrible to have to learn the couple of dozen words one needs to get by in the Ukraine? Far more terrible are all these mindless 'orientations,' 'evacuations,' 'demobilizations,' and 'democratizations' that now litter our Slav speech." (*Teffi v strane vospominanii*: LP Media 2011, p. 215)

38 The actress Vera Ilnarskaya (1880–1946) was married to Lolo, a writer with whom Teffi sometimes collaborated. She published the journal *The Spotlights and Life (Rampa i zhizn')*. See note 8.

39 A salty East European dish made from minced meat, anchovies, or herring, together with onions.

40 Teffi's train did indeed pass through Gomel, which lies about 300

kilometres to the north of Kiev, in what is now Belarus. Shavli (or Siauliai), however, lies in present-day Lithuania, not far from the Baltic; it could not possibly have been on their route. Gooskin's geography is confused.

41 "Out!" (German).

42 Olyonushka's first two words mean, "The exceptions are…" She then comes up with a number of verbs that are exceptions to some grammatical rule.

43 "This was in Schöneberg" (a part of Berlin).

44 *Schon* means "already"; *nun* means "now."

45 At the end of the nineteenth century Jews constituted nearly forty percent of the population of Odessa. The ever-alert Gooskin, with his colourful way of speech, answers perfectly to the Russian stereotype of a Jewish Odessan businessman. The quintessential Russianness of his first name and patronymic is therefore unexpected. It is this that makes everyone laugh.

46 Anatoly Durov (1865–1916) and his elder brother Vladimir (1863–1936) were famous trainers of circus dogs. Unlike most trainers before them, who had relied on pain and fear, they used mainly positive encouragement—the carrot rather than the stick.

47 From April until November 1918, the Ukrainian Head of State was titled "the Hetman."

48 Bolshevik propaganda during these years often pictured capitalism and counterrevolution as a hydra—a monster with many heads.

49 The main street in Kiev, used as a promenade.

50 Leonid Sobinov (1872–1934) was a well-known tenor; he remained in the Soviet Union. Fyodor Kurikhin (1881–1951) was a well-known actor; he too remained in the Soviet Union. Yury Ozarovsky (1869–1924) was an actor, director, theatre critic and drama teacher; he died in Paris. Vlas Doroshevich (1864–1922) was a journalist and writer of short stories; after living in the Crimea from autumn 1918, he returned to Petrograd in May 1921 and died there in February 1922. According to the literary historian Yury Kaplan, as many as eighty newspapers, magazines, and almanacs opened in Kiev at this time (Haber, chapter 6). It was widely felt that the realistic theatre had had its day, and there was a vogue for cabarets, sketches, and short

plays of all kinds. Teffi's graceful witty playlets—the best-known of which was *The Woman Question* (1907)—were very popular. Teffi's daughter Valeria writes: "She personally worked on the staging of her plays, giving the actors very valuable directions and often sketching the designs for the costumes with her own hands." (Edythe Haber, chapter 3)

51 The Stray Dog was a café in Petersburg, a famous meeting place for writers and poets. Between January 1, 1912, and its closure on March 3, 1915, nearly all the main poets of the time—regardless of their political or artistic affiliations—gave readings there. Part of Teffi's story "The Dog" (included in *Subtly Worded* [Pushkin Press, 2014]) is set there.

52 Most likely, this was the actress Maria Zan'kovetska (1854–1934), a key figure in the revival of a Ukrainian national theatre.

53 During her three months in Kiev, from October 7, 1918, until January 1919, Teffi published at least twenty articles and sketches, gave public readings, and helped to arrange for the production of several of her plays, as well as writing a new one-act play for the opening night of a new theatre (*Teffi v strane vospominanii*, pp. 11–13). Many thoughts, images and anecdotes from these articles—and from the three or four articles she published in Odessa between January and April 1919—reappear in *Memories*, in most cases treated with greater sophistication.

54 Symon Petlyura (1879–1926), a writer, journalist and socialist politician, was the leading figure in Ukraine's unsuccessful struggle for independence. After the February 1917 revolution, he joined the Ukrainian Central Rada ("council"), which in June 1917 proclaimed Ukraine an autonomous republic. Soon after this, however, the Germans occupied Ukraine and established a puppet government led by Pavlo Skoropadsky, who was officially known as "the Hetman" (a historic title that had not been used since the seventeenth century). When the Germans withdrew, Petlyura, now heading the five-member directorate of the Rada, seized power. Petlyura then had to confront both the Reds and the Whites. When the White armies, which had occupied Ukraine and replaced Petlyura's government at the end of 1918, withdrew in the autumn of 1919, Ukraine fell under Soviet

authority. During the Russo-Polish War of 1919–20 Petlyura allied with the Poles. The Poles repelled the Red Army from Poland itself but failed to secure independence for Ukraine.

55   Mikhail Milrud (1883–1942) had previously, like Teffi, worked for the *Russian Word*. He was on the editorial board of *Kiev Thought*. From 1924 he edited a Russian-language newspaper in Latvia. Arrested in 1941, he died in the Gulag.

56   Ilya Vasilevsky (1883–1938) was a prominent journalist. Together with his wife, he left Kiev for Odessa and then Constantinople. Vasilevsky later returned to the Soviet Union in 1923. He was shot in the purges: http://www.bulgakov.ru/b/belozerskaya/

57   In Dostoevsky's *Crime and Punishment* Sonya Marmeladova is driven by poverty to prostitute herself. After going out onto the streets for the first time, she comes back home, wraps herself in a *drap de dames* (a very fine kind of fabric) shawl, and lies down on the bed with her face to the wall.

58   Count Alessandro di Cagliostro (1743–1795) was a famous Italian fraudster, Freemason, and occultist, supposedly gifted with magical powers.

59   Lenin's biographer, Robert Service, thinks it unlikely that Lenin ever had any contact with Duclos (personal email, April 2015).

60   In November 1918, Teffi published an article titled "Armand Duclos" (*Teffi v strane vospominanii*, pp. 188–91). Much of it is about the arguments between those who believed in Duclos's clairvoyant powers and those who saw him as a trickster. In the last fifteen lines, however, Teffi strikes a different note. After emphasizing how everyone, no matter what their social position or political allegiance, asks Duclos essentially the same simple questions about love and happiness, she continues:

> Always the same: we want to hold our little human happiness and take it away with us. To a place where no one will steal it from us.
>
> Yes, the most ambitious, most ascetic, most ideologically committed builder of a new life, just like a simple stonemason, feels the need to come back home in the evening. To light his lamp, open his book, and smile into affectionate, loving eyes.

> Armand Duclos! Brilliant clairvoyant! Look closely—will we
> yet meet happiness and be able to hold onto it? Surely we must!
> How pitiful we all are.

61 Vladimir Vinnichenko (1880–1951) was a leading Ukrainian writer
and nationalist politician. He was the chairman of the council of
five, "the Directorate," that ruled much of Ukraine in late 1918 and
early 1919. Petlyura was a member of this Directorate, as well as
commander of its army.

62 The Hetman, Skoropadsky, had been supported by the Germans.
When the Germans withdrew, many of his officers and soldiers
deserted and went over to Petlyura and the Directorate. See note 54.

63 The Kiev Pechersk Lavra. This cave monastery, founded in 1051
by Orthodox monks from Mount Athos, is believed to contain the
uncorrupted bodies of saints from the days of Kievan Rus, the
medieval Slav kingdom that embraced Christianity in 988. Present-
day Russia, Ukraine, and Belarus are all descended from this first
important kingdom of eastern Slavs.

64 In "Slain Servants of the Lord," an article published in Kiev in December
1918, Teffi wrote:

> Horror, and words about death, no matter with how much emotion
> they are pronounced, no longer disturb us. They are now our simple,
> everyday vocabulary, as normal for us as "health" or "money."
> They do not call up any vivid, or painful, image in our minds.
> "Where's A?"
> "Seems he's been shot."
> "Where's B?"
> "Seems he's still alive."
> We all seem to be alive, or maybe we seem to have died.
> There in that "seems" we sway, like ghosts in the mist on a
> moonlit night.

65 A woman's perfume, created by Jacques Guerlain in 1908.

66 Alexey Grishin-Almazov (1880–1919) was, during much of 1918, in
command of the White armies in western Siberia. He then moved to

the south of Russia. In December 1918, the French, then in control of Odessa, appointed him military governor.

67 Vladimir Burtsev (1862–1942) was a historian and journalist who served time in prison under both the tsarist and Soviet regimes. His newspaper *The Common Cause* went through several different incarnations: in 1909–10, 1917, 1918–22 and 1928–33.

68 A once-famous novel by Semyon Yushkevich (1868–1927). It is set largely in Odessa.

69 An infamous Odessa gangster, Jewish revolutionary, and Soviet military leader.

70 The Moldavanka was a poor part of Odessa, with a reputation for criminality. The writer Isaak Babel was born there, and it provides the setting for his "Odessa Tales," a cycle of stories about the life of Jewish gangsters.

71 This paragraph is, in effect, a condensed version of "The Last Breakfast," the last article Teffi published in Odessa. See appendix, p. 231.

72 Fyodor Blagov (1886–1934), the last editor of the *Russian Word*, emigrated to China, where he worked for Russian newspapers in Harbin and Shanghai.

73 Maximilian Voloshin (1877–1932) was a leading figure among the Russian Symbolist poets of the early twentieth century. For over a decade his large house in Koktebel, where he both wrote and painted, was a refuge for writers and artists of all political and artistic persuasions. Among his hundreds of guests were Maxim Gorky, Nikolay Gumilyov, Osip and Nadezhda Mandelstam, and Marina Tsvetaeva. In 1924 the house became a "House of Creativity" for Soviet writers, the first of the many such closed-access hotels that were a central part of the Soviet cultural world. In spite of a number of facile professions of faith in Russia's purification through suffering, Voloshin's poems about the Civil War and the subsequent Red Terror in the Crimea are courageous and incisive. Voloshin was steadfast in his refusal to accept any ideology as absolute truth. A poem titled "Civil War" ends:

> And from the ranks of both armies
> I hear one and the same voice:

> "He who is not with us is against us.
> You must take sides. Justice is ours."
> And I stand alone in the midst of them,
> amidst the roar of fire and smoke,
> and pray with all my strength for those
> who fight on this side, and on that side.

Voloshin's belief in the power of his words—what Marianna Landa refers to as "his Dostoevskian faith in the divine spark in the soul of the abominable criminal, and his Symbolist belief in the magic of the poetic word"—seems to have been unshakeable; his personal appeals to Red and White officials and commanders, on behalf of individuals in trouble, and his verse-prayers addressed to God, on behalf of his country, have much in common. Voloshin believed he could affect the course of events—and sometimes he did. That he escaped arrest and execution is astonishing. See *The Penguin Book of Russian Poetry* (Penguin Classics, 2015, ed. Robert Chandler, Boris Dralyuk, and Irina Mashinski), pp. 175–180. For a somewhat more critical view of Voloshin, see Ivan Bunin, *Cursed Days*, pp. 82, 112. Much about Voloshin evidently enraged Bunin. In a diary entry for April 16, 1919, he writes, "Voloshin visited us […] It was monstrous! He said he had spent all day with Severny, the head of the local Cheka, who has a 'soul like crystal.' That's just what he said: 'like crystal.'" (ibid. p. 85) Nevertheless, Bunin's wife writes in her own diary, September 6, 1919, "Valya [Kataev] lashed out at Voloshin. For some reason he can't stand him. [Bunin] defended Voloshin, saying that though his verse is wordy, something genuine and personal shines forth from it. 'There are too few Voloshins around for you to be negative toward him. How well Voloshin has sung of his country. How very good are his portraits.'" (Thomas Gaitan Marullo, *Ivan Bunin: Russian Requiem* [Ivan Dee, 1993], p. 346.)

74   Grigory (or Grishka) Otrepyev, popularly known as "The False Dmitry," was a monk who claimed to be Dmitry, the murdered son of Ivan the Terrible. He reigned for eleven months during 1605–6.

75   Yelizaveta Kuzmina-Karavayeva (1891–1945) was elected deputy mayor of the southern Russian town of Anapa in 1918. When the Whites

captured the town, she was put on trial as a Bolshevik but acquitted. Her judge, Daniil Skobtsov, who had once been her teacher, then married her; their marriage (her second) fell apart in the late 1920s, but her writings are often published under her married name of Skobtsova. In 1932, in Paris, she took monastic vows, assuming the name of Mother Maria. During World War II she helped many Jews to escape the Nazis, often by providing them with baptismal certificates, but she was eventually sent to the Ravensbrück concentration camp. In March 1945, a week before the camp was liberated by the Red Army, she was sent to the gas chamber; according to one testimony, she voluntarily took the place of a Jewish woman. In 2004 she was canonized as a saint by the Orthodox Patriarchate of Constantinople. See also *The Penguin Book of Russian Poetry*, pp. 188–89 and p. 547, note 22.

76 In the Russian Orthodox Church a metropolitan is a high-ranking clergyman, senior to an archbishop and second only to a patriarch.

77 Admiral Alexander Kolchak (1874–1920) established a right-wing government in Siberia in late 1918 and was recognized as Supreme Commander by the other leaders of the White forces, not only in Siberia but also in the south of Russia.

78 In June 1917, mutinous sailors of the Black Sea Fleet decided to confiscate their officers' weapons. Rather than surrender his ceremonial cutlass, Kolchak threw it into the sea. It was later returned to him, with a respectful message.

79 Teffi's first books, both in fact published several years before the beginning of the War, were two volumes titled *Humorous Stories*, in prose, and *Seven Fires*, in verse. The latter is divided into seven sections: "Sapphire," "Amethyst," "Alexandrite," "Ruby," "Emerald," "Diamond," and "Topaz." The poet Nikolay Gumilyov reviewed *Seven Fires* enthusiastically, describing the poems as "literary in the best sense of the word" and referring to the "mask that Teffi wears with a solemn grace and, it seems, with a barely noticeable smile." Quoted in Nadezhda Teffi, *Almaznaya Pyl'*, (Moscow, 2011) p. 8.

80 This stone was first discovered in April 1834, on the sixteenth birthday of the future Tsar Alexander II. Green or bluish-green in daylight, it turns a soft shade of red under incandescent light. "The bloody sunset" refers to the tsar's assassination in 1881.

81 Alexander Yakovlev (1887–1938) was a painter and graphic artist. Like Teffi, he worked for both *Satirikon* and *New Satirikon*, as well as many other journals. In the summer of 1917, he went to study in the Far East. After travelling through Mongolia, China, and Japan, he settled in Paris. Teffi mentions his wife Bella Kaza-Roza in the first chapter of *Memories* (p. 9 and also note 9).

82 Friedrich Martens (1845–1909) was a Russian diplomat and lawyer who made important contributions to the field of international law. Valerie Sollohub, the widow of Martens's grandson Count Nicholas Sollohub, writes, "I fear this story must be apocryphal. Professor Martens died in the daytime, in Livonia, on the railway station platform, unbeknown to his wife who was at their country house, Waldensee, with the telephone out of order. From the depths of the country she would not have been sending servants out with opals nor, indeed, was she inclined to buy precious stones; she left all that kind of thing to her husband." (Personal email, May 2014. There is no knowing whether Konoplyov's story is his own invention or Teffi's.)

83 Mikhail Kuzmin (1872–1936) was one of the finest poets of his time. He also wrote plays and composed music. In 1906, he published *Wings*, the first Russian novel with an overtly homosexual theme; two large editions sold out at once.

84 The Triple Entente was the alliance that, from 1907 until the end of World War I, linked France, Russia, and Great Britain—a counterweight to the "Triple Alliance" of Germany, Austria-Hungary, and Italy. There were French forces in Odessa in early 1919, but the French intervention in Crimea and southern Ukraine was brief, badly planned, and unsuccessful (See Ivan Bunin, *Cursed Days*, p. 77–78, notes 2 & 3). Teffi's characters are vainly hoping to see British or French ships bringing reinforcements to protect them from the advancing Red Army. In an article she published while still in Kiev, in December 1918, Teffi makes fun of the way people all of a sudden began excitedly talking about "pennants." The Russian equivalent, *vympel*, is rarely used, and Teffi professes not to know whether it means "a rag," "some kind of stick or pole," or "an assistant to a ship's captain" (Teffi, *V strane vospominanii*, pp. 203–06).

85   Ivan Bunin (1870–1953) remained in Odessa after it fell to the Bolsheviks in April 1919. The Whites, however, recaptured the city in August and Bunin was able to leave Russia in January 1920. He settled in France, where he and Teffi became close friends. In 1933 he became the first Russian to be awarded the Nobel Prize for Literature. He was married to Vera Muromtseva (1881–1961). Alexey Tolstoy (1883–1945), nicknamed the Comrade Count, was a gifted but opportunistic writer, best known for his science fiction and historical novels. He settled in Paris in 1920 but returned to the Soviet Union three years later; he was awarded a Stalin Prize three times. His wife Natalya Krandievskaya (1888–1963) was a poet and memoirist; the couple separated in 1935. Sergey Gorny (the pen name of Alexander Otsup [1882–1948]) was a poet and satirist; during the Civil War he served as an engineer in the White navy. Pyotr Nilus (1869–1943) was a Russian Impressionist painter. From 1920 he lived in Paris, initially sharing a house with Ivan Bunin. Alexander Pankratov (1871–1922) was a journalist; like Teffi, he had worked for the *Russian Word*.

86   "The Last Breakfast" is included in the appendix. And see note 71.

87   The soldiers' strange words are probably derived from the Arabic Hamdullah ("Praise Allah"). As for their "fierce teeth," Teffi uses the word *kannibal'skie*, which can mean "cannibalistic" but which was also used more generally in the sense of "brutish" or "savage." People at this time tended to think of cannibalism as more widespread than it was. Russians, most of whom had little contact with sub-Saharan Africa, may have been particularly prone to this misapprehension. Our thanks to Boris Dralyuk for his help with this note.

88   "Your tongue will lead you to Kiev" is the Russian equivalent of the English "He who has a tongue goes to Rome." That is, if you ask enough questions, you will receive an answer.

89   On April 3, 1919 the French government decided to evacuate all French troops and the city's civilian administration. This caused widespread panic. The evacuation was largely completed by April 6, though there was probably no military necessity for such speed.

90   Here we are translating *khlopotat'*, a common Russian word for which there is no English equivalent. Elsewhere, in passages where Teffi draws less attention to this verb, we have translated it in different

ways: "apply for," "try to obtain," "procure," etc. In "Moscow: the Last Days," an article she published in Kiev in October 1918, Teffi explains the word: "Incidentally, there is no equivalent to this idiotic term *khlopotat'* in any other language in the world. A foreigner will say, 'I'll go and get the documents.' A Russian, 'I must hurry and start to *khlopotat'* with regard to the documents.' The foreigner will go to the appropriate institution and obtain what he needs. The Russian will go to three people he knows for advice, to two more who can 'pull strings', then to the institution—but it'll be the wrong one—then to the right institution—but he'll keep on knocking at the wrong doors until it's too late. Then he'll start everything all over again and, when he's finally brought everything to a conclusion, he'll leave the documents in a cab. This whole process is what is described by the word *khlopotat'*. Such work, if carried out on behalf of a third party, is highly valued and well paid" (*Teffi v strane vospominanii*, pp. 167–70).

91 Alexander Kugel (1864–1928) was a critic. In 1908 he co-founded The Crooked Mirror, a Petersburg theatre that specialized in parodies and put on two of Teffi's plays. He remained in the Soviet Union, still directing this theatre, till his death.

92 Not as nonsensical as one might think. Some French units did indeed refuse to fight the Bolsheviks and there were revolutionary movements on board some of the ships: http://militera.lib.ru/h/civilwar_blacksea/02.html

93 Founded in 1436 on an archipelago in the White Sea, the Solovetsky monastery was for many centuries the most important monastery in northern Russia. In 1923 the Soviet authorities turned it into a special prison and labour camp—the prototype for the vast system later known as the Gulag. Teffi visited the monastery in summer 1916 (Haber, chapter 6).

94 Known as the Angel of Blessings, Barachiel is often portrayed holding a white rose against his chest, or with rose petals scattered on his cloak; the petals symbolize the blessings he bestows.

95 Prayer belts are wide belts with the words of prayers woven into them, intended to be worn or to be hung on the wall.

96 The True Cross was thought to have been made of pine, cedar, and cypress; more generally, cypress is one of the oldest symbols of

mourning. The Solovki monastery and the Pechersk Lavra, the cave monastery in Kiev to which Teffi says goodbye in chapter 12, were the two most important of all Russian Orthodox pilgrimage sites. That Teffi tells us about devotional objects from each site is significant; the tiny icon in a bottle from the Lavra and this cypress cross are almost the only personal possessions she describes in *Memories*—an embodiment of the Holy Russia she would never see again. Her story "Solovki" (first published in émigré journals in 1921 and republished in the 1924 volume *Evening Day*) was important to her; she considered it one of her best (See N.A Teffi, *Nezhivoy Zver'* (Moscow: Lakom, 1999), p. 9).

97 The engineer "V" was in reality Alexander Otsup, see note 85. He and Teffi remained close friends until his death. In a letter to Teffi (February 5, 1948) he refers to their meetings in Kiev in late 1918—in particular to Teffi's bout of Spanish influenza—and to this last day in Odessa. For the most part, his account tallies with Teffi's. http://kfinkelshteyn.narod.ru/Literat/O_Sergee_Gornom.htm#prim30

98 Lermontov, "The Ghost Ship."

99 "Ataman" Nikifor Grigoriev (1885–1919) had earlier fought on the side of Petlyura and the Directorate, but by 1919 he had allied with the Bolsheviks. He captured Odessa only a few days after the French evacuation.

100 Venedikt Myakotin (1867–1937) was a Populist politician; expelled from Soviet Russia in 1922, he became a professor of history in Sofia in 1928, then lived his last years in Prague. Fyodor Volkenstein (1874–1937) was a lawyer, writer, and journalist; he remained in the Soviet Union. Alexey Ksyunin (1882–1938) was also a journalist, at one time head of the Russian press bureau in Constantinople. Alexey Titov (dates unknown) was a chemical engineer and Populist politician; he emigrated to Paris. Ilya Ilyashenko (1859–1920), deputy minister of justice from 1913 to 1917, was executed by the Bolsheviks in 1920.

101 These lines by Vladimir Mayakovsky were well known. Mayakovsky recalled reports of sailors singing them as they marched on the Winter Palace in 1917 ("Tol'ko ne vospominanii", in V.V. Maiakovskii, *Polnoe sobranie sochinenii* (Moscow, IMLI, 1955–61) v 12: Stat'i, zametki i vystupleniia, p. 149–59).

102 This song became popular among soldiers and sailors, both Red and White, during the Civil War. Like many traditional songs, it proved remarkably adaptable to varying political requirements.

103 Nikolay Yevreinov (see notes 9 and 23) wrote about how art should take its inspiration from life. Haber comments on this scene, "Teffi compares the sight to theatrical experiments of the recent past, except in this case it was not a performance; life itself forced the actors to play the role, as it would compel them again and again to reinvent themselves in emigration."

104 Stenka Razin, a Russian folk hero, was the Cossack leader of a major revolt in 1670–71.

105 A quote from "The Reaper" by Alexey Koltsov (1809–42).

106 A quote from "Dubinushka" ("The Club"). Originally written by V.I. Bogdanov, this was refashioned to make its sentiments more revolutionary. The famous bass Fyodor Chaliapin included it in his repertory.

107 Fyodor Volkenstein (see note 100) had separated from his wife, Natalya Krandievskaya (see note 85), in 1914. Krandievskaya subsequently married Alexey Tolstoy and emigrated with him and her son by Volkenstein—the little boy referred to here—only to return to the Soviet Union in 1923. This boy, who became a physicist, is the anonymous friend to whom Stalin's daughter, Svetlana Allilluyeva, addressed her "Twenty Letters to a Friend."

108 An allusion to a famous "gypsy song" by the poet Apollon Grigoriev. It begins: "O speak to me, you at least, my seven-stringed friend!"

109 Albert Zabel (1834–1910) was a teacher, a composer, and the main harpist at the Mariinsky Theatre.

110 Both the Hebrew and Church Slavonic bibles, unlike the King James Bible, include instructions of this kind before the main text of each psalm.

111 *Novoe Vremya*, a Petersburg daily newspaper, published 1868–1917. Under its last editor, A. S. Suvorin, it was considered extremely reactionary. The Bolsheviks closed it down the day after the October revolution.

112 A cold soup made from *kvas* (a slightly alcoholic drink made from fermented bread) and the leafy tops of various root vegetables, often with the addition of some kind of sturgeon.

113 Like many of Teffi's poems, this poem, written on the *Shilka*, was set to music by the émigré singer, Alexander Vertinsky (1889–1957), who titled it "Song about the Motherland." Vertinsky returned to the Soviet Union in 1943 but remained the object of official disapproval until long after his death.

114 The most likely meaning of these words is "Beautiful woman!" *Guzel* means "beauty" in Persian and in many Turkic languages. *Kari* is a Turkish word for "spouse," but it is also used, somewhat disrespectfully, to mean "woman." The soldiers are, of course, African, not Turkish—but much of northern Africa had once been a part of the Ottoman Empire.

115 Where are you, old man? (French)

116 The soldiers' song from *Les Huguenots*, a once extremely popular and successful grand opera by Giacomo Meyerbeer.

117 Tsarist Russia in many ways followed the German educational system. A gymnasium is a secondary school with a strong emphasis on academic learning, similar to a British grammar school or a prep school in the US.

118 Teffi's younger sister Elena Lokhvitskaya (1874–1919) was the closest to her of her many siblings. She too wrote both poetry and plays. In 1922, soon after receiving the news of Elena's death, Teffi wrote in a letter to Vera Bunina, "I feel complete emptiness. It's as if, because of this news, a wind has passed over my earth and swept everything away. I haven't spoken, I've grown thin and black in four days." *Diaspora*, 1 (Paris–SPb, 2001), 365.

119 The Greens were armed bands of peasants who, at one time or another, fought both Whites and Reds as they tried to protect their villages from reprisals and requisitioning. After the defeat of the Whites, they constituted the last remaining military challenge to the Bolshevik regime. In late 1920 a Green army under the leadership of the Socialist Revolutionary Alexander Antonov numbered as many as 50,000 and controlled a large part of the province of Tambov.

120 A small town, now a holiday resort, about fifteen miles from Novorossiisk.

121 Now known as Trabzon, this town in northeastern Turkey was occupied by the Russians at the end of World War I.

122 To this day, there is a large cement factory in Novorossiisk, one of the oldest such factories in Russia, founded in 1882.

123 This is inconsistent with Akyn's earlier account on page 171: "He had once got so very angry... that he had 'torn his throat.'" Teffi may have intended the reader to understand that she herself heard different stories about this cook—or, more likely, this is simply a mistake on her part.

124 Fyodor Batkin (1892–1923) fought in World War I, first as a volunteer in the Belgian army, then in the Russian Army. During the summer of 1917, as the leader of the "Black Sea Delegation" set up by Admiral Kolchak to combat defeatism, he gave impassioned patriotic speeches in Moscow and Petrograd.

125 The flag of the Russian navy.

126 The evening edition of *The Stock Exchange Gazette*, an important Petersburg daily newspaper, published 1861–1879 and 1880–1917. Teffi was a regular contributor.

127 After fighting for the Whites, Batkin emigrated to Turkey. There, in 1920, he was recruited by the Cheka. In 1922, however, after returning to Russia without authorization, he was arrested and shot.

128 Bobchinsky and Dobchinsky are comic characters in Gogol's play *The Government Inspector*. Like Tweedledee and Tweedledum, they are inseparable, always appearing on stage at the same time.

129 A private school in Petersburg.

130 Leonid Andreyev (1871–1919) wrote plays, novels, and short stories. Konstantin Arabazhin (1866–1929) was a literary critic and editor. Akim Volynsky (1861–1926) was a critic and art historian. For Meyerhold, see note 23.

131 A comedy first performed, to considerable acclaim, in 1909.

132 In an article published in 1950 about her participation in a benefit evening for the poet Konstantin Balmont (1867–1942), Teffi describes this train journey a second time:

> I was travelling at night, in a coach packed with men who were only half alive. They were sitting on one another, standing, swaying, lying side by side on the floor; they were like corpses. A terrifying old man was leaning heavily on my shoulder. His mouth was wide

open, and I could see only the whites of his eyes. He was crushing me. The carriage was airless and stinking. My heart was pounding violently, then missing a beat. I felt I was going to suffocate, that I would not last until morning, and I closed my eyes.

And then, deep in my soul, I heard the music of a sweet, naïve, childish poem:

There was dancing in the castle
and the sound of music…

Balmont!

And the stinking, wheezing coach disappeared. There was only music, the circling of moths and, from the castle pond, the flash of a magic goldfish.

From the goldfish in the pond
came a sweeter music…

I recited the poem and began again. Like an incantation.

Dear, sweet Balmont!

We reached our destination early in the morning. Blue and motionless, the old man was carried out. It seemed he had died. As for me, I had been saved by the magic of verse.

I told the audience about this miracle, looking all the time at the corner of the hall where Yelena [Balmont's most loyal devotee] was still quietly weeping (*Moya letopis'*, p. 242).

133 Osip Runich (1889–1947) left Russia in 1919; he then lived in Italy, Germany, Latvia, and South Africa. Alexander Koshevsky (1873–1931) was a famous singer in musicals; he remained in the Soviet Union.

134 Anton Denikin (1872–1947) was the commander-in-chief of the White forces in southern Russia from December 1918 until April 1920.

135 Pavel Novgorodtsev (1866–1924) was a liberal political philosopher and lawyer; he emigrated in 1921 and died in Prague. For Myakotin see note 100, for Volkenstein note 100 and 107. Pyotr Ouspensky

(1878–1947) was a follower of the spiritual philosopher George Gurdjieff (1866–1949).

136 In the Song of Solomon 4:1, Solomon says to a woman referred to as the Shulamite, "Behold, thou art fair, my love; behold, thou art fair; thou hast doves' eyes within thy locks: thy hair is as a flock of goats, that appear from mount Gilead."

137 Ksenya Mikhailovna G (1892–1919) was an anarchist who, after the October Revolution, joined the Bolshevik Party. Her independence of mind led to her being sent out of the way, to Kislovodsk, where she worked as an investigator for the Cheka. After the Whites captured Kislovodsk, she was arrested, sentenced and hanged. "G" was the pseudonym adopted by her husband, whose surname was Golberg.

138 Mamont Dalsky (1865–1918) was a tragic actor, famous for his interpretation of the lead role in *Edmund Kean or The Genius and the Libertine* by Alexandre Dumas. In his novel *The Road to Calvary*, Alexey Tolstoy writes, "When the Revolution began, Dalsky saw in it an enormous stage for tragic drama… He brought together isolated groups of anarchists, took over the Merchants' Club and declared it the House of Anarchy."

139 The steamer is named after Grand Duke Alexander Mikhailovich (1866–1933), the brother-in-law of Tsar Nicholas II.